REPORTING

THE NEWS

REPORTING
THE NEWS

by PHILLIP H. AULT

Executive Editor, Associated Desert Newspapers of California;
former United Press London bureau manager and war correspondent,
and assistant managing editor, Los Angeles Mirror-News

and EDWIN EMERY

Professor of Journalism, University of Minnesota; former United
Press San Francisco bureau manager, and editorial writer, St. Paul
Dispatch and Pioneer Press

New York · Toronto 1959

DODD, MEAD & COMPANY

Foreword

THE ROLE of the reporter grows constantly in importance as the complex pressures of life increase in this day of astounding scientific advances, social readjustments, and split-second communications. For those who enter it properly prepared mentally and technically, the profession of journalism offers a stimulating career of deep significance to our society.

With this in mind, the authors have undertaken to examine the reporter's function, and to discuss the techniques of newsgathering and writing that he needs. Our aim has been to produce a book that is practical and realistic. We have sought to base it upon the best principles and practices of contemporary journalism, in the hope that it will be accepted with equal validity in the classroom and the city room.

We wish to thank the following for their cooperation in extending permission to reprint news stories and other materials: the Associated Press, United Press International, New York *Times*, New York *Herald Tribune, Wall Street Journal,* Chicago *Daily News,* Chicago *Tribune,* St. Louis *Post-Dispatch,* Los Angeles *Mirror-News,* San Francisco *Chronicle,* Detroit *Free Press,* St. Paul *Pioneer Press,* Minneapolis *Star* and *Tribune,* Tulsa *Tribune,* Louisville *Times,* Indianapolis *Star,* Cleveland *Plain Dealer, Washington Post and Times Herald,* Milwaukee *Journal,* Cleveland *Press,* Miami *Herald, Journalism Quarterly, Nieman Reports,* and the Bell Syndicate, Inc.

Illustrations showing reporters in action were supplied by the

United Press International, the Associated Press, and the Minnea-polis *Star* and *Tribune*. Other photographs were generously sup-plied by these same three organizations and by the Chicago *Sun-Times*, Winona (Minn.) *Daily News*, San Francisco *Chron-icle*, Milwaukee *Journal*, *Christian Science Monitor*, Washing-ton *Post and Times Herald*, Louisville *Courier-Journal*, Chi-cago *Daily News*, the New York *Times* Studio, the United Fea-ture Syndicate, and the Columbia Broadcasting System.

The authors wish also to thank the newspapermen and women whose stories were used, and the photographers whose pictures appear in the book.

Finally, we wish to acknowledge the helpful criticisms and suggestions given by Professors Kenneth Stewart of the Univer-sity of Michigan and Richard L. Disney, Jr., of the University of Wisconsin, who reviewed the manuscript.

PHILLIP H. AULT *and* EDWIN EMERY

Contents

Part One: NEWS AND THE AUDIENCE

Part Two: WRITING THE NEWS

Part Three: THE TECHNIQUES OF REPORTING

Part Four: VARYING THE WRITING

Illustrations

NEWS

AND THE AUDIENCE

Chapter 1

The Reporter's Key Role

What Is Reporting?

News reporting has become an integral part of our contemporary civilization. Hardly any American lives through a day without receiving news in some form—from his newspaper, from radio and TV broadcasts, or through the more leisurely and comprehensive articles in magazines and other printed media.

Collecting and presenting this news is the business of a large group of specially trained men and women. Their task is fascinating, unpredictable, and demanding; the product they handle is perishable and mercurial.

The term "news" is broad and elastic. It covers such diverse events as a crucial United Nations Security Council meeting whose decisions may determine war or peace, a bus accident, the election of a new member to the town library board, the murder of a society leader, and a discovery in the fight against cancer.

The men and women who make newsgathering their career are of many talents and temperaments, although they share certain qualifications necessary to their craft. They perform a variety of functions. Some are concerned with reporting the news, some with handling it as copy desk men and news editors, some with interpreting it as editorial page writers and news specialists. Others concentrate on the mechanical problems of presenting news to the world.

3

The reporter is the most important of these experts; he is the heart of the newspaper and of the electronic media newsrooms. As William Rockhill Nelson, founder of the Kansas City *Star*, once put it, the reporter "is the big toad in the puddle. We could get along pretty well without our various sorts of editors. But we should go to smash if we had no reporters."

A definition of reporting broad enough to cover all media of information can be made in a single sentence:

Reporting means gathering information of interest to other people and presenting it to them accurately in a way which makes them understand and remember it.

Several fundamental questions arise out of that definition. What interests people? How does the reporter go about gathering such information? What techniques can he or she use to present news so that its meaning and significance are brought home clearly to the reader? The purpose of this book is to answer those questions in a realistic way and to show how news reporting functions in a high-speed world in which important developments can be flashed around the globe within a few seconds.

What Makes a Good Reporter?

Before going into a detailed study of newsgathering and writing, we should examine the seven qualifications required for a person to succeed as a reporter. A young reporter who has developed these qualifications should be able to make his or her way successfully, no matter what branch of newsgathering he or she enters. They are:

1. *An inquisitive mind.* The true reporter seeks information about any situation to which he is assigned because he feels a personal challenge to learn the full story of what is happening and why.

2. *Imagination.* A reporter must be able to grasp what a news situation means and where it may lead. He must also have the ability to realize what it is about this situation that other people—his audience—want and need to know.

3. *Tenacity.* He must be willing to work diligently and to

explore all possible avenues for pertinent information, to overcome obstructions and wade through masses of dull routine in
search of his story.

4. *Unswerving devotion to accuracy.* Distribution of misstatements, intentional or accidental, through the media of public information is a disservice. This may harm those involved in
the news situation and mislead those who receive the reporter's
faulty version of what happened. Carelessness is a cardinal sin of
reporting.

5. *Interest in his fellow humans.* News comes from people
and is reported to people. The good reporter needs a sympathetic interest in the activities of his news sources and curiosity
about why people behave as they do. The more he knows about
what interests other people, the better the job he can do in providing that information. He must have a desire to serve society
through a significant professional career.

6. *Good general knowledge.* A reporter handles assignments
involving many fields of activity. The more intelligently he asks
questions, the better the story he obtains. If he doesn't have
background information about a situation, he should know where
to obtain it.

7. *Ability to tell his story well.* A reporter's ingenuity and
perseverance are largely wasted if he cannot communicate his
information to his audience. The end result of all his efforts must
be a story which conveys the news to his readers clearly and
comprehensively.

This list of qualifications may look frightening to the beginner
who is starting to prepare himself or herself for journalism work.
"How can I ever expect to meet all those requirements?" he or
she asks. But take another look; they aren't nearly so forbidding
as they seem at first. We all possess a certain degree of inquisitiveness, imagination, tenacity, and interest in other people. In
training to be a reporter, you must concentrate on sharpening
these instincts. Accuracy is much like Thomas Carlyle's definition of genius: "an infinite capacity for taking pains." The basis
of a good general fund of knowledge is acquired in school; the
very fact that you are attending classes shows that you realize
the need for this. But remember: Learning must be a continuing

process after you have left school. In fact, for a news-minded person it should never stop. One purpose of this course is to teach the fundamentals of good news story writing, as practiced on the finest newspapers in the country.

Examined in this light, the list isn't so overwhelming. In fact, you are actually started on your way toward being a good reporter already.

Reporters are made, not born. A "nose for news" does not grow long and powerful automatically, like an elephant's trunk. It can be developed and trained by anyone who has a spark of imagination and the determination to develop it. Some students catch the knack of news reporting and writing quickly; others develop their skills only through laborious trial and error.

Some general tests for interest and aptitude in journalism include these: a record of work on high school or college newspaper or yearbook staffs; an interest in following the news; a liking for writing, early demonstrated; a liking for the social sciences or literature; a desire for creative service to society. In vocational interest tests, the would-be journalist usually scores well in the "author-lawyer-journalist" cluster. High ratings in clerical skills indicate reliability and interest in the detail work which sometimes falls to the journalist.

These guideposts are not infallible, however, and no one who is interested in journalism should turn away without fully experimenting with its possibilities. For journalism is many things, and it offers opportunities in many different professional fields to men and women with varying interests and talents developed out of a basic communicator's background.

Who Uses Reporting Skills?

The art of reporting is used far more widely than most people realize. It is quite evident that reporters play key roles in newspaper offices, radio and television newsrooms, news magazine offices, and in press association bureaus where news is gathered for these mass media. The use of reporting skills reaches much farther, however, into areas of journalistic work not directly concerned with handling the spot news developments of the day. Reporting is a basic skill for all communicators —magazine article writers, technical writers, news photographers, advertising and sales promotion personnel, public relations men and publicity men, and media researchers.

Writers of nonfiction articles for magazines do a reporting job before they write. And indeed, the fiction writer who is trained in reporting is likely to be more successful than his competitor who is not. News magazines such as *Time, Newsweek,* and *U.S. News & World Report* have large reporting staffs; but general magazines such as *Life, The Saturday Evening Post, Reader's Digest, Look,* and *The New Yorker* have staff reporters, too. Free-lance writers do exacting reporting jobs in the articles they submit to these and hundreds of other magazines. The men and women who edit the thousands of employee publications for industrial companies all report and interpret news.

Technical writing is a field of growing importance in our modern society. Science, engineering, medicine, agriculture, home economics, and business are some of the areas in which specialized and interpretive writing is needed. Before a technical writer can tell his story, however, he must gather his facts, do his organizing and interpreting, and decide what his reading audience can or should absorb about the subject.

News photography is a specialized form of reporting in which the camera replaces the typewriter. Newspapers, magazines, and television stations all seek constantly for photographers who know not only the skills of their craft, but what is newsworthy and how news is gathered. A "reporter-photographer" is a prized staff member, particularly for smaller newspapers.

Future advertising men and women usually question their need for learning reporting skills. They think of advertising as a sales operation and of advertising copy as being persuasive and exciting. But much advertising copy is informative in nature, and more often then not the advertising copywriter, the promotion writer, and the direct mail writer are drawing upon basic reporting skills. New products, new styles, new engineering achievements, new uses for products are all advertised. The advertising manager of a men's specialty clothing shop, for example, cannot hope to compete with the dominant department store in terms of repetitive advertising or price advertising. He has limited space in which to make his message count, and he stays one jump ahead by emphasizing new design, new fabrics, new buying trends. He thus is using the reporter's tools to sell a product. So is the department store advertising copywriter who goes to see a new model refrigerator before she writes her copy. So is the advertising agency account executive who undertakes extensive merchandising research about his client's product.

The fields of public relations and publicity writing attract many persons, the majority of whom have had previous experience with news organizations. Public relations is the management function which evaluates public attitudes, identifies the policies and procedures of the company or organization with the public interest, and executes a program of action to earn public understanding and acceptance. Publicity thus becomes a tool which the company uses to explain itself. Reporting experience is obviously needed in much public relations work. Information programs which are essentially reporting jobs are carried on in countless places—the Voice of America, federal government bureaus, state government offices, universities and colleges, community chests and social work organizations, business and trade associations, chambers of commerce, and industrial companies.

Media research is another growing field of specialization. The mass media need to know much more than they do about their own procedures and techniques, about public attitudes and opinions, about their audiences' reading, listening, and viewing habits and preferences. The media researcher understands and uses statistical tools, but he also understands and uses reporting skills in many of his activities.

In short, then, news is the heart of journalism and reporting is its basic skill. Fact-finding, story organizing, and effective writing are the specific elements to be mastered.

Starting Professional Careers

Many journalism students find it hard to believe that they will be accepted for professional work after graduation. This is a natural enough doubt. Yet journalism school records across the country show that graduating seniors do go directly into responsible work for the various media with substantial success.

The largest single group enters reporting. Many who later make the finest records get their start on small dailies or weeklies, where they must handle many aspects of reporting and editing and where they have the greatest opportunity for personal self-development and overcoming any natural tendency toward shyness. Those who go directly from school into large metropolitan papers face the danger of being restricted indefinitely to a limited job, such as overnight police reporter, without the opportunity to experience the broader aspects of news work.

Other journalism graduates fan out in smaller numbers into a variety of starting jobs. Some sell advertising for newspapers, a basic experience for advertising careers; some become newsmen or production men for radio and television stations; some join magazine staffs or edit a small publication; some become advertising copywriters for companies or stores; some join news desks of newspapers or become press association writers; some become news photographers.

Ten to fifteen years later some have become key persons in journalism. Our beginner now works as a science news writer, a city editor, a press association bureau chief, a magazine managing editor, a weekly newspaper owner, an advertising agency vice-president, a television news director, a Washington correspondent, a foreign correspondent, a newspaper advertising manager. These are not idle fancies; they are examples taken from journalism school records.

Newspapers Are Fundamental

The bulk of reporting work is done by newspapers and the press associations which supply them with national and foreign news. Many writers who go into other media, such as those just mentioned, have their training on newspapers. Often they are heard to say proudly, as though displaying a badge of distinction, "I used to be a newspaper reporter myself." The principles and methods they learn in the city room are useful to them in their more specialized fields. Therefore this book is

focused upon the daily newspaper, which remains the fundamental method of news dissemination in this country.

In later chapters, where newspaper operations are discussed
in detail from the reporter's viewpoint, staff alignments and functions are explained primarily in terms of the large city newspaper.
Smaller newspapers usually follow the same basic patterns, tailoring their staffs and assignments to the particular size and needs
of their communities. The differences are of degree rather than
principle. Police terminology and legal procedures vary from one
state to another. An effort has been made to present these subjects on as general a basis as possible, but minor changes of
phraseology may be necessary in some regions.

Development of the Reporting Concept

Reporters existed before the printing press was invented
some five hundred years ago, for man always has wanted and
needed to know the news. But organized methods of gathering
and printing news remained largely undeveloped even after
the first newspapers appeared in Europe at the close of the
sixteenth century. Newspaper editors in both Europe and colonial
America gleaned nonlocal domestic news and foreign news from
the columns of other papers. None had local news reporters as
we know them today.

Gradually American newspaper publishers sought to improve
their newsgathering status. By the 1830's the responsiveness of an
enlarged reading public, improved communications facilities, and
better printing processes resulted in the founding of a popular
newspaper press.

The penny press, as it was called, was the first to place major
emphasis upon reporting. In addition to dispatches on important
national and world events, it advanced a category of news called
"human interest"—stories with appeal based on writing skill
rather than necessarily upon news value. Local police reporters
augmented the budget of sensational or popular news—stories
involving the human passions, crime, violence, and the doings
of the famous and infamous.

Benjamin Day's New York *Sun* of 1833 was the pioneering

paper in this country in these respects. James Gordon Bennett, founder of the New York *Herald,* taught his competitors how to make news of economic and political significance popular through excellence of factual reporting and emphasis upon speed of transmission and "exclusiveness." Horace Greeley's New York *Tribune* and Henry J. Raymond's New York *Times* contributed an emphasis upon news interpretation. By the time of the Civil War, American newspaper editors had learned how to go out and get the news and how to present it in a fairly comprehensive and interesting fashion.

Gradually the newspaper developed the threefold function we know today: to inform, to express editorial opinion about the day's news, and to provide entertainment.

The coming of the telegraph permitted newspapers to organize press associations for cooperative newsgathering and distribution of nonlocal news. The New York morning newspapers founded the first Associated Press in 1848 to share the costs of collecting foreign news from the European newspapers which arrived by ship at East Coast seaports. With the laying of the Atlantic cable, the American press associations began making exchange agreements with European news agencies. They also developed domestic news coverage, spurred by the impact of the Civil War upon news reporting and newsgathering.

Industrialization and urbanization changed the face of America during the latter half of the nineteenth century, and its newspapers entered an era known as that of the "New Journalism." Increased concentration was placed on impartial gathering and reporting of the news. Newspaper editorial opinion became more independent of partisan pressures. Planned crusading in the community interest appeared in the news and editorial columns, and content was popularized further through style of writing, headlines, and pictures.

Joseph Pulitzer, with his St. Louis *Post-Dispatch* and New York *World,* was the best-known architect of the "New Journalism." He and other publishers of the period emphasized reporting because they had been reporters themselves—Charles A. Dana of the New York *Sun,* who emphasized the human interest element; Henry W. Grady of the Atlanta *Constitution,* who advanced the art of interviewing, along with Dana; Melville E. Stone of the Chicago *Daily News*. Others were essentially managers of news enterprises—Edward Wyllis Scripps and William Randolph Hearst with their newspaper chains and Adolph S. Ochs, who rebuilt the New York *Times* into a great newsgathering machine.

Reporters became stars by the turn of the century. Colorful and able men like Will Irwin, Lincoln Steffens, Jacob Riis, and Richard Harding Davis became nationally known. The "muckraking" reform era offered an opportunity to men like Steffens who wished to write about public affairs for a national magazine audience. Another group of men became known as "yellow journalists" because they took part in a wave of circulation-building sensationalism designed to attract new groups of readers. The "romance of reporting" was never more compelling to eager young men and women than in the decades preceding and following 1900.

Reporting Today

Events soon made the business of reporting the news far more complex. World War I and the postwar years, the great depression of the 1930's, and World War II brought enormous changes in American society. The mass media assumed new responsibilities for interpreting the news and raised their professional standards to meet this challenge. The modern press associations of the twentieth century demanded highly skilled staff men; radio and television each in its turn searched for reporters and news analysts of marked ability; the news magazines appeared to give reporters further professional opportunities. The leading newspapers, which traditionally had provided the training grounds for reporters, were aided by colleges and universities whose departments and schools of journalism were well established by the 1930's.

Newspapers, both large and small, found they needed men and women with both sound liberal educations and technical training in journalism if they were to cover the variety of news events and public issues which confronted them. Editors no longer wanted merely colorful writers as reporters. Some of the glamour of the "happy-go-lucky days" disappeared, but the authentic glamour of a socially responsible calling appeared. Today's newspapers are staffed predominantly by college-educated men and women who may be called upon to do specialized reporting of public affairs, education, business, science, and other types of serious news. Yet newspapers have learned that contemporary audiences also desire a sprinkling of light, whimsical stories and human interest articles to balance their news diet. The all-around reporter must be able to handle many kinds of stories competently, even though he is a specialist in some field.

What the Reporter Encounters

The young man or woman who becomes a newspaper reporter enters a unique world. Probably it is unlike anything he or she has encountered in life. Because newspapers deal with facts, the reporter at times finds himself in the midst of situations which are laden with violence, heroism, hatred, shock, sentiment, happiness, sorrow—the entire gamut of emotions in the human being.

Although he must walk hand in hand with unpleasantness, he also has the opportunity to report and frequently to assist in the innumerable constructive affairs of his community. By his skill with words he can make known the efforts and goals of men and women engaged in the work of government, welfare agencies, schools, charities, business and social activities. His field of interest embraces every aspect of his city's multitudinous activities.

At times his sensibilities will be shaken. Many of the sheltered viewpoints about life that he has had since childhood will be shattered. He will rub shoulders with men and women who believe that laws are made only to be circumvented; he will see death in distressing forms. Nobody spreads a blanket of niceties and soft phraseology over the rough facts of existence for his benefit, although he must perform that service for his readers.

It is his job to walk daily through the tumultuous emotions of life and report them to thousands of readers. They depend upon him for a balanced and honest report. As their eyes and ears he observes the daily grist of history and does his best to put it down on paper in the truest, most interesting form he is able to command.

Almost any newspaperman will tell the beginner that his is the most fascinating business in the world. Most of them believe what they say. Certainly it provides more contacts with human activities and a larger portion of stimulation than almost any other business. There is a thrill in being close to events as they happen. The reporter who approaches his job with curiosity about his fellow human beings and sympathy for them can find rewards in the business far surpassing those of his weekly pay check.

It is a mistake, however, for the beginning reporter to believe that his life will be a constant round of supercharged excitement. His daily work is marked by much routine and monotony, as is any job; the reply from his news sources that "there's nothing happening today" is heard far too often for his satisfaction. Yet he must keep diligently at his rounds, building his contacts and expanding his knowledge for the day when the big story does occur.

Reporting is highly competitive. The best reporter is one who fights with all the tenacity and ingenuity within his power to get an important fact into print first. He is competing not only against rival newspapers and other news media, but against the vast intangible forces which wittingly or unwittingly conceal the facts he wants. Very little news is handed to the reporter on a platter; even when it appears to be, he must keep looking beyond the obvious to see if there is a story behind the story. Frequently there is.

It is easy for a reporter to become cynical. From his privileged position he discovers that some of the personalities he has always respected have feet of clay and that at times a very thin line exists between right and wrong. Some newspapermen never recover from this disillusionment. But the successful ones gradually build a faith of their own in the essential goodness of people, putting the unpleasantness and dishonesty they see around them into perspective against the larger mass of constructive work and

good deeds which go on in any community endlessly, and often
with too little publicity.

Above all, the reporter develops a sense of pride in his work.
He finds his deepest satisfaction in the knowledge that he is helping to tell the people of his community what they as free citizens
have the right to know.

Chapter 2

Elements of News

Definition of News

"What's the news?" is a common question. Every reader asks it subconsciously as he picks up his newspaper from the doorstep or the newsstand at a corner. When he turns the dial to a newscast he wonders the same thing: "What has happened in the world that I'd like to know about?" The profession of journalism exists for the purpose of supplying the answers, every day of the year, for millions of readers and listeners.

Before the reporter can reply to this perennial query, however, there is another question to which he must have the answer. "What *is* news?"

What are the elements in a set of facts which make it newsworthy? Probably the subscriber who looks at the front page of his newspaper cannot define accurately what he means when he asks, "What's the news?" But the reporter needs to know what his audience is seeking. He cannot operate efficiently unless he is aware of the kinds of information to gather.

A definition of news might read:

News is a report of an event, containing timely (or at least hitherto unknown) information which has been accurately gathered and written by trained reporters for the purpose of serving the reader, listener, or viewer.

Accuracy, timeliness, and "reader interest" thus become the primary qualities of a report which is considered newsworthy. Serving the reader means providing him with information which he needs to regulate his life—information which affects him as an individual, either directly or in a more remote way, stimulates him by arousing his emotions, or entertains him. If the weather forecast in the morning paper predicts rain, he dresses accordingly. If the city council votes to build a new city hall, he knows that his tax bill will go up slightly. If a revolution breaks out in a Middle Eastern country, he realizes that his son or some other relative wearing an American uniform may be dispatched to that far-away land before the trouble is settled.

Accuracy

Accuracy is all important. When an event is taking place, men and women turn to the news media to get a correct and honest report. One of editor Joseph Pulitzer's famous commands was "Accuracy! Accuracy!! Accuracy!!!" He meant, first of all, to get the facts straight and to report facts rather than rumors. He also meant to report the event objectively—to get both sides of the story, to exclude human bias insofar as possible, to avoid partisan presentation calculated to deceive the reader. But he meant, finally, that the reporter should, when necessary, interpret the meaning of the event in terms of its relation to a larger situation or to other events. A report which does not meet these tests of accuracy is unworthy of being called news.

Timeliness

News is a perishable commodity, sped to the marketplace to be sold for a price. The purchaser of a newspaper or news magazine pays the circulation rate to read the latest news. The sponsor of a radio or television newscast pays to have his advertising message told to an audience attracted to hear or see the latest news. The advertiser in a newspaper or magazine, of course, is paying for the use of space adjacent to the same news. Each of the press associations which serve these mass media justifies its existence by striving to deliver the news ahead of its competitors.

This fight to be first becomes so intense that a press association bureau in London once received a glowing cable of congratulations from its office in Buenos Aires because it had delivered news of an important British election to Argentina *fifteen seconds* ahead of its competitor.

Timeliness is not the only element which determines the profit-making ability of news media. But they are distinguished from other sources of information by this characteristic. Being "first with the news" is their business. In the relatively few cities where direct competition between newspapers exists, beating the opposition is a constant objective and tying with the opposition is a necessity. Newspaper and television reporters vie with each other to get the news first. Sometimes little more than professional pride is at stake, since the news item involved is of minor importance to the reader or listener. But without the impulse to "get it now" those in the news business would become slack. Even where there is no competing medium, the truly professional newsman regards the factor of timeliness as one of his primary obligations. His readers have paid for news, not recent history.

Accuracy must not be sacrificed in the rush to be first with the news. Throughout the history of journalism, newsmen have sought to solve the problem presented to them by the twin commands of "accuracy" and "timeliness." The injunction "Get it first, but get it right" is a splendid one, but it is not always easy to obey it. The larger aspect of accuracy, which involves proper interpretation of an event, comes into play here. To obtain a full interpretation reporters sometimes work for weeks before they break a story to the reading public. But at other times the competition to tell the news forbids waiting, and as a result the news media are subjected to criticism for telling only one side of a story or for printing an inadequately interpreted account.

The reason for putting accuracy first should be obvious to anyone. Accuracy without promptness is better than promptness without accuracy, but neither combination will win any plaudits for a reporter.

In the office of an afternoon newspaper, rewrites of news published in morning papers and reports of early morning events are due in time for the first edition, not the second edition. The afternoon paper aims to publish today's news and some of yesterday's late news, along with predictions of things to come. The morning paper covers yesterday's and last night's news. The weekly newspaper and the weekly news magazine make the news as timely as possible in covering the period since previous publication. Nothing is as dead in a newspaper office as a story which should have been in the previous edition, but wasn't. Radio and television—with their early morning, noon, early evening, and late evening newscasts—work at an even faster pace.

Timeliness is not always measured by the hands of a clock, however. A local interview will be timely if it can be presented in the same edition with a related story carried on the press association wire. A streak of mistaken weather forecasts will make an interview with the harassed weatherman timely. Historical features are more timely during a city's centennial year than during its 99th or 101st years—especially the latter. Baseball stories become timely in early spring; football stories in August; and so on.

It should be pointed out that timeliness does not always operate as a factor in determining newsworthiness. There are feature interviews and human interest stories which are interesting whenever read. Although this is true, the reporter should never assume that such stories will wait for him indefinitely. Many a reporter has read unhappily in a rival paper the story he intended to do sometime. The same injunction applies to a story which deals with an event of the past, the outcome of which has remained unknown. A story confirming unmistakably the manner in which Adolf Hitler met death in 1945 would still be news. But the reporter who obtained the information would be well advised to rush his account into print before a competitor somehow obtained the same facts. In that sense, timeliness is always a factor in the world of news.

Reader Interest

People have many different reasons for becoming interested in specific terms of news. Also, there are numerous tests by which a reporter can determine whether an accurate and timely set of facts he has collected will make a good news story. The trained reporter instinctively runs this information through his mental assay furnace to see how well it passes these tests.

Wilbur Schramm, in his essay entitled "The Nature of News" (published in *Journalism Quarterly* in 1949 and reprinted in *Mass Communications,* a book of readings edited by Schramm), says it is self-evident that the reader, viewer, or listener expects to be rewarded. Some news, Schramm says, gives the reader the pleasure of an immediate reward. This is human interest or exciting news of transitory interest: features, sports, society, accidents, disasters, crime, sex. Other news—called "hard news" by editors—is concerned with unpleasant reality. The reader is informed about important situations which will affect him later and thus anticipates a delayed reward. Delayed reward, Schramm says, can be expected from news of public affairs, economic matters, social problems, science, education, weather, and health.

In short, some news is offered readers, listeners, and viewers primarily because it is interesting. Other news is offered primarily because it is significant. If the news is both interesting and significant, it makes a big story, indeed.

Three important concepts which affect the degree of reader interest attached to news should now be treated in detail. They are significance, proximity, and prominence.

Significance

News is judged to be significant when the event has consequences for readers which they can understand by reading the story. A bumper wheat crop can be reported simply as a matter of facts: there will be so many more bushels of grain than in previous years. But a significant news story will go beyond this. How will the crop affect the government's agricultural programs? What, in turn, will be the political effects? What will happen to the price of wheat, and consequently how will general farm economy fare? How about the consumer?

The story of the release of atomic energy by man, given to the world in August 1945 when the first atomic bomb was dropped at Hiroshima, is a classic example of news of incalculable significance. A strike in automobile factories which supply the nation has more consequence than a strike in an industry serving one immediate area—except in that area. Americans have learned the hard way that a politico-military crisis in Manchuria, Ethiopia, Indo-China, Egypt, or Algeria can have great consequence in Rapid City, South Dakota. Unfortunately we have not yet learned that news of socio-economic events in India, Southeast Asia, and China should be followed as closely as similar news coming from the traditional centers of influence in Western Europe.

Proximity

An editor of the Kansas City *Star* once remarked that "the farther away from Kansas City it is, the less it is news." This sounds dangerously provincial, but properly applied the concept of geographical proximity has validity. Local news is the backbone of virtually all news operations. Even the *Christian Science Monitor* and the *Wall Street Journal,* our two nationally circulating newspapers specializing in significant news, are careful to include regional-interest news in their various editions. Radio and television stations have local and regional news programs as well as national network news shows.

Excellence in local and regional news coverage has been a primary reason for the economic success of such great newspapers as the Milwaukee *Journal,* the St. Louis *Post-Dispatch,* the Louisville *Courier-Journal,* the Washington *Post and Times Herald,* and others known for their high news standards and opinion leadership. Papers which have developed their own foreign news staffs—the New York *Times,* New York *Herald Tribune,* Chicago *Daily News*—have also competed intensely in local news. The average American daily newspaper, which has a circulation of not more than 10,000 copies and serves a town of about 20,000 population and its surrounding trade area, regards proximity of events as a matter of high importance in selection of news. So does the average small-town radio station. The weekly newspaper's mission is to give the local news, and it looks for what is called the "local angle" in everything it prints.

The Continuing Study of Newspaper Reading—a study of 138

newspapers from 1939 to 1950 conducted by the Advertising Research Foundation—offers an insight into the pulling power of local news. A summary lists the individual stories receiving the highest percentage of readership in the particular issues under study. The best-pulling story during the normal postwar years, combining scores for both men and women, appeared in the Lima, Ohio, *News*. The headline read: "Judge Smith Dies Suddenly in Home." It received 86 per cent readership by men and 91 per cent by women. Of the eleven top stories for men, eight were local in nature; of the eleven top stories for women, seven were local in nature.

Readers identify themselves with news about other persons in their own communities and with news of their communities, regions, and states. A tornado 100 miles away is more intensely interesting than one 1000 miles away—and, of course, the newspaper can throw its own reporting resources into the story 100 miles away. Inevitably, much local news is concerned with individuals, groups, governmental bodies, and businesses whose activities are of interest only in their home town. Only the local paper can let them read about themselves and their neighbors, and this is the local paper's secret of success. The success of rapidly growing dailies in the outskirts of such metropolitan centers as New York and Los Angeles in recent years, and the similar growth of suburban weeklies outside Detroit and other cities, is evidence of this simple journalistic truth. During the 1950's the largest mass-circulating metropolitan dailies tended to decline in percentage of total newspaper circulation, and the circulation of smaller community dailies increased because they could reach closer home to their readers.

Proximity should not be regarded entirely as a matter of geography, however, important as that factor is. "Sameness" might describe another reader-interest element. A city which has an aviation company building planes is interested in the subject of plane building wherever the events take place. Growers of oranges in Florida are interested in news of the California orange groves. Newspapermen, doctors, professors, and business executives are interested in their counterparts in other areas. As the communications barriers of the world shrink each year and as interdependence of areas and peoples becomes more pronounced, geographic proximity tends to be interpreted more generally. But such news will only augment the basic staple of geographically local news.

Prominence

The Judge Smith who died in Lima, Ohio, was prominent locally, and sudden death is always shockingly newsworthy. Thus a combination of factors accounted for the phenomenally high readership of his obituary. People who achieve prominence are interesting subjects of news stories, and their public and private lives always have been subject to public curiosity. Our news coverage of presidents, royalty, movie stars, and millionaires is nothing new. The ballad singers who antedated newspaper editors learned to sing about princesses and kings, their loves and sorrows. Let the town's leading businessman or professional man slip, and people cluck, "He's not so great." Let him win an award and people say, "Isn't that wonderful?" It was always thus.

Community groups are well aware of the pulling power of prominence. They borrow the names of prominent citizens for their committee lists, expecting the newspaper to run a story for this reason. They get a prominent speaker for their luncheon meeting, knowing that his name will make the speech report more newsworthy, as indeed it might. Newspapers need to exercise caution in paying too much attention to the doings of prominent folk at the expense of not mentioning more average readers, but they cannot ignore the basic interest the mass of readers have in well-known persons.

Once a person has achieved prominence or notoriety he is always newsworthy. People want to hear the end of every story, and the Charles A. Lindbergh who became the first man to fly from New York to Paris in 1927 will always be interesting. The once-great baseball star or opera singer who dies in obscurity has a final story printed about him or her in most newspapers.

People of prominence also figure in the news because they are in a position to make news. What a United States senator thinks about an issue of public importance is far more newsworthy than what an average citizen thinks because the senator casts a crucial vote in Washington. Ex-senators find their opinions do not rate so much attention or space for this simple reason.

Human Interest

Sometimes a newspaper runs a front page story about someone who lives far away, who is not prominent, and who has done something which is not particularly newsworthy in point of timeliness. But to the reader, the story is "just plain interesting" and that is reason enough for running it. Probably the story has what is called "human interest" qualities either because of the way it was written or because of what the story tells.

Helen MacGill Hughes, author of the classic book *News and the Human Interest Story*, points out the emphasis placed on this "human interest" quality throughout journalistic history. The human emotions may be involved: love, hate, sorrow, laughter, suspense, sympathy. Conflict and progress are two contending forces in the news stream. Births, marriages, and deaths are the "vital statistics" of life, and death particularly is a subject of deep human concern. Unusualness in the circumstances of otherwise ordinary events holds interest for us.

Joseph Pulitzer put it this way in a memo to his reporters: Cover the news of St. Louis incessantly. Look for the significant news. But look also for the "original, distinctive, dramatic, romantic, thrilling, unique, curious, quaint, humorous, odd, apt to be talked about" news. Pulitzer, himself a reporter before he founded the *Post-Dispatch*, did not have to read about elements of human interest to know what was "apt to be talked about" and was therefore news.

Stories involving the emotions are our oldest type. A humorous bit, a light story about young lovers, a story which can make us hate, a tale of quiet sorrow, a misadventure which evokes sympathy: these can be as interesting if told from afar by a press association writer as if written locally. The skill of the writer counts a great deal. If, of course, the persons involved are prominent, interest is enhanced. One of the greatest suspense stories of all time—because it involved royalty, sex, and conflict—was

Celebrities + Emotion + Sex
"Dammit," cried the Duchess, "take your hand off my kne

the day-by-day drama which ended in the abdication of King Edward VIII in favor of life as the Duke of Windsor with "the woman I love."

Conflict is often interesting, and newspapers are sometimes criticized for emphasizing it. Actually, if properly handled, progress is just as interesting a theme as the ordinary stories of conflict. People want to feel they are making progress, collectively if not individually, and advances in science, education, the arts, medicine, and other fields are interesting as well as significant. News sources have to work harder to demonstrate that their stories of progress are as worthy of news space as their fight stories. But perceptive reporters will learn to gauge the true news values of both types of events.

Readership surveys show that babies and very old persons make as interesting picture subjects as beautiful women, despite popular emphasis upon what is called "cheesecake." Animals are always interesting subjects. Fala, President Franklin D. Roosevelt's dog, became as well known as top officials of the government. The San Francisco *News*, during the height of the closing days of World War II, took time out to run a page one, column-length picture of a mother giraffe and its baby, just born at the local zoo.

There is nothing wrong with human interest in the news. Unless newspapers have reporters who can inject qualities of human interest into their writing, they will not hold reader attention. Readers want some entertainment along with the fare of significant news, and whatever they are offered should be written as interestingly as possible. Stories involving people invariably interest readers more than abstract situations. When a situation can be told in terms of people, so much the better. If a reporter is assigned to do a story about how strikers are living without pay in a prolonged labor dispute, an account of one typical family's experiences is more effective than a generalized statement and as important to include as the statistical summary for the group. Similarly, an increase in gas rates is a major story since most readers use gas, but an illustration of how the rate change will affect two or three families' gas bills in dollars and cents will make the story even more interesting and understandable.

Summary

News is an accurate report of a timely event which proves to have interest or significance for the reader, listener, or viewer. In a perfect society, all citizens would read and understand full accounts of significant events, and "human interest" elements would not be perverted into mere sensationalism. But there is no such society, and the news media must be responsive to their audiences. The media also produce the news under obvious limitations: news which they want to tell is not always available, despite their efforts; space in the newspaper and time on the air are limited, and hard choices must be made between newsworthy topics; reporters and editors must follow routines of collecting and printing news which sometimes produce a mediocre grist that passes for news. Future chapters will develop in much greater detail the explanation of how the reporter applies what he knows about the elements of news in his daily work.

Chapter 3

The Audience

Serving the Reader

If a reporter had a motto to hang behind his typewriter it would read: "Serve the reader." The newsman's task is to tell the reader what he needs and wants to know, and to do it in a way that pleases him. The free press guarantee in our Constitution ensures the publication's right to print what it desires, and it does so to protect the people's right to know. Thus the reporter carries a heavy responsibility to serve his reader; unless he does so, he is unworthy of his profession.

From an economic standpoint, too, mass media can exist only so long as they enjoy the acceptance of their audience. The disappearance of several long-established newspapers from the metropolitan scene in recent years can be attributed largely to the fact that they failed to keep step with their readers' needs and could not attract enough new readers to cover their constantly rising cost of operation.

When a reporter sits down at his typewriter with his notes, he should ask himself several questions. Who are the readers of my newspaper? Which of them are likely to be interested in this story? How can I attract the largest possible percentage of them to read what I am about to write?

Often a reporter, impressed by the significance of the story he has been covering, mutters to himself, "A lot of people ought to know about this!" To put his story across to the maximum number of readers, the reporter should keep an image of his potential audience in mind. The newspaper in which his story appears will come into the hands of many kinds of people—the businessman reading on the bus while coming home from work, the housewife who wipes dishwater from her hands before she sits down to read, the retired plumber sitting on a bench in the city park, the teen-age boy who devours the baseball standings and then glances through the main news section, the attractive secretary whose thoughts are primarily of romantic things, the men waiting in the barber shop for a haircut. His is a heterogeneous audience. The same is true for news broadcasters on radio and television.

Reader Selectivity

None of these people will read all the stories in the newspaper. Most of them don't have the time to consume every word, or think they haven't; more important, there are many stories in every issue which fail to interest some of the readers. Nobody tells each person what he must read, and so he chooses only those stories which interest him. This is the basic principle of reader selectivity.

To see this principle in operation, ask half a dozen people—your family or a group of friends—to go through a newspaper with you after they have all read it. Have each one point out the stories he or she read in full, glanced at only long enough to get the gist, or passed over entirely. Compare their choice with your own. You will find an extremely wide range of selections, each governed by the individual's tastes, needs, experience, and interests.

Since there are so many kinds of readers in a newspaper's audience, and the reporters and editors who produce the publication must try to serve them all, the paper obviously must print many kinds of news. If his story is exciting enough, and laden with human emotions, the reporter who tells it well can expect to capture a large percentage of those readers. But many other stories in the paper are equally essential, even though they attract a small fraction of the total reading audience. The story may be read by only 5 per cent of the newspaper's subscribers, but to that 5 per cent it is extremely important. Therefore a newspaper must publish a budget of news and features as heterogeneous as the audience which receives it.

The Continuing Study of Newspaper Reading summary showed that among readers of 138 newspapers studied, men read an average of 14 per cent of all the items in a paper, and women read an average of 11 per cent. Only one-fourth of the stories were read by 30 per cent or more of the potential audience; one-fourth had 4 per cent or less leadership. Although reporters are always looking for the big story, they are usually writing for splinters of the potential audience. Their challenge is to present these limited-interest stories in a manner which will attract the largest possible number of readers.

Radio and television newsmen are in a different position. Their audiences listen or watch, intently or indifferently, for the entire time of the newscast. These are mass audiences without much power of selectivity. Items of limited appeal cannot be used except at the peril of boring and losing a good deal of the audience. Radio and television must concentrate on those stories which received 30 per cent or more of the newspaper readers' attention. Nor do they have the time to present more than a fraction of what the newspaper presents in its available news space.

Readers, being people, are a peculiar and unpredictable lot. A large metropolitan daily recently made a survey of former subscribers to find out their opinions about the paper. A substantial number had become dissatisfied because they felt the paper printed too much sensational crime and sex news. Some said the paper should print more "hard news" about national and international affairs; some had dropped their subscriptions because they couldn't find the advertising they wished to read, while others complained about too much advertising; some had quit because of the newsboy; some wanted more sports news; some felt a lack of news about their suburb; some just didn't have time to read the paper. From among these, the housewife who sent in this comment must have frustrated the conscientious editors: "You have a fine newspaper. As soon as we are not so busy with the Cub Scouts we will subscribe to it again."

Weekly newspapers, with their concentration on local news appeal in smaller communities, are more thoroughly read than are small dailies, and they, in turn, get a higher average readership per item than do the big metropolitan papers. The sheer bulk of a metropolitan paper is one factor explaining this situation. Other factors which lower the average readership per item are diversity of the news offerings and diversity of the audience.

Audience Diversity

In competitive cities substantial differences among the newspaper audiences are apparent. The character and aims of each newspaper attract certain kinds of readers who find that it gives them more of the particular information they desire than does its rival. Some newspapers are intentionally tailored to an audience through the kind of news stories featured and the political positions taken in the editorial columns. In other instances, the paper's character develops instinctively as a reflection of the personalities of the men who publish it.

The audiences of the sedate New York *Times* and the tabloid New York *Daily News* will serve as examples. One would be mistaken if he assumed much more than that *Times* readers want to be more fully informed than do *Daily News* readers. Both papers have readers in all educational and economic levels. The *Daily News* serves several times as many readers as does the *Times,* and it achieved its huge circulation by emphasizing human interest and entertainment aspects which attract the most casual of the city's readers. But it still prints enough news to be the despair of its competitors. The *Times,* with its slogan, "All the news that's fit to print," is not unaware of the importance of human interest and entertainment appeal and satisfies enough readers on this score to maintain a healthy position.

In the vast majority of towns and cities where weekly or daily newspapers are published, everyone reads the same paper. This does not mean that people do not have access to other news media. They hear radio news and see television news; some subscribe to a paper from another city; some subscribe to news magazines. One fairly sizable group of people in any community will follow the news through all of these means and, in addition, will read other magazines and books and watch educational television. This group is drawn from various educational and economic levels; its only cohesiveness is found in a common interest in being informed. Certainly these persons make up a special and demanding audience for the local newspaper. Those who read or hear a minimum of news anywhere make up another special audience which wishes mainly to be entertained.

Reader Selectivity in Operation

Some examples of reader selectivity can be given from readership survey results of a large metropolitan morning newspaper. Virtually every reader read at least part of one story on page one (97 per cent) and at least part of one story on the remaining pages of the first section (92 per cent). The local news page opening the second section had a 72 per cent score on the same basis. In sports, 79 per cent of the men and 20 per cent of the women read at least part of one item, for an average of 48 per cent. In women's news, 79 per cent of the women and 24 per cent of the men read at least part of one item, for an average of 53 per cent. By contrast, 66 per cent of the men and 79 per cent of the women read at least one comic strip, for an average of 73 per cent, and 94 per cent of the women and 62 per cent of the men saw at least one display advertisement, for an average of 79 per cent.

But what about individual stories? The lead story on page one, judged most important news of the day, drew 30 per cent readership (45 per cent of the men, 18 per cent of the women). It was about international affairs and dealt with a military crisis in the Middle East. Another story on page one, placed in the left top position, drew the best readership: 72 per cent (76 per cent of the men, 69 per cent of the women). It was a state story with the headline: "Farmer Crawls 2 Miles, Surrenders in Shooting." Seven stories and two pictures on page one out-drew the lead story in readership. So did stories back on pages 8 and 9. So did Ann Landers' advice column on page 16. So did a local columnist. And so did the classified ads, as a group.

Does this mean the editors used poor news judgment? Not at all. It means the audience exercised reader selectivity. The lead story was by all odds the most significant and important story of the day. Its headline was seen by 60 per cent of the readers ("Egypt Rushes Troops to Aid Syrian Defense"). Only 36 per cent went on to glance at the story; 30 per cent read part of it; 14 per cent read all of it. The rest decided, correctly enough, that war would not break out and went about their other reading.

In other years, readers of the same newspaper read the lead story in greater numbers: 87 per cent, 60 per cent, 55 per cent, 43 per cent, 39 per cent. The story which drew 87 per cent readership was about a South American man who New York doctors had decided might be more than 150 years old! The 60 per cent readership story was about a 7-inch rain which had flooded downtown Chicago—an out-of-state story for the newspaper publishing it. The pull of human interest is amply demonstrated in these instances.

What about the stories with less than 10 per cent readership, which amount to half of those published? For a big metropolitan paper, 10 per cent means 30,000 to 40,000 readers, assuming even two readers for each copy. A story or advertisement drawing only 1 per cent readership had at least 1000 readers for each 100,000 copies. Perhaps you have been the subject of a news story in your local paper; if so, you were surprised by the large number of persons who made it known that they had seen the item, no matter how small it was. Readers who didn't know you skipped the item, but somehow a lot of readers who did know you saw it. The same reader response is true for other limited-interest items.

Writing for Different Audiences

Let us suppose that a writer has all of the information about a plant which will use atomic power to produce electricity. If he writes a story for a scientific journal he will have an audience well informed about the subject, one which will want quite a bit of technical information and will not need much simplified explanation. If he writes a story for *Science Digest*, he still will have a "sophisticated" audience which will be interested in technical details. If he writes a story for the *Reader's Digest,* he will have a potential audience of eleven million readers; the magazine will want to emphasize the human interest element of progress and will want more background explanation of peaceful use of atomic energy. The same will be true if he writes a story for the nearest metropolitan newspaper. Technical information will still be included, but it will be subordinated so that only those readers who wish to continue through the entire story will reach it.

The same principles can be applied in writing other stories for newspapers. The opening paragraphs of a story about a legislative hearing on a tax reform bill should contain summaries of the information the reporter thinks will be of interest to the largest number of readers. More intricate details of how the bill will affect smaller groups should await coverage in the lower part of the story. More readers would be induced to read international news if some of the unfamiliar names of persons and places could be omitted from the story's opening and introduced later on. This can sometimes be done without reducing the effectiveness of the story or outraging the sensibilities of the minority of readers who are highly informed on international events. Casual readers who stop after a few paragraphs would thus get the gist of the news, and thorough readers would learn the details. When a casual reader stumbles over something he doesn't understand, he quits reading, and the reporter's goal is to keep him reading.

Simplicity of writing is increasingly being recognized as a key to better readership. One press association even carried on a campaign among its reporters to "write it as you would tell it to your wife!"

Because readers exercise the power of selectivity, however, reporters often write briefly and directly to a limited audience. The education writer at times will want to present information to the widest possible audience; at other times his story is of interest only to those who are his regular readers and he will make little attempt to interest others. The business writer has a lot of routine earnings statements of corporations to report to his regular readers; once in a while one of these statements has interesting enough implications (rapid growth, sharp earnings increase or surprising decline) to warrant a different type of story written for general readership. Women's news reporters and sports reporters usually write for consistent groups of readers. But they, too, will watch for opportunities to enlarge their audiences when the right story comes along.

Summary

We have now reached the point at which you will want to begin writing. There will be more discussion of the elements of news and of writing for the audience, with specific examples of writing styles and reporting techniques. If you remember that you are not writing for yourself, but for a segment of the reading audience, you will be better able to judge such elements as timeliness, proximity, prominence, significance, and human interest.

Part Two

WRITING THE

NEWS

Chapter **4**

The Basic Story Form

The Inverted Pyramid Story

Writing "news style" does not seem very hard. The experienced reporter glances at his set of facts and the words of his opening paragraph fall into place, one by one, in his mind. The order of the remaining paragraphs is quickly resolved. He slips his copy paper into his typewriter and writes something like this:

James B. Reston, Pulitzer prize-winning Washington bureau chief for the New York Times, will speak on "Politics and the Reporter" at 8 p.m. Monday in Scott auditorium.

Reston's appearance on campus is sponsored by Sigma Delta Chi, professional journalistic fraternity, as a part of Journalism Week.

Winner of the 1945 and 1957 Pulitzer prizes for national reporting, Reston is widely known for his coverage of political and diplomatic news from the nation's capital.

He will describe problems faced by reporters who bring the stories of national political campaigns to their readers, George T. Brown, Sigma Delta Chi chapter president, said yesterday.

Reston has been a member of the Times staff since. . . .

The "experienced reporter" who might have written such a story is a college junior. Four years before he was fumbling with words and paragraphs for his high school newspaper. Now he is writing in much the same form as the five-year veteran on the downtown daily. He knows how to do the newspaper's bread-and-butter story, even though he as yet lacks the skill and experience to report and write in the wider range of the professional.

What he has done is to gather his facts and organize them into the most common of the newspaper's story forms. It is known as the "inverted pyramid" form.

His opening paragraph is called a summary lead. A "lead" (sometimes spelled "lede") is simply the opening of a story. A true summary lead tells the reader the essence of the important news in a single paragraph in contrast to modified summary leads which carry the same information in the first two or three paragraphs. In either case, the rest of the story expands upon and explains the information given to the reader in the lead.

From the lead the copy desk writes a headline: "Reston to Speak on Campus Monday." The reader sees the bigger type of the headline. *Who is Reston?* he wonders if he does not recognize the name. *What* will Reston be saying? *When* will he speak—afternoon or evening? *Where?* The reader's four questions are answered in the first paragraph of our summary lead story. If he is interested he reads more, and he discovers *why* Reston has been invited to the campus and *more about who* he is *and what* he will say.

Suppose the night editor of the college paper is unable to run more than four paragraphs of the story underneath the headline. The essential news has already been told to the reader, even if Reston's biography disappears. If only three paragraphs can be used, the story still tells the reader the "who, what, when, where, and why" and something additional about the "who." If only two paragraphs will fit, just the additional "who" is lost. And if only one paragraph can be slipped into the type form, the reader at least knows *who* will speak about *what, when,* and *where.*

These are the reasons from the newsman's point of view for using the summary lead and the story form known as the "inverted pyramid." If you placed a pyramid upside down over the block of type which forms this news story, the wide base would cover the lead paragraph and the narrow point would reach the last sentence. The area of the pyramid represents news interest, and as the story is cut from the bottom the least possible area of the pyramid disappears. What is most important, a coherent story is left at each point where the news editor or the makeup editor might decide the story must end. The headline writer has found the essence of the story in the opening sentences. The most interesting facts have been told within the space allotted to the story.

The reader also finds this style of writing news helpful. He usually spends only 30 or 35 minutes paging through a full-sized metropolitan daily. A headline beckons; the eye rests on the opening lines of body type. A newspaperman speaking about politics? Disinterested, the reader looks over instead at the picture in the next column. Interested, he reads a second paragraph, a third, or perhaps the entire story.

Is the story the most interesting which could be written about Reston and his campus appearance? Undoubtedly not. It does not reflect Reston's personality; the reader does not get the feel of the work of a Washington political reporter; the human interest element is not emphasized.

But the story does the job it is intended to do. The reporter has gathered the necessary facts and has organized them for reading ease. Within the space allotted him, he has made words count. He has used facts, not generalities, to identify Reston. He might have called him "a well-known member of the Washington staff of the New York Times" in his opening sentence, but he has learned not to waste words that way. "Pulitzer prize-winning Washington bureau chief for the New York Times" takes no more space and offers the reader evidence of the validity of the later qualitative phrase, "widely known."

As an initial announcement of the coming lecture, the story tells the reader what he wants to know. If the reporter and his editors feel a second story is justified, perhaps they will find out more about Reston and his journalistic accomplishments. Under what circumstances did he win his Pulitzer prizes? How does he go about his work? When he arrives on campus, the reporter can interview him. A feature interview story will make the reader feel he knows something about the man behind the name.

But all this coverage may not be justified if the paper is to tell the reader the rest of the news each day. Journalism students will be most interested in Reston; after them political science students, some faculty members, the local readers of the New York *Times*, and so on. How big a slice of the total readership of the paper do they represent? What other important or interesting news is breaking these same days?

These are the problems which brought about the rise of the "news style" which is based upon the use of the summary lead and the inverted pyramid form of story. Much of the news must be told briefly and succinctly. This never means that it is to be told dully. Within this precise form which he often uses, the reporter strives always to use the words which will be most interesting, to tell the facts which are most valuable to the reader, to put together an easily read and understandable story.

Where the Basic Story Form Began

If you have listened to radio or television newscasts more regularly than you have read newspapers, you might well be saying, "Why write that way?" Why not say something like this:

A Pulitzer prize-winning Washington newsman will speak on our college campus Monday. He is James B. Reston of the New York Times. His eight o'clock talk will describe the way reporters cover national political campaigns. . . .

Newspapers are behind the times, you might be thinking. They are using a basic story form which is out of date.

It is true enough that the summary lead dates back to the 1880's. Before that time newspapers usually presented the news in chronological style—each event following the other in time sequence even though the climax of the action came after several columns of type had been set. There had been men such as Lawrence A. Gobright of the Associated Press who, faced with tremendous news, had simply blurted it out over the telegraph:

WASHINGTON, Friday, April 14, 1865—The President was shot in a theater tonight, and perhaps mortally wounded.

But even though headline writers were seizing upon the important news and using it in series of heads running down the column, the reporter was not following their idea of getting the gist of the most important facts into easy view.

Then came the revolution in newspaper-making known both to the newsmen of the times and to journalistic historians as the "New Journalism." In the industrialized America of the latter part of the nineteenth century, new reading audiences developed in the growing cities and towns. Newspaper publishers such as Joseph Pulitzer with his St. Louis *Post-Dispatch* and New York *World*, Melville Stone with his Chicago *Daily News*, Edward Wyllis Scripps with his Cleveland *Press*, and William Randolph Hearst with his San Francisco *Examiner* and New York *Journal* followed a new trend. They recognized that the basic function of the press was to provide widespread and impartial reporting of the news. They saw that a mass-read newspaper, appealing to a variety of audiences, needed to be popular in content and style of writing. They emphasized clear, simple, and understandable writing. And as they included a greater variety of news and feature stories in their papers, they were forced to develop brief, succinct coverage of much of the day's news.

So the rambling, loosely written story, often depending upon the chronological form of the storyteller, began to give way in the competition for newspaper space. By 1894, when Edwin L. Shuman wrote the first American textbook in journalism, *Practical Journalism*, he declared that "the style followed almost universally in large American newspaper offices at present" was to write a first paragraph containing the "marrow of the whole story." In a 1903 edition, Shuman listed the famous "5 W's"—who, what, where, when, and why—as questions to be answered in the first paragraph. Later "how" was added as an alternative to "why."

Cementing the summary lead and inverted pyramid form into American journalism was the growing influence of the press associations. The Associated Press of the nineteenth century and its twentieth century competitors, the United Press and the International News Service (now combined as United Press International), delivered news to the newspaper offices, first by telegraph and later by teletype printers. Space on the wires was limited; competition to deliver the news first was keen. The press associations found the summary lead technique ideal for presenting the gist of a story—if it were important news and a newspaper's press deadline was at hand, the single paragraph could go into the paper. The inverted pyramid form of story likewise served the press associations' purposes admirably, whether they told stories within 100-, 200-, or perhaps 500-word limits, or let more important stories run at length. Wire editors could more easily select the length of story they could use, without extensive rewriting.

Modifying the Summary Lead

But as in the case of all formulas for writing, this one could be misused. The trouble came when a slavish effort was made to get all the "5 W's" and perhaps the additional "how" into the opening paragraph. Too many inadequately trained and uninspired news writers failed to see that to be interesting they should place chief emphasis upon the one or two "W's" which were most essential and eye-catching in a particular news situation. Then they could work details of the remaining "W's" into the second or third paragraphs, if not the first. In other words, a good news writer exercises his power of selection among these essential points in the interest of attractive reading, but gets them all in early in the story.

The all-inclusive summary lead, lacking any emphasis upon the one or two most important of the "W's" and containing too much detail about all five, became the curse of modern journalism. A typical example is this New York *Times* lead of 1898:

The West End Hotel and seven cottages at Rockaway Beach were destroyed by fire which started shortly after 11 o'clock last night in the hotel. The hotel was a four-story frame structure at the corner of Grove, Hammells, and Ocean Avenues. It contained 200 rooms and was owned by Paul Hauk, who lives in Seventy-fifth Street. He purchased it three years ago, paying $70,000 for it. He has since made extensive repairs and largely refurnished it.

This is an example of careful reporting, but some of the detail could have been saved for the body of the story. A modern lead might read:

Fire destroyed the 200-room West End Hotel and seven adjoining cottages at Rockaway Beach late last night, causing property losses of at least $70,000.

As late as 1933, a leading textbook on news writing printed this as an example of a good lead:

Twenty-eight persons were injured, six of them seriously, today in a collision of two trolley cars, one bound south and the other north in Broad Street. At Bridge Street the south bound car jumped the tracks and ran head on into the other car.

By today's standards this example includes too much of the "where" and the "why," or "how." The city desk would edit the lead to read:

Twenty-eight persons were injured, six seriously, today when two trolley cars collided head on at Broad and Bridge Streets.

The deleted details would appear, of course, later in the story.

The impression should not be left that all news writing over the years was bad. The same edition of the New York *Times* which carried the Rockaway Beach fire story had five paragraphs of a fragmentary news story under the headline "The Maine Blown Up." The story began:

HAVANA, Feb. 15—At 9:45 o'clock this evening a terrible explosion took place on board the United States battleship Maine in Havana harbor.

Many persons were killed or wounded. All the boats of the Spanish cruiser Alfonso XII are assisting.

As yet the cause of the explosion is not apparent. . . .

Considering the fact that the cause of the explosion aboard the Maine was never conclusively determined, and excusing the "when" opening, this was good reporting and writing.

The Associated Press lead from Versailles on June 28, 1919, remains a dramatic bit of writing because it put the emphasis on one "W":

> Germany and the allied and associated powers signed the peace terms here today in the same imperial hall where the Germans humbled the French so ignominously 48 years ago.

There are Edwin L. James' concise opening words of May 21, 1927, from Paris to the New York *Times:* "Lindbergh did it." And the lead of another *Times* great, Frederick T. Birchall, on December 10, 1936, which treated momentous drama so deftly:

> Sometime Saturday morning, perhaps even as soon as tomorrow night, Edward VIII will cease to be a King and Emperor. He has made his choice between a woman and a throne and the woman has won.

Finally, the powerful simplicity of a 1941 United Press lead:

> HONOLULU, Dec. 7—War broke out with lightning suddenness in the Pacific early this morning when waves of Japanese bombers attacked Honolulu and the great United States naval base at Pearl Harbor.

And, similarly, of Merriman Smith's UP lead of April 12, 1945, from Warm Springs, Georgia:

> Franklin D. Roosevelt, President for 12 of the most momentous years in this country's history, died of a cerebral hemorrhage at 3:35 p.m. today in a small room in the "Little White House" here.

By this time the influences of radio news writing and of systematic analysis of news writing style had begun to modify the form of the conventional news story. Radio could not concentrate all of the essential details in one opening paragraph, nor could it elaborate on details in the way newspapers could. If radio newsmen did this, listeners could not follow the news. Newspapermen reasoned that some of radio's simplicity would also make for easier reading.

So by definition the word "lead" came to mean the opening of a story, not always just the first paragraph. More and more news-papers encouraged reporters to discriminate in selecting the emphasis to be placed upon treatment of the "5 W's" and the "H." But none of these essential elements was to be omitted en-tirely, and all were to be adequately treated in the opening 100 words or so of the usual inverted pyramid story. That kind of story still remains the bread-and-butter story of journalism, and the beginner should mind his W's and H religiously until he de-velops the skill and sense of news selectivity of the more experi-enced reporter.

The 5 W's and H

News usually takes the form of "who did what?" or "what happened and why?" Newspapers by their nature need to in-clude the "when" and "where." And in action stories "how" be-comes a major element. This seems simple to grasp and put into practice. But the ability to do so depends upon an understand-ing of news values, a sense of what will constitute reader interest in the particular incident, and quite a bit of practice in ferreting out the necessary facts and learning to put them together in a readable series of sentences and paragraphs.

Who sometimes is a single person—a man elected president of a chamber of commerce or a labor union, for example. In such a case the person's name is clearly the "who" element, together with necessary identification. Sometimes only a single person is involved in a story, but his identification is more interesting and important as the "who" element than his name—a city policeman is arrested for selling liquor without a license. In this case the proper name undoubtedly will wait until the second paragraph (had it been the police chief, he would have made the lead para-graph by name). The fewer the readers in the total audience who will recognize a name, the more likely it is the reporter will use an indefinite or generalized "who" identification.

Sometimes "who" is several persons—the five victims of a traffic accident, or the four students who have won scholarships. Sometimes it is an organization, a corporation, or a nation's people. Sometimes "who" is missing or can be identified only in nonpersonal terms—when a spontaneous fire destroys a building, "fire" serves as the "who" in the formula.

What overshadows "who" whenever the event is interesting or significant to readers regardless of those taking part in it, or whenever the persons involved are identified only generally. "What" usually is the result of action by a "who"—and in stories where there conceivably can be more than one "who," complications set in for the reporter. He solves the question of priority by deciding which "who did what" is the more interesting to the reader. Or, having found the most interesting and important "what," he locates the proper "who."

When fits into a lead paragraph as unobtrusively as possible, probably in the shortened form of "today," "yesterday," or "tomorrow." It serves as a badge of timeliness for the ordinary story. If it is important for the reader to know, a more exact accounting of "when" is given later in a story. Very rarely does a story *start* with the "when" element—when it should, your news sense should cry out the fact. ("Midnight tonight is the deadline for income tax payments.")

Where is the identification of proximity and can become merely "here," "city," or "local" in home-town stories. But readers often have a real interest in an exact "where"—the precise location of a fire or an accident, the place of a meeting, the route of a parade. Again, very rarely does a story *start* with the "where" element, although it may be a featurized element in the lead paragraph.

Why is often described as "the rest of the story" in many instances involving action. A mob riots in a foreign capital—why? The price of fuel oil advances—why? The favored candidate loses in an election—why? The lead of such a story attempts to set the tone and indicate to the reader that he will find out "why" if he completes the story. Sometimes "why" is the feature of an action story—a bee stings a driver who then wrecks his car. So the story will start with the "why" because it is different.

How most often is the meat of the action story. The team won, 13-7, on a last-second pass—the pass is the feature "how" of the lead and the long build-up to the climactic moment is the story of the entire game. Sometimes, however, "how" is a single fact. In the following story, the reporter's failure to include the "how" leaves the reader slightly baffled.

Two leather criss-cross buttons led to the arrest this morning of an 18-year-old Pasadena youth, just three hours after a young mother was stabbed in the bedroom of a girl friend she was visiting for the night.

Pasadena police booked Reynaldo Moreno, 18, of 68 Hurlbut St., on suspicion of burglary. He was linked to the case by two buttons, found at the scene of the stabbing, which match the remaining buttons on a leather jacket found at his home.

Estella Acosta, 22, of 1030½ S. Fair Oaks Ave., told police she and her child had gone to the home of Rachael Contreras, 21, of 48 Allesandro Pl., to spend the night.

Shortly before 4 a.m. Mrs. Acosta was awakened by someone standing over her in the bed she was sharing with Mrs. Contreras.

The man snarled at her: "Shut up or I'll knife you."

As she started to struggle, he plunged the knife at her, cutting a deep gash in her hand that required eight stitches to close. The man then turned and fled, Mrs. Acosta told Officers C. Lawrence and Don Breidenbach.

Investigators found the two leather buttons near a kitchen window that had been forced open to gain entry.

The reporter has answered carefully all the "W" questions but not the "how." How did the police happen to search Moreno's home, out of the thousands of homes in Pasadena? How did they happen to suspect him? Did he know one of the two women, for example? A basic element is missing from the story.

Let us again identify the "W" elements of the story about newsman Reston which appears at the opening of this chapter. They are:

Who—James B. Reston, Washington bureau chief, New York *Times*

What—will speak on "Politics and the Reporter"

When—8 p.m. Monday.

Where—Scott auditorium

Why—lecture sponsored by Sigma Delta Chi as part of Journalism Week.

The reporter decided to emphasize the "who" element by starting with it. He felt the reader would be interested in the fact that Reston twice had won a Pulitzer prize and decided enough readers would recognize the honor involved to justify featuring it. So "Pulitzer prize-winning" was added to the lead.

The "when" and "where" elements are important in an advance story of a news event, so the reporter decided to give the exact details in his first paragraph. That made the opening paragraph long enough, and "why" became the second paragraph. The third and fourth paragraphs expanded the "who" and "what" elements, which are the major elements of the story.

There are 27 words in the first paragraph:

James B. Reston, Pulitzer prize-winning Washington bureau chief for the New York Times, will speak on "Politics and the Reporter" at 8 p.m. Monday in Scott auditorium.

The reporter added only commas and connectives to the essential "W" elements. His 27 words carried him into the third line of his typewritten copy, and it will take seven lines of ordinary newspaper body type to print them. There are no set rules about lengths of lead paragraphs, but this one is slightly above average length. So the reporter resisted adding more words. It reads easily, and the story is well organized, so he resisted shortening the lead.

Sometimes the reporter's first paragraph will be just a few words long; sometimes it will run as many as 35 to 40 words. But these will be exceptions. Generally he will need somewhere between 15 and 30 words to write his opening paragraph clearly and interestingly, most likely 20 to 25 words. A good rule for the beginner to remember is that if he gets into a fourth line in his typewritten copy, he had better re-examine his analysis of the "5 W's" and the relative emphasis he has placed upon them. If he gets to a fifth line, he has gone too far. (These are typewritten lines averaging 60 characters in length.)

For example, had our reporter not exercised caution he very

well could have ended up with an opening paragraph of 54 words such as this:

> James B. Reston, chief of the New York Times' Washington bureau and winner of the Pulitzer prize for national reporting in 1945 and 1957, will speak on "Politics and the Reporter" at 8 p.m. Monday in Scott auditorium as a part of Journalism Week activities, George T. Brown, Sigma Delta Chi fraternity chapter president, announced yesterday.

The reader can still get through this paragraph, and understand it, but with greater difficulty. In the newspaper, this lead would cover 14 lines of body type—an unattractive and harder-to-read solid block of gray.

Identification

The reporter must identify adequately each person, group, or organization mentioned in a story. The conventional identification is familiar to all readers: name, age, address. Occupation frequently is an essential or interesting identification. In the Reston story, for example, occupation replaces age and address as the suitable identifying element.

Why the emphasis upon age and address? Because the reader wants to know, and because such identification helps him decide whether or not he is acquainted with the person involved in the story. "John M. Brown, 31, 4119 Sixty-first Ave. S., was injured . . ." is a line familiar to all readers. If the reader knows two John Browns, he can decide more readily which of the two is involved when he sees the middle initial, age, and address. If the story mentions that this Brown is a painter, the reader is further aided. If he does not know a John Brown, but he does live down the block on Sixty-first Ave., the reader feels a sense of identification with the accident victim.

Proper identification often involves more than these rudimentary elements. In the Reston story, "Washington newspaperman" would not be as helpful or interesting a phrase to use as "Washington bureau chief for the New York Times," even though it is shorter. And the phrase "Pulitzer prize-winning" identifies him as a leader in his profession. References to previous newsworthy activities of persons or groups help the reader to associate the current news with his knowledge of the past.

The reporter must exercise some caution in making identifications. They must be pertinent to the subject matter of the news event. During and after World War II, some newsmen were quick to identify any man arrested for a crime as a "GI" or "ex-GI" or "veteran," if he was or had been in service. "Teenager" is another blanket identification which annoys readers when its use in combination with unpleasant news is not an essential element of the story. Racial and religious groups in the population suffer when a racial or religious identification is used even though it is not needed to tell the story properly.

Time and Place

Most publications have a uniform method of telling the reader the "when" and "where" elements if they involve an hour, day, and specific location. Usually the information is presented in that order: "8 p.m. Monday in Scott auditorium." The designations "a.m." and "p.m." are usually preferred; "o'clock" requires a further explanation of morning or evening time. Newspapers have style books which instruct the reporter on such details, and all reporters follow the rules so that readers will not be subjected to a variety of style details in the same copy of the paper. "Time before place, hour before day" is a common rule and a good one for the beginning reporter to learn.

Authority

If the reporter is an eyewitness to a news event, he does not need to cite authority for the facts he presents to his readers. He sees a fire; he obtains the names of those injured, in firsthand reporting circumstances; he interviews witnesses. But if he asks the fire chief for an estimate of the amount of property damage, or the hospital how seriously the victims are judged to be injured, then he will need to cite the authority for each of those opinions.

In an ordinary news story a reporter never makes a statement involving opinion or judgment without citing the source of the statement. If he does, the statement of opinion appears to the reader to have become the opinion of the newspaper itself. For example:

> Spinach isn't all it's advertised to be and soap can't wash lies from a child's mouth, *the American Medical Association said today.*

Without the concluding italicized phrase, the statement would appear to be that of the newspaper publishing it . . . and spinach growers might write letters of complaint to the editor which actually should be addressed to the AMA.

Two other simple examples:

> You may possibly see Sputnik III tonight if you happen to look at the right place at the right time, *University astronomy spokesmen said.*

> Schools should not be criticized for trade courses or for emphasis on what is carelessly called "life adjustment," *Dean E. W. McDonald said yesterday.*

Newspapers are also careful always to attribute weather predictions to the weather forecaster, who should take the blame if rain ruins the picnics.

The Associated Press requires its correspondents to begin their stories with the name of the source if the material involves charges or controversial statements. Not all news organizations are so strict, but they do insist that the source be clearly indicated. "Police said" is a familiar attribution of authority in crime stories, for example. If a district attorney announces he will seek an indictment against a citizen, he properly is cited as the source of the news. If a politician makes a charge of a controversial nature, it is vitally important that the reader be able to judge its validity by what he knows about the politician in question.

Announcements of important actions are usually attributed immediately to the authority for the news: "President Eisenhower said today that he will ask the Congress to take action . . ." is a familiar opening of stories from Washington. Or,

"Mayor Smith said today he will appoint Robert W. Johnson as fire chief. . . ."

But there is a line where citing of authority ceases to be a requirement, at least for the lead paragraph. Publicity writers are prone to start their stories with the name of the company president, who is announcing the promotion of a district manager to a vice-presidency. Clearly the "who" is the man being promoted, and the phrase "was announced today" often replaces the name of the company official making the announcement. Announcements of meetings, speeches, conventions, and similar events never require the citing of authority for the facts which the reporter has collected. In the story about newsman Reston's speech, the name of the Sigma Delta Chi chapter president who supplied the news is included in a lower paragraph as a courtesy to the news source (newspapers should show thanks for the assistance given their reporters and editors) rather than as a needed element.

Organizing the Lead

The basic story form, we have seen, includes a number of elements in the lead material:

1. The answers to the questions which the reader will have: who, what, when, where, why and how? One or two will be more important, depending upon the news situation. The reporter will exercise judgment as to how much detail concerning each of the "5 W's" is needed, but no essential element will be omitted, and all the "W's" will be covered early in the story.
2. The feature of the story, if there is one which will make the lead more attractive to the reader.
3. The authority on which the news is printed, if needed.
4. Adequate identification of persons or organizations mentioned.

The reporter makes certain that he has obtained this necessary information and checks himself for accuracy. Then comes the problem of writing. The first paragraph should give the gist of the essential news; it should be the most interesting and most informative 15 to 30 words possible; it should be easily read; and it should lead smoothly into the next paragraphs of the story.

Here is a news story taken from the columns of a prize-winning high school newspaper which will illustrate the problem faced by any beginner when he or she sits down to type out a story. In what order should the "who," "what," "when," "where," and "why" be presented? Indeed, is there more than one "who" or "what"? Somewhat baffled by the information he had gleaned from an announcement, the young reporter backed into the story this way:

> *On Wednesday, March 19,* at the monthly meeting of the Mothers' Club, there was presented the annual spring luncheon and style show. The purpose of the affair was to provide Central High's mothers with an afternoon of relaxation and a glimpse at the latest styles in women's clothing.
>
> Several of the mothers served as models to show the clothes to 300 members of the club in the gymnasium. They were Mrs. George H. Dickinson, Mrs. Edward W. Casey, Mrs. John C. Wilson, Mrs. Mark S. Madden, Mrs. Willis R. Lindsey and Mrs. Ralph T. Jones.

"When" clearly was not the most important fact for the high school newspaper which printed this story on April 2. But it offered the baffled writer a way to begin. He also molded his story into the passive voice ("there was presented," "the purpose of the affair was to provide") rather than the active voice which the newspaper tries to use. He used that needless phrase, "the purpose of the affair was," and he included a pointless opinion that it was an "afternoon of relaxation."

Nor would "where" be a good opening, for the story then begins:

> *Central High's gym* was the scene of the annual spring luncheon and style show of the Mothers' Club on Wednesday, March 19. . . .

When we try "who" a better, even though quite routine, lead emerges:

The Central High Mothers' Club held its annual spring luncheon and style show on Wednesday, March 19, devoting its monthly meeting to obtaining a glimpse of the latest styles in women's clothing.

"What" and "why" provide two other possible openings:

The annual spring luncheon and style show of the Central High Mothers' Club took place. . . .

Latest styles in women's clothing were shown at the annual. . . .

It is time to take another look at the original story. Isn't the most interesting "who did what" the fact that several mothers served as fashion models at the style show? How can we work this into the lead, in order to make the story more attractive? A "what" lead now develops this way:

Latest styles in women's clothing were worn by members of the Central High Mothers' Club who served as models at the group's annual spring luncheon and style show on Wednesday, March 19, in the school gymnasium.

Here is a summary lead which includes all the information contained in the first paragraph of the original story except the discarded fact that the club meets every month, plus the feature material and the "where." But it is 36 words long, and the facts are strung out along a series of connectives: "in . . . by . . . of . . . as . . . at . . . on . . . in."

Let's count the names given in the original story. The "several mothers" who served as fashion models become "six." Now another "who" lead becomes possible:

Six Central High mothers became models for an afternoon last month to show 300 Mothers' Club members the "new look" in women's fashions.

Latest styles in dresses, hats and coats were exhibited at the Club's annual spring luncheon and style show held Wednesday, March 19, in the gymnasium.

The six mothers were. . . .

Our new lead contains only 23 words. The reporter has done a little investigating about the subject of fashions and has improved his vocabulary. He has decided that the details of "when" and "where" can be left for the second paragraph ("where" is implied in the opening paragraph—Mothers' Club meeting). He now takes his pencil and crosses out "Wednesday" since the day of the week is no longer important to the reader.

One thing is certain. No two reporters given the original story would have come up with the same version in their rewrites, let alone the exact version just worked out here. That is one of the things which makes journalism interesting.

One more example, taken from another prize-winning high school newspaper. Here the reporter has written a 45-word, one-paragraph story:

> The monthly meeting of the Benildus Club will be held at 7 p.m. Monday, March 24. The guest speaker will be Father Hamm, a Maryknoll missionary. He will show films on the work of a missionary and will tell about the life of a Maryknoller.

The reader finds out everything except where the Benildus Club meets. But the fact that a club meets every month is scarcely the most interesting opening for the story. A 28-word inclusive summary story would read like this:

> Films depicting the work of a missionary will be shown Benildus Club members by Father Hamm, a Maryknoll missionary, at 7 p.m. Monday, March 24, in room 302.

Another version five words shorter than the original, but using two paragraphs, could read:

> The work of a missionary will be described in film and words at the next meeting of the Benildus Club.
> Father Hamm of the Maryknoll order will be the club's guest at 7 p.m. Monday, March 24, in room 302.

Which of the three versions is the most readable, most attractive to the reader? Probably the third.

The Body of the Story

The reporter has an obligation to fulfill, once he has interested the reader in scanning his lead material. By the way he has shaped his lead sentences and has suggested interesting facets of the story, he has led the reader to expect more.

In the story about the Reston lecture at the opening of this chapter, for example, the reader who has finished the first two paragraphs is expecting to find certain additional information in the next paragraphs. He wants to know more about the Pulitzer prizes or about what Reston does in Washington (told him in paragraph three). He needs more indication of what Reston will talk about than the general topic "Politics and the Reporter" (told him in paragraph four).

Unhappily, however, the reader is not always treated so logically by the reporter. The third paragraph in some versions of the Reston story might have become a quotation from the journalism school dean about the virtues of Journalism Week. There would be no objection to putting such a statement at the close of the story, but it should not come between the reader and his desire to know more about the main facts of the story. The reporter must always be on guard against following an interesting tangent which intervenes between the lead material and the orderly expansion and explanation of that material in the paragraphs which constitute the body of the story.

Here is a brief item from an afternoon daily which illustrates orderly development of the body of the story:

> A boy pulling a red wagon was killed by a truck at 12:45 p.m. today as he stepped off the curb at Riverside and Twenty-second Aves. S.
>
> He was identified tentatively as Ralph Sennett, 9, son of Mrs. Leonard Sennett, 2924 S. Seventh St.
>
> Mrs. Sennett was on the scene within a few minutes but was overcome by emotion and did not look at the body, which had been covered by police. She identified the boy's wagon.
>
> The truck was driven by Alfred F. Hammond, 60, 1617

N. Fifth St., a rubbish hauler. Hammond said he did not see
the boy in time to stop. He was held by police for investigation.

Paragraph one gives the reader the who, what, when, and
where; the second paragraph develops the "who" element in
detail, and paragraph three explains the reason for the tentative
identification. The final paragraph identifies the second "who"
—the truck driver—and tells what the paper knows about the
"why."

Notice the tiny feature of the story: "A boy pulling a red
wagon . . ." And notice that the wagon reappears in the third
paragraph. In an accompanying picture the crushed and over-
turned wagon was shown beside the covered body of the boy.

The lead previously quoted about spinach and soap offers another example of proper story handling. This lead paragraph has
two elements—"spinach isn't all it's advertised to be" and "soap
can't wash lies from a child's mouth." The reporter uses his second paragraph to explain how the American Medical Association
happened to take a stand on these two issues. His third paragraph develops the subject of spinach, which appears first in the
lead; the final three deal with child psychology and the soap
treatment:

> Spinach isn't all it's advertised to be and soap can't wash
> lies from a child's mouth, the American Medical Association
> said today.
>
> The A.M.A. magazine, "Today's Health," tore into the
> spinach legend and soap as a truth serum.
>
> "Potatoes, squash and carrots contain more iron per por-
> tion than spinach," the magazine said. Dr. William Bolton,
> associate editor of the magazine, said the spinach story boils
> down to its being "a filling food" with a low calorie content.
>
> Elizabeth B. Hurlock of Bryn Mawr, Pa., past president
> of the American Psychological Association's division on psy-
> chology teaching, said the thing to do when a child lies is
> to find out why he's telling untruths—not wash his mouth
> out with soap.

She said a child lies for two reasons: To escape punishment and to win approval.

Washing a child's mouth out with soap, or spanking him, or making him confess in front of others does not help the situation one bit, she said.

Note how the transition from the subject of spinach to that of soap is accomplished by starting the fourth paragraph with the name of the second authority being quoted by the reporter. A whimsical little bit, but it appeared on page one of several metropolitan dailies, because it was concise and well-organized, and because it dealt with two subjects imbedded in America's folklore.

In the example which follows, a "who will do what" announcement immediately called for a "why and how" emphasis. The first three paragraphs give the gist of the news; the next two explain "why" in brief; the next three tell "how"; and the story then returns to the "why" emphasis. Certainly the reader who was affected by the news wanted to know the reasons why.

More than 1300 students registered in the College of Science, Literature and the Arts must take a newly required senior college composition examination this spring.

J. W. Buchta, associate dean of SLA, yesterday announced registration for the examination will take place in 225 Johnston Hall throughout next week.

A passing grade on the examination is required of all SLA students who entered senior college last fall or later, Buchta said.

"SLA faculty last June adopted the examination requirement and added it onto the Freshman English requirement," Buchta explained.

"The point was to emphasize to students that good writing is important throughout college and after college, not just during the freshman year."

Examinations will be held May 20, 21, 22 and 24, Buchta said. A student registering next week at 225 Johnston will select four theme topics from a list made up by the department in which he is majoring.

At examination time he or she will be assigned one of the four topics, Buchta said. The student will be allowed an hour to write 300 words without aid of books or notes.

Examination judging will be done by SLA students' major departments, Buchta said. Those who fail will be required to complete a noncredit, one quarter composition course before graduation.

Buchta explained two purposes which the SLA faculty saw in requiring a senior college composition examination:

1. Writing for one hour won't make a student a good writer, but it will emphasize that his responsibility for good writing does not end with freshman English. The student in physics, sociology, history and other subjects will recognize that good writing makes a difference in his major work and, later on, in his job.

2. Major departments will be involved and will share responsibility for student performance in composition and rhetoric along with English and communications faculty members.

SLA students served on the committee which recommended the new requirement, Buchta pointed out.

Note that in the story just quoted, the authority for the news is carefully stated throughout the article. The dean's name opens the second paragraph, as the news source for the opening summary statement. It reappears in each paragraph which follows, except for three paragraphs which are linked to a preceding paragraph as part of a running quotation. In the two sections of the story where "why" is being developed, the phrase "Buchta explained" is used as a transitional aid.

Many additional examples of well-organized news stories appear in later chapters. The student just being introduced to problems of news writing should observe two things:

There is a basic story form which emphasizes orderly presentation of the news in a concise and logical series of paragraphs.

Each news situation, however, determines the emphasis placed upon each of the news elements in a story. There is no rigid pattern to be used over and over again, but rather there are general principles to be absorbed and applied in an infinite variety of reporting situations.

This is true whether the story concerns a campus lecture, a street accident, the food value of spinach, or the death of a President of the United States. Rarely has a reporter written the last-named story, and perhaps Merriman Smith's account for the United Press of the death in office of Franklin D. Roosevelt should be quoted further as an example of a lengthy running-action story of momentous importance which follows the basic news pattern. Smith's job was to write the general summary account, among the many stories which were being written about the death of the President and the chain of events which followed. The country was stunned by the news; for security reasons Mr. Roosevelt's whereabouts had not been known exactly during wartime; the state of his health had not been a news subject. Note how Smith anticipated these reader interest factors as he put together his story for the morning newspapers of April 13, 1945:

President Roosevelt Is Dead

WARM SPRINGS, Ga., April 12 (UP)—Franklin D. Roosevelt, President for 12 of the most momentous years in this country's history, died of a cerebral hemorrhage at 3:35 p.m. today in a small room in the "Little White House" here.

Death came only two and a half hours after he had been stricken by a severe headache.

Mr. Roosevelt had been in Warm Springs—which he liked to call his "second home"—since March 30.

Most of the week preceding he had passed at his home in Hyde Park, N.Y.

He was 63 years old and had served as President longer than any other American.

News of Mr. Roosevelt's death came from his secretary, William D. Hassett, who called in three press association reporters who had accompanied the President here and said:

"It is my sad duty to inform you that the President died at 3:35 (central time) of a cerebral hemorrhage."

News Sent to Capital

Simultaneously, the word of the President's death was telephoned to the White House in Washington. It was announced there, at 5:44 p.m., by Stephen T. Early, his secretary and confidant since he first took office in 1933 to become the only President in the nation's history to be elected for more than two terms.

A funeral service will be held in the East Room of the White House at 4 p.m. Saturday. Burial will be at Hyde Park on Sunday, at a time yet to be set.

The body will not lie in state.

[*At this point Smith had completed the essential coverage; now he turned back to a detailed account of the final days and hours at Warm Springs, the first several paragraphs of which follow.*]

The President had passed a leisurely two weeks in Warm Springs, and at no time was there any indication that he was sick, beyond the fact that he had not made his usual visits to the Warm Springs swimming pool, where in 1924 he began his lifelong battle to overcome the withering effects of infantile paralysis.

Went for Long Rides

Almost daily during his stay he took long automobile rides in the Georgia spring sun. He had been keeping up constantly with developments in Washington and abroad by telephone and through official papers flown to him every morning.

Relaxed, in fine spirits, President Roosevelt had sat in front of the fireplace in his cottage here, posing for a portrait artist, N. Robbins of New York City.

It was 1 o'clock.

Suddenly he said: "I have a terrific headache." These were said to be his last words.

At 1:15 p.m. he fainted.

At 3:35 p.m. he died, without having regained consciousness, of what was described medically as "a massive cerebral hemorrhage."

Only three persons were with the President when he died. One was his personal physician . . .

Summary

Journalism has a basic story form which is used more often in reporting the news than any other form. It is known as the inverted pyramid form and it utilizes the principles of the summary lead. In using it, the reporter should observe these rules:

1. The "5 W's" and "H"—who, what, when, where, why, and how—are adequately covered early in the story. The most important of these news elements are emphasized in the opening paragraph.

2. The body of the story further explains and expands upon the essential news, in concise and orderly fashion.

3. There is adequate identification of authority, or source of the news, and of persons or groups mentioned in it.

4. The most interesting news element is featured, if possible, to make the story more attractive to the reader.

5. The reporter's goal is to be interesting, not dull; to tell the facts which will be most valuable to the reader; and to put together an easily read and understandable story.

Chapter 5

Paragraphs and Sentences

"Can He Write?"

A person who wants to be a reporter should have a good command of language. The best writer in the world would fail miserably as a reporter if he lacked news sense, reportorial judgment, and the desire to go out and get the news. But the best reporter in the world is going to be in trouble if he can't get his subjects and verbs to agree, if his sentences and paragraphs lack unity and clarity, and if he is weak in spelling.

Writing skill is a prerequisite throughout the journalistic world, of course. Newspapers, magazines, radio and television stations, advertising agencies, and publishing houses all very early ask this question about a job candidate: "Can he write?" They really are asking two questions. They want to know if he possesses the imaginative qualities which are so necessary in journalism and which distinguish a good writer from a dull one. They also want to know if he has mastered the essentials of effective writing.

Good journalistic writing is simply good writing. There is no such thing as "journalese," a term of scorn sometimes applied to the work of the newspaperman. Writing which is called "journalese" is simply bad writing; the faults include careless organization, sloppy sentences, poor word choices (slang and clichés), and incomplete coverage. Neither the journalism professor nor the newspaper editor tolerates bad writing, any more than does the English composition teacher.

There are some conditions which the journalistic writer must meet, however, which do not apply to the theme writer or the essayist. These conditions sometimes make the beginning journalist feel that there is real conflict between what he does in the reporting laboratory and what he does in the composition classroom. But the conflict is more apparent than real. A student who comes well-trained in composition and rhetoric should have little trouble in the world of journalism.

The basic newspaper story form emphasizes word economy, relatively simple sentence structure, and short paragraphs. But placing emphasis on these factors does not mean that the reporter abandons other principles of good writing. Variety in vocabulary usage is not barred by emphasis on word economy; in fact, newspapers encourage their writers to use the most effective word, stipulating only that a definition of effectiveness includes reader comprehension. Short declarative sentences are the workhorses of journalism, but unless the writer achieves some variety of sentence structure and length, his story will be dull and unacceptable. Nor do all paragraphs need to be the same monotonous length.

Paragraphs

Undoubtedly some readers of this book were surprised by the brevity of the paragraphs in the news stories quoted in the previous chapter, even though everyone reads newspapers. Not until a reader stops to analyze newspaper stories does he really notice the difference in paragraph organization, as compared to the style practiced in books and magazines. The essay-type paragraph contains a topic sentence which sets the stage for the unified development of a topic or thought. When the thought or topic has been developed, the essay writer ends his paragraph—but not until then, whether he has written 20 words, 50 words, or 300 words. The newspaper reporter, however, rarely writes a paragraph as long as this one. His average paragraph is 20 to 25 words in length.

The reporter writes this way because the newspaper column is a little less than two inches wide. Average body type runs about five words to the line, and eight lines to an inch of type. The narrow column width and the small size of the type require frequent paragraph breaks so that some white space will relieve the gray and unattractive appearance of the type mass. Paragraph indentations catch the reader's eye and carry him along through the story at the rapid pace which most newspaper readers maintain.

So the reporter breaks up his thought units by subtopics. He maintains unity and coherence by using the same devices the essay writer utilizes: transitions, reference words and phrases, variation of sentence order. These devices make his one- and two-sentence paragraphs hang together, just as they act to guide the reader through the longer single paragraph of the essay. That is why the casual newspaper reader doesn't particularly notice the difference in paragraph organization.

The two stories from the Minneapolis *Tribune* which follow are set in standard newspaper column width. The one on the left has a better variety of paragraph lengths and is more attractive to the reader. In it, note particularly the division between paragraphs three and four and the transitional "but." Paragraph three is the topic sentence for the two paragraphs. The same technique is used to create paragraphs five and six, whose topic sentence is the first sentence of paragraph five. Paragraph eight becomes a topic *paragraph* for the three which follow; this is a favorite device of newspaper writers.

OWATONNA, Minn.—This southeastern Minnesota community didn't have to go looking for industry.

Industries—a variety of them—literally grew up here: Jewelry, insurance, specialized farm equipment, food canning and maintenance tools, to mention a few.

No one is exactly sure how Owatonna came to be blessed with such diversity.

But no one is displeased with the "blessing." The variety of manufacturing enter-

Private and public spending will exceed $67,000,000 before the lower loop redevelopment in Minneapolis is finished.

If the program goes as its sponsors hope, the job will be finished in 1963. At that time, the marketable part (about 35 acres) of the 70 acres of land to be bought and cleared by the housing and redevelopment authority will have been sold back to private owners.

Buildings—principally office structures—will have been put up on most sites. An ex-

prises have combined with the healthy agriculture of Steele county ("land of the sure crop") to produce stability and solid growth.

Even so, efforts are under way to attract more industry. The chamber of commerce is funneling its efforts through a newly strengthened industrial committee.

And Don Reigel, publisher of the weekly Photo News, is stumping editorially for formation of an industrial development corporation.

"This is a big item in Owatonna's future," said Reigel. "More farmers are coming into the city as a result of the technological revolution. We must have jobs for them, or they'll move on."

The combination of thriving industry and agriculture has given Owatonna steady growth since the end of World War II.

Row upon row of attractive modern homes testify to a growing population—up 52 per cent since the 1940 census to a present total of 13,225.

Retail stores on streets branching off from the town square are doing an estimated 20-million-dollar volume annually, a 28 per cent increase since 1948.

And checkbook spending, as measured by bank debits, was over 177 million dollars last year, up 66 per cent from a decade ago.

ception may be the land sold for automobile parking. In some cases, owners of such land may still be operating simple parking lots in 1963, waiting for enough demand to develop to justify erection of parking ramps.

Forecasts of the program's timing, and how much it will cost, gained interest last week as the public part of the job neared final approval.

The authority expects to get formal notice early this week that the federal urban renewal administration (URA) is generally satisfied with the proposed redevelopment plan. This will open the way for submission of the plan to the city council and for preparation of a final valuation of land to be taken.

Completion of these final formalities—probably by Sept. 1—will satisfy the last requirement set up by URA, and the authority will be free to start spending $14,270,690 for purchase of land and buildings.

(Over-all cost of buying and clearing land and installing public improvements will be $19,277,548. Net cost after sale of land will be $13,689,681. Of this latter amount, URA will contribute $10,267,261, the city, $3,422,420. The city will pay 100 per cent of some other costs, bringing its total share to $4,244,360.)

Although it may be late. . . .

The good writer, then, merely needs to learn to "paragraph his paragraphs," for news writing. He must remember to bump his typewriter back for the next indentation more often, and with somewhat more variation. Actually, every skillful writer knows the devices so commonly used by the reporter: variety of paragraph length, use of topic paragraphs as transitional devices, interjection of brief sentence-paragraphs, use of direct quotes, and so on. He just doesn't have to use them as consistently.

Reporters' paragraphs have another common characteristic. "Start right out saying something," is the way the veteran explained this to the youngster. Most of the paragraphs in the two stories just quoted start with significant or key words. In the Owatonna story, this is less true because more transitions are used between paragraphs, but the final three paragraphs serve as examples of opening-word emphasis. In the other story, about redevelopment in Minneapolis, virtually every paragraph starts with a key word or word group.

Transitions

The effort to begin paragraphs with significant or key words is made with the idea of catching the eye of the reader. An emphatic opening to a sentence tends to carry the reader along through the paragraph. The writer of the Minneapolis redevelopment story relied heavily upon this journalistic writing device. In doing so, he used a minimum of the transitional devices employed in writing to indicate continuity and to urge the reader to continue.

The writer of the story about Owatonna, as has been pointed out, used a substantial number of opening transitions. The word "Industries" which begins the second paragraph is a key word, but it also is a transitional word referring back to the final word of the first paragraph. "But no one," the opening of the fourth paragraph, refers back to the opening of the third paragraph. The openings of paragraph five and six, "Even so" and "And," are transitional devices. The eighth paragraph begins with a transitional statement referring back to the fourth paragraph, "The combination of thriving industry and agriculture." The rest of the sentence, "has given Owatonna steady growth since the end of World War II," leads the reader into the next three paragraphs. "And" opens the last quoted paragraph as a transition.

Which of the two writers was more effective in carrying his

readers along through the story? Most critics of present-day newspaper writing style argue that reporters too often forget the necessity for providing transition. Professor Theodore Morrison of Harvard University, writing in the publication of the Nieman Fellows, the *Nieman Reports,* said on this point:

"A skillful and needed transition is not a mere formality. It distributes emphasis, makes a distinction, sets relative importance in order, puts a rib on the skeleton, or generalizes the particulars and illustrations. In a good deal of newspaper writing, transitional sentences seem to be forbidden."

The common-sense rule should be this: When a transition is needed, it should be supplied at the opening of a sentence or paragraph; when a transition is not needed, the reporter should endeavor to begin the sentence or paragraph with a key word to achieve emphasis.

Transitions which refer back to earlier material can often be key words as well. They thus do double duty. They reduce the amount of effort expended by the reader as he seeks to absorb the news and they encourage him to continue the story. In the example which follows, these "double duty" words are set in boldface type, while other transitional words are italicized.

WASHINGTON (AP)—The National Association of Manufacturers (NAM) today urged Congress to make labor unions subject to the anti-trust laws, to ban compulsory unionism, and to bar use of union funds for partisan political purposes.

Donald J. Hardenbrook, New York, chairman of *NAM's* industrial relations committee, told a Senate labor subcommittee that revelations of the Senate rackets investigating committee "have shocked the sensibilities of thoughtful citizens."

Hardenbrook, vice president of Union Bag-Camp Paper Corp., said regulation of union internal affairs—proposed in several bills before the *subcommittee*—might become less necessary if his far-reaching proposals were adopted.

Another witness, Theodore Iserman, New York attorney

specializing in labor relations matters, also urged action in *the three fields cited by Hardenbrook.*

Iserman, who said he had represented many employers in labor cases, asserted "the need for the reforms I favor has been clear for years."

However, the subcommittee has indicated it is not going into some of the major issues raised by Hardenbrook and Iserman.

The issue of application of anti-trust laws to unions. . . .

Only two of the italicized transitions are not referring back to earlier material. These are the two in the fourth and sixth paragraphs, both of which open with transitions because the subject matter has changed. "Another witness" signals that a new source is being quoted. "However" indicates the differing point of view of the subcommittee.

Other transitions and connectives serve to indicate to the reader that a comparison is being made, a result is being given, an illustration is being cited, or a fact is being added. Inverted pyramid stories which do not follow chronological sequence often need transitional expressions such as "earlier" or "later" to help the reader keep the sequence of events straight. Some others of these familiar journeymen not already cited include "meanwhile," "in addition," "finally," "for example," and "more recently." Anyone who listens to radio news will recognize some old friends among these words, and newspaper writers can indeed profit by being attentive to the use of transitions in radio news broadcasts.

Sentences

Good sentences have unity; they are easily understood; they transmit to the reader the emphasis which the writer intended; and in concert they have sufficient variety to be attractive to the reader. Unity, clarity, emphasis, and variety are key words in all books on grammar.

Unity means the state of being one, or singleness. A properly written sentence containing a single statement which represents a complete thought is obviously unified. But unity also means the reference of all the elements to a single main idea. Complex and compound sentences containing two or more statements achieve unity only when they are written so that the reader is able to grasp a single main idea.

If, for example, two statements in a sentence are not closely related, sentence unity is violated and the reader is confused: "The natives of the country wear wooden shoes and are naturally hospitable." Not many would-be reporters make such an obvious error. But a good many have trouble with some aspect of the principle of subordination. When two statements are coordinate in importance they are written in a coordinate form; but when one statement is less important, it must be subordinated if the reader is to grasp the main idea easily. The worst sin, of course, is to put the main idea in a subordinate construction, as a dependent clause or a participial phrase.

An example of incorrect subordination of a coordinate idea would be writing "Educated at Harvard, he became a professor at California in 1950" instead of "He was educated at Harvard and became a professor at California in 1950." An example of failure to subordinate a less important statement would be: "The school board meeting ended at 9 p.m., but none of the members would discuss the decision reached." A better version would be: "None of the school board members would discuss the decision reached at the meeting, which ended at 9 p.m." An example of improper subordination of the main idea would be: "He was walking through the alley behind the house, when he saw the body of the dead girl." The "when" should open the sentence, or the two parts should be reversed.

Clarity is lost when the writer changes the pattern of his sentence by failing to observe rules of grammar. The literate reader expects to find parallel construction within a sentence. And he does not expect to find dangling modifiers, inconsistent enumerations, or widely separated subjects and verbs.

Parallel construction means that for a like meaning there must be a like construction; the same grammatical forms and parts of speech must be used in pairs or series. Some examples of errors in parallel construction are italicized in the following sentences:

"Johnson denied the *murder* and *dumping* the body in the ditch." (Noun and gerund are not parallel.)

"The dean said he would appoint a committee *to review* the salary scale and another *for studying* promotion policies." (Infinitive and gerund are not parallel.)

A dangling modifier is a modifier which cannot be connected immediately and unmistakably with an antecedent in the same sentence. Dangling participles, gerunds, and infinitives create some of the "slips that pass in the dark" in newspapers; they also annoy the reader. The most usual mistake is to open a sentence with a modifier which implies a subject and then not to follow with the subject. Some typical danglers are:

"After considering the problem, a vote was taken." (The subject of the modifier, "they," is missing.)

"To hold the paper in place, the thumb must be placed against it." (The subject of the modifier, "you," is missing.)

A sports reporter ruined an otherwise good baseball story for sensitive readers by managing to combine a dangling modifier and nonagreement of subject and verb in a single sentence:

"But that last Spartan effort had the fans on their feet. After disposing on the first two batters in easy fashion, an infield error and a hit batsman was followed by a single by pinchhitter Ron Bietz." This atrocity appeared in a metropolitan newspaper. The reporter meant to say something like this:

"But that last Spartan effort had the fans on their feet. After Roberts had disposed of the first two batters in easy fashion, one Spartan was safe on an infield error and another was hit by a pitched ball. Pinchhitter Ron Bietz then hit a single."

Inconsistent enumeration occurs when a necessary "and" or "or" is omitted. "The new journalism building has offices, reporting and editing rooms." The sentence needs an "and" after "offices," instead of a comma.

Wide separation of subject and verb is not an outright error, but it can be confusing to the reader. Rules of good writing call for the verb to follow the subject as closely as possible. Long sentences which open with a subject and close with a verb are always suspect. This is especially true if the intervening clauses are set apart by commas: "Johnson, who had been following the debate closely, and who had encouraged Smith to speak after speaking himself earlier on the motion, now again rose to answer." Two sentences would be better.

Emphasis is sought by the news writer in order to give prominence to the central idea. The reporter wants the reader to see the key word or words and to understand the thought or fact being emphasized. He can do this by proper subordination of minor facts or ideas, a technique already discussed. He can do this also by writing sentences with emphatic openings and by using the active voice rather than the passive voice.

Sentences are weakened when they open with such statements as "There are," "It was decided that," and "The purpose of the meeting was . . ." The important idea comes farther along in the sentence where the reader has less chance to focus upon it. Particularly in reading shorter sentences the reader glances at the first word or group of words to gain his impression. It is true that in writing long sentences, one can achieve emphasis by placing important material at the end. But since most newspaper sentences are short, a strong opening is the common rule. Subject-and-verb beginnings are typical of newspaper style.

The passive voice is less emphatic than the active voice. Sometimes it should be used, particularly when the thing done is to be emphasized: "Richard Smith has been appointed chairman . . ." or "Increased telephone rates were approved today by . . ." But more often the active voice should be substituted for the passive to achieve emphasis. For example, "The mayor received the report" is preferable to "The report was received by the mayor." "Five students took the test" is preferable to "The test was taken by five students." "Ronald Anderson received committee endorsement" is preferable either to "Ronald Anderson was endorsed by the committee" or "The committee endorsed Ronald Anderson," an active form which does not emphasize the name.

Verbs are extremely important in achieving emphasis. Action verbs are the mainsprings of sentences. The reporter uses strong simple verbs whenever possible, and he is careful to include a liberal number of verb forms in his longer sentences. He uses verbs, not adjectives, to give his writing strength ("the fire roared," not "a fierce fire"). He combines simple verbs with simple adverbs to encourage readability.

Variety of expression is gained by using common sense in following the general rules for journalistic writing: sentences and paragraphs often have emphatic openings; sentences are likely to have subject-verb beginnings; sentences usually are short; paragraphs generally contain only one or two sentences. Variety is achieved by judicious deviations from these general patterns.

Sometimes it is preferable to open the sentence with a prepositional phrase, a noun clause, or a subordinate clause in order to achieve emphasis. Transitional devices are needed at times for paragraph and sentence openings, and they give variety to the story when they are used. Not all sentences contain information which deserves emphatic treatment; those which do not can vary from the regular pattern in their construction.

Compound and complex sentences naturally occur in all writing and provide change of pace in stories composed mainly of simple sentences. Sentences containing semicolons offer variety but are used less often in news writing than in essay writing. Interrogative sentences sometimes fit the subject matter of a story; imperative and exclamatory sentences are suitable less often. When they are, they offer deviations from the declarative sentence pattern.

Sentence and paragraph lengths vary, too. In the story about the town of Owatonna reprinted earlier in this chapter, the number of words in each sentence varies from 8 to 26. The number of words in each paragraph varies from 11 to 34. Lengths of sentences and paragraphs fluctuate in the story as follows:

Words in sentences: 11, 23, 14, 8, 25, 10, 14, 19, 10, 14, 10, 19, 26, 26, 23.

Words in paragraphs: 11, 23, 14, 33, 24, 19, 34, 19, 26, 26, 23.

One of the two-sentence paragraphs combines 8-word and 25-word sentences; the other, 10-word and 14-word sentences. The paragraph containing three sentences of direct quotation material has a 10-14-10 pattern.

There is nothing wrong in having occasional 30-to-40-word sentences in news stories. A careful explanation of a scientific term might, for example, require that many words and might be best stated in a single sentence. One would be foolish to attempt to cut some of the words or to divide the sentence. The reporter likely can use one or two shorter sentences in the following paragraph and thus restore the average. On the other hand, if the reporter uses a series of quite short sentences to reflect the feeling of action, he generally will follow them with medium-length or longer sentences. He thus avoids a monotony of rhythm.

No one can learn in "one easy lesson" the general principles of writing which have been discussed in this chapter. Paragraph organization, use of transitions, sentence unity, and achievement of clarity and variety are all subjects requiring a great deal of instruction and practice. The journalist puts additional emphasis upon certain characteristics of writing to achieve his purposes. He is particularly conscious of such factors as word economy, use of emphatic openings, variation of sentence and paragraph lengths, and use of strong verbal forms to promote ease of reading and understanding. He has only a limited space in which to tell his story, and his story is competing with many others for the reader's attention. So he combines various suggestions made to him about effective news writing with what he already knows about general principles of writing, in ways which seem best in each specific news story situation.

Formulas to Test Readability

Several researchers have developed "formulas" which can be used by the writer to test the probable readability of his stories. The basic principles of the various formulas come from the experience of writers over the years; that is, they test readability by measuring such things as word length, sentence length, human interest content, and word familiarity. Formulas should be used as yardsticks against which writing can be checked, not as rigid patterns into which all writing should be molded.

The Flesch formulas were devised by Dr. Rudolf Flesch, author of *The Art of Readable Writing* and other books. One formula measures reading ease by finding the average sentence length in words and the average word length in syllables. The other measures human interest by the average percentage of "personal words" (pronouns, nouns that have masculine or feminine natural gender, and the collective nouns people and folks) and average percentage of "personal sentences" (quotations of spoken sentences; questions, commands, requests addressed to the reader; exclamations).

Dr. Flesch's yardstick for "standard" writing becomes not more than 150 syllables per 100 words and not more than 19 words per average sentence; at least 6 personal words per 100 words and 12 personal sentences per 100 sentences. You rate "very poor" if you have more than 186 syllables per 100 words, more than 27 words per average sentence, and have no personal words or personal sentences. The Associated Press and many newspapers and magazines have used the Flesch formulas as yardsticks to check over-all readability and to stimulate individual writers whose styles varied widely from the average.

The Gunning formula for determining "Fog Index" was devised by Robert Gunning, author of *The Technique of Clear Writing* and consultant to the United Press and various publications. It is based upon average sentence length in words and the percentage of words of three syllables or more in a given passage. Actual determination of the "fog index" is a more complex matter. Gunning also gives weight to the human interest factor.

The Dale-Chall system, advanced by Edgar Dale and Mrs. Jeanne S. Chall of Ohio State University, uses average sentence length but also takes into account reader familiarity with words by using a list of 3000 words familiar to fourth graders. This prevents a word like "tort" being scored as more readable than a word like "vacation."

Students of writing will want to take formulas such as these into account and learn more about them. But in addition the news writer can check his readability by reviewing these points periodically:

1. Look at your paragraphs. What about variety of length and average length? Remember that four lines of average typing make a longish paragraph.
2. Look at your sentences. How many have emphatic openings? What is the average length? How do they fluctuate

in length? Do simple declarative sentences occur fairly often?

3. How often have you used transitional devices, including words which refer back to earlier statements? Have you helped the reader move from one thought to another?

4. What about your verbs? Do strong simple verbs carry your action? Do your longer sentences contain ample numbers of verb forms?

5. What about word economy? Are vague or unneeded words and phrases eliminated? Have you said it in the shortest, most direct way?

6. Do your sentences have unity? Do they transmit to the reader the emphasis you have intended? Can the reader move along through your sentences and paragraphs and grasp the information you have to offer him?

If your writing passes muster on these points, you are on your way to becoming a reporter who will be read.

Chapter 6

Varying the Basic Story Form

The Need for Variety

The basic news story, we have seen, is written in traditional pyramid fashion. The necessary "5 W's" and "H" elements are covered adequately early in the story. Sometimes these news elements fit into a summary lead paragraph; in other situations only the most important are emphasized in the opening paragraph. The body of the story explains and expands upon the essential news. Its concise and orderly pattern reflects the principle of decreasing reader interest.

How does the reporter obtain variety in his writing if he uses this basic story form more often than any other? One important way has already been discussed. The reporter should not fall into the habit of writing a summary lead for every story. A summary lead is called for when a simple set of facts should be told briefly. But on many other occasions the reporter will find he wants to emphasize one or two of the "W's" in a modified summary lead.

We have suggested that the reporter should play up the feature of the story, if there is one, to make his writing more attractive to the reader. This might be one of the "W's," or it might be some other element. Sometimes it is called "the angle"—what is it that makes this story different? Playing up the feature insures variety, even though the basic story form is followed.

Various writing techniques can be used in fashioning lead paragraphs. Ordinarily the subject-verb declarative sentence is selected. But sometimes different sentence order is called for by the nature of the story. Interrogatives, direct address, brief dramatic phrases, and other writing devices also can be used appropriately to vary the openings of basic news stories.

Finally, some stories by their nature insure variety in manner of presentation to the reader. If the reporter has a multiple set of facts to tell, he organizes his story in a different way than if he has only a single important fact to relate. When he covers a speech, the reporter again varies his manner of presentation, even though he still follows the basic story form.

In this chapter we are discussing ways of making the basic story form interesting to the reader. We are still dealing with the inverted-pyramid structure which calls for telling the essential news early in the story. It is vital that beginning reporters master this basic form; it is equally important that they learn to use it imaginatively. Good reporters possess the gift of imagination, and there is always the danger that as beginners they will feel the basic pyramid form shackles their expression of imagination. This must not happen if the reporter is to be interesting rather than dull. Proper organization of the lead and body of a story requires imagination; so does playing up the feature, varying the sentence construction of leads, or allowing for the more complex nature of some pyramid style stories.

Later in this book, once the problems of reporting the news have been thoroughly explored and the basic story form has been established, it will be time to look at different styles of news writing and different story forms: feature story writing, human interest and color writing, specialized news writing, and such story forms as the chronological and suspended interest types. Compared to the basic story form, these are more easily learned, and the problem of "making it interesting" is less demanding. The man or woman who wants to become a versatile and top-flight reporter will concentrate on learning to use the bread-and-butter pyramid form in the most imaginative way before he or she turns to other story forms and writing styles which complete the repertoire of the journalist. For the true mark of the professional is his or her ability to handle the grist of the news swiftly, clearly, and interestingly.

Playing Up the Feature

There are countless ways to play up the feature of a story. A reporter is told that at a city-wide Boy Scouts meeting one program bit will be the honoring of a lawyer who has been in scouting for 40 years. He decides this is the most interesting item on the program and writes:

A Charleston lawyer who has been in the Boy Scout movement ever since he joined a troup 40 years ago will be honored tonight at a city-wide Scouts conclave.

A courthouse reporter finds that the occupation of a defendant offers a feature angle for an otherwise routine story, and writes:

A bookkeeper ended up in court today because he couldn't keep his checkbook straight.

Joseph G. Donovan, 47, employed by the Smith Construction Co., was charged in Superior Court with passing three checks without having sufficient funds to cover them.

Donovan, who lives at 719 Delaware St., explained he had made a $100 error in subtraction on a check stub. Judge James Delaney withheld sentencing pending further investigation.

Two religion reporters watching a ceremony in Pittsburgh found different features to include in their leads reporting the merging of two major Presbyterian church groups into a new denomination. Leaders of the two groups marched through the city streets in processions which met at a street corner. There the moderators of the two groups clasped hands to signal the union. Rain was falling throughout the ceremony. The two leads follow:

A handclasp on a street corner today joined together three-fourths of the nation's Presbyterians into a new church denomination.

Three-fourths of the nation's Presbyterians were united in a new church denomination today as their leaders met in a baptism of rain.

Baseball writers always need to find the circumstance which makes today's story different from yesterday's. An Associated Press sportswriter added the feature to his lead this way:

PITTSBURGH(AP)—The league-leading San Francisco Giants exploded with their bats *and tempers* today to whip the Pittsburgh Pirates, 5 to 2 and 6 to 1.

A 15-minute fight in the fifth inning of the first game. . . .

A Chicago *Daily News* reporter found an apt verb to feature in this story about a high school class which built a complete house:

A group of North Chicago teen-agers have hammered out a unique building success story.

They constructed a complete three-bedroom home as part of their North Chicago High School building trades classes.

The 19 boys spent a year working three hours a day to do the job.

Under the direction of Norbert Holz, building trades instructor and a journeyman carpenter, the students erected a one-story home with redwood siding at 1817 Elizabeth, North Chicago.

Having covered the essential "W's," the reporter then continued with the details of the story in essentially a pyramid style.

The *Daily News* stresses brief leads, one-sentence paragraphs, and feature angles. In another of that paper's stories, the reporter used a brief quote to build an unusual lead for an otherwise pyramid-style bit of writing:

A handsome, new red and pink home for "soup, soap and salvation" was dedicated Friday.

The $1.8 million glass and tile home is the Salvation Army's territorial headquarters for 11 Midwestern states.

A pine tree was planted in front of the building at 860 N. Dearborn. The roots were covered with earth from the 11 states.

Salvation Army Commissioner John J. Allen spoke of the "spiritual bit" of the Army's work in "dispensing soup, soap and salvation." Allen, former central territorial commander, gave the dedication address.

Mayor Daley thanked the Salvation Army "for giving Chicago such a beautiful structure."

Three hundred persons gathered on the sidewalk at Dearborn and Delaware place for the ceremonies. A Salvation Army band played. . . .

Here are some other lead paragraphs, written for inverted pyramid stories, which illustrate the possibilities of playing up the feature.

A bee buzzing about the head of one driver caused a three-car collision on Hwy. 36 today. Three persons were injured, none seriously.

A showdown between two quarreling aldermen is expected when the City Council takes up the question of taxicab licenses at its weekly meeting tomorrow.

An Austrian who has spoken English only two years will compete with three other Penn State students in next week's interclass oratorical contest.

Varying the Lead Construction

All of the lead sentences quoted so far in this chapter have been declarative sentences. Sometimes the reporter wishes to emphasize a feature element which does not belong in the main clause, or which is better stated apart from the "who did what" of the main part of the sentence. Conditional clauses and various phrases can be used to open leads, as these examples show:

Because he ignored a policeman's command to halt, a Denver teen-ager was in City Hospital today with a bullet wound in his leg.

Although the company's gross income reached a new high last year, International Combine made a smaller net profit than in any recent year, President Franklin W. Greene reported today.

As though a debut in itself weren't enough excitement, most debs these days get an extra dividend—a trip to Europe.

For the third time in as many weeks, thieves broke into a grocery store at 517 N. Broadway last night and helped themselves to food and cash receipts.

After a frantic three-hour search by relatives and neighbors, three-year-old Deborah Williams walked up to her back door yesterday and announced, "I'm back."

Disregarding the protests of 27 householders, the City Council today ordered removal of 45 shade trees to permit widening of Elm St.

A word of caution: Remember that these are examples of deviations from the usual declarative sentence pattern. The reporter had a purpose in each case; he wished to emphasize a particular point which he felt would command the interest of the reader. The beginner who needlessly avoids the subject-verb summary statement will find his copy edited.

Interrogatives, direct address, and other writing devices can sometimes be used to make leads attractive. The reporter who wrote the following story for the Minneapolis *Tribune* decided he had no strong news peg for a summary lead. His story had feature characteristics but still tended to fit the inverted-pyramid structure. So he used a direct address question as the opening of a modified summary lead in which the essential "W's" were covered in the first four paragraphs.

More Than 1,000 Prizes

Housewife Finds Formula
For Winning Contest Prizes

By John C. McDonald

Can you tell in 25 words or less why you like a certain brand of soap or toothpaste or flour?

Lucille Pearson, a Minneapolis housewife, can—and does.

A home, a husband and four children haven't prevented Mrs. Pearson, slight and on the sunny side of middle age, from finding time to win prizes in more than a thousand contests.

Two scrapbooks filled with clippings and letters attest to her prize-winning talents. So do a piano, a refrigerator, an electric stove and other furnishings of the Pearsons' white stucco home at 2922 Girard Ave. N.

Mrs. Pearson has won so many prizes she can't remember them all, but she recalls an indeterminate number of wrist watches, vacuum cleaners and diamond rings, a half-dozen radios, and countless other valuable items. Her husband, Stanley, liked a $1,000 cash prize for a limerick most.

"I've won a watch and two radios in the past couple of weeks, first prize in a national contest which will give me a pair of nylons every month for life and"—here she smiled —"$10 for a statement about why I like beer."

She entered her first contest about 10 years ago after jotting down the rules for it while listening to a radio program. Her observations on the merits of a soap powder won her an electric dishwasher and a desire for more competition.

Her next endeavor was a short story in a confessional magazine contest. She didn't win a prize, but the magazine bought her story.

After that, there was no stopping her. She sold a few more magazine stories, but she discovered that she hadn't enough time to write fiction. She turned once more to contests.

"I do most of my writing around 11 or 12 o'clock at night after the kids are in bed and the house is quiet," she says.

"I've entered all sorts of contests and I've won all sorts, too, but I prefer short statements, essays, letters, limericks. I can't enter all the contests I see, so of course I pick the ones in which I think I'll have the best chance."

Mrs. Pearson attributes much of her success to the fact that she obeys contest rules implicitly, tries to submit exactly what the sponsor wants. She estimates that fully one-third of all contestants are weeded out because they don't observe the rules precisely.

Contesting must be either hereditary or contagious. Even the Pearson children win prizes. They use their own ideas, and their mother helps them with punctuation and final polishing.

The popularity of contests is proof that large numbers of people enter them, particularly housewives. The lead the reporter used undoubtedly attracted far more readers than any summary lead which would have attempted to say that Mrs. Pearson had won more than a thousand contests during the past ten years, including several during the past two weeks.

Another example of the use of direct address is this brief lead written at a time Congress was changing postal rates, including the rate for mailing first-class letters. The lead covered the most important news for the average reader; the next paragraph quickly indicated the range of other postal rate changes reported upon in detail later in the story.

WASHINGTON(UPI)—It'll cost you 4 cents to mail a letter, starting Aug. 1.

Familiar sayings can sometimes be incorporated into leads effectively. Here are examples taken from the openings of inverted pyramid stories.

A judge's conscience won out over the letter of the law in St. Paul federal district court Thursday.

Silence is golden, especially when you are in court, Frank McNutt discovered yesterday.

The role of the Good Samaritan was played once again by a Toledo motorist last night.

A note of caution: Misuse or overuse of this device can lead to the appearance of outworn, trite phrases in stories. Some reporters get a few "household" phrases fixed in their minds and overwork them badly.

One more story from the Chicago *Daily News* illustrates how a reporter can enliven a routine story. The assignment was to cover the departure of a Russian dance company which had performed in Chicago during the past week. Through little touches of writing and through careful reporting of details, the reporter achieved reader interest. He used a dialogue lead.

Russ Dancers Leave for Coast, Bid Chicago 'do Svidaniye'

By Nicholas R. Shuman

"Very good city. We Chicago very much like."

So saying, the Russian Moiseyev dance company left the city Thursday—by plane and by train—to cross the American steppes.

They open in Los Angeles Saturday night and in San Francisco May 31.

Twenty-five of the dancers, and that many more American musicians accompanying them, boarded the Santa Fe Chief for the trip.

The rest of the company, 76 persons, took an American Airlines coach flight out of Midway airport. This group included the "balletmeister," Igor Alexanderdrovich Moiseyev.

The dancers were given their choice of transportation. Those on the Chief were there because they wanted to see more of the country.

"We will see nine states—your great mountains and your farms," said Victor Sudakov, 26, in Russian.

As the company parted at the Bismarck hotel, the plane riders joshed the train people.

"We will all be bronzed by the sun by the time you get there," one girl said, laughing.

"You will be sick in bed with sunburn," came the retort.

Both groups boarded chartered busses for the rides to the Dearborn st. station and the airport.

They were overloaded with luggage and locally bought packages. Bread and sandwich meats peeked out from the tops of some bags.

Olga Tverdochleba, 20, and pretty, dropped a bag of oranges and apples on the bus. Blushingly, her blond pigtails waving, she scurried to pick them up.

Asked if they would like to come back to Chicago, Tanya Vasileva, 25, another blond, and Anatoly Borzov, 29, nodded eagerly.

Sudakov added, with a broad grin, "If you invite us."

Multiple-Fact Stories

Planning the lead and organizing the body of a story become more difficult when the reporter has a number of facts or incidents to tell, based on the same event.

A city council or a school board, for example, may take several actions at a single meeting. A political convention may generate three or four important developments in one day which the political reporter must relay to his readers at the breakfast table next morning. A storm or disaster story may have several important facets to treat.

The reporter may decide to "wrap up" the important developments in a single paragraph and use the next few paragraphs to tell more about each of the items in his lead, before expanding into the body of his story. For example, this story covers three developments in a political crisis.

PARIS(UPI)—Gen. Charles de Gaulle, summoned to Paris by President Coty to try to form a new government, left for home early today after meeting secretly with parliamentary leaders in an attempt to whittle down opposition to his return as premier.

There was no immediate indication of the results of de Gaulle's midnight meeting with Andre le Troquer, president of the National Assembly, and Gaston Monnerville, president of the Senate.

De Gaulle left for his country home in Colombey-les-deux-Eglises after the rendezvous. The parliamentary leaders were expected to report to Coty within hours on results of the conference.

Coty summoned de Gaulle to the capital Wednesday night, as the country's political crisis reached a climax. . . .

If one action seems more important than others, the reporter may describe it in the first paragraph and summarize the other actions in his second paragraph. The body of the story will then carry the details in the same order that the actions have been listed.

Harry R. Zimmerman was appointed city purchasing agent by a unanimous vote of the City Council today. He succeeds John P. Wilson, who died April 17.

In other actions, the council approved sale of city water to the suburb of Glen Valley, ordered an inquiry into enforcement of restaurant sanitary regulations, and approved three new liquor licenses.

The "1-2-3" device also serves to give the reader an overview of the important developments in a story before he begins to read the details.

Three overnight developments faced delegates to the Republican state convention today as they prepared to meet at noon to ballot on candidates for the gubernatorial nomination.

1. Gov. Luther Bronson set rumors at rest by issuing a flat

statement saying he would "not accept renomination under any circumstances."

2. Martin county delegates swung their support to Lt. Gov. Gomer Smith in an early morning caucus.

3. Supporters of Rep. Charles Kennedy claimed they had the backing of the Bronson organization, and jubilantly predicted victory for the 33-year-old lawyer from Priceville.

In a swiftly breaking story, the reporter sometimes lets the various developments fall into place in an orderly pattern—not necessarily chronologically in terms of actual occurrence, but accomplishing that effect for the reader. In this story written for the New York *Herald Tribune* in 1945, Washington correspondent Bert Andrews had a big story to tell:

Truman Takes Oath of Office In White House Ceremony

WASHINGTON, April 12—Harry S. Truman, 60 years old, became the 33rd President of the United States at 7:09 p.m. today, taking the oath of office from Harlan F. Stone, Chief Justice of the United States.

The quiet, bespectacled man from Independence, Mo., picked up the heavy burdens of the war, the coming peace negotiations and the gigantic reconversion problems at a brief swearing-in ceremony in the Cabinet room of the White House.

As his first official act after stepping from the comparative obscurity of the Vice-Presidency into the glaring limelight of the world's biggest job, President Truman announced a get-on-with-the-war policy.

For his initial statement as President, Mr. Truman authorized Jonathan W. Daniels, White House press secretary, to quote him as follows:

"The world may be sure that we will prosecute the war on both fronts, east and west, with all the vigor we possess, to a successful conclusion."

He quickly implemented these words with four deeds.

First he authorized Edward R. Stettinius, Jr., Secretary of State, to announce there would be no postponement of the San Francisco Conference of United Nations on international organization, despite President Roosevelt's death.

Next he requested all members of the Cabinet of President Roosevelt to remain in office, and they promptly acquiesced.

Then he disclosed he would

confer promptly, probably to-morrow, with America's military leaders, headed by General of the Army George C. Marshall and Fleet Admiral Ernest J. King.

Finally he said, through Mr. Daniels, that he would hold his first press conference early next week.

Mr. Truman was called to the White House . . .

Speech Stories

Abilities of reporters can be measured by the way in which they handle speech stories. Writing a speech story from the text of a manuscript is a hard job. Writing one from notes taken at the speech itself is an even more demanding job. You will be told more later about the reportorial function. It is important that you not be struggling with the techniques of writing —story organization, proper use of quotes, etc.—at the time you should be concentrating on reporting what the speaker said.

The lead of a speech story usually is a summary statement. It tells the reader the essence of the main theme of the speaker's message. The lead material (first two or three paragraphs) also identifies the speaker, tells where and when he spoke, and under what circumstances.

If the speaker discusses two or three major issues—as in a political campaign, for example—there probably is no single main theme. Then the reporter decides which one of the major statements should be featured in the lead, and he very early summarizes the others, as in a multifact story.

Once the lead material has been completed, the reporter must develop the explanation of the main theme. Several paragraphs will probably be devoted to this block of the story. If there are secondary themes listed in a summary secondary lead paragraph, they will then be developed, one by one. It is vitally important that the lead material be expanded immediately because the reader wants to know what basis the speaker had for saying what he did.

Transitions are very important in speech stories. They are used to carry the reader from one thought to another, and from one subject to another. The reporter must remember to maintain adequate identification of the speaker throughout his story by using his name or "he said" in each paragraph or series of related paragraphs.

Direct quotations make a speech story much more readable and convincing. They need to be alternated with indirect quotations, which are summaries by the reporter of what the speaker said. A direct quotation is carried within quotation marks; an indirect quotation is not. The reporter must have a quite exact version of what the speaker said in order to use the quotation marks. He may make minor deletions or word changes, however, provided he has not changed the speaker's style or the essence of what he said. In the indirect quotation, the reporter must be just as accurate in reflecting what the speaker said, but he may use his own language to report the speaker's ideas. The reporter uses indirect quotations to summarize longer portions of the speech, or illustrations, and direct quotations to reproduce the speaker's exact words on major points. The reporter always should have direct quotations to back up his lead statements.

The rules for punctuating quotations are the same in news writing as in any other writing, but they seem to give reporters a lot of trouble. The same is true of attribution of the statements to the speaker. Here are some points to remember:

Indirect quotations often start with the source; direct quotations almost never do. Attribution of the direct quotation should be made as early as possible, however, usually at the close of the first sentence.

Direct quotations which represent a block of several paragraphs can "run open." The first paragraph opens with quotation marks, and there must be a set preceding and following the attribution of source. The second paragraph and succeeding ones open with quotation marks, but remain unclosed, until the writer reaches the end of the final paragraph of his block of quotation material. Then he uses closing quotation marks. A common fault of reporters is to open a direct quotation and forget to close it.

Summary paragraphs are often used as transitional paragraphs introducing blocks of direct quotations. It is obvious that if the reporter is switching from one of the speaker's thoughts to another, he will indicate this to the reader by changing writing style and will avoid at all costs running right on with direct quotation material.

Watch how these general rules are applied in the following sample speech story:

Yale Professor Answers
Criticisms of Public Schools

The United States needs to restore the proper perspective to criticism of education, John S. Brubacher, professor of philosophy of education at Yale University, said yesterday.

Dr. Brubacher opened Education Day festivities with a convocation address to several hundred faculty and students in Northrop Auditorium.

He cited four current "shot gun" criticisms of education, attempting to bring each into historical perspective. Never, he said, has such criticism been so severe and continuous as since World War II.

Dr. Brubacher attributed this in part to "emotional tensions" growing out of the cold war and an attempt to find a scapegoat for the nation's troubles.

The first of the four criticisms currently leveled at education, Dr. Brubacher said, is that today's schools neglect the talented student and pamper the mediocre one.

"I resent the implication that other groups should be neglected in order to favor the talented student," he answered.

"It would be better to have a balanced system than to educate the few at the expense of the many. Perhaps we have neglected the talented students, but we must not neglect those of somewhat less talent whom we have taken care of so handsomely in the past half-century."

A second criticism, Dr. Brubacher said, is closely related to the first. This is that school standards are low.

"It's not so much this," he said, "as that standards today are different than in an earlier period when we had one standard for all.

"Many people feel that because we try to motivate studies—to make them interesting—this is a lowering of standards.

"Current comparisons of American and European educational standards are often not fair in that they neglect the fact that most European education is for a highly select few."

Another "shot gun" charge being made is that the school curriculum is anti-intellectual, Dr. Brubacher continued. Those who make this charge point to the "mental discipline" emphasis of 19th century education, he said.

"But while the 19th century school course was decidedly intellectual, it also was arid and barren," he declared. "More functional courses were introduced to correct this—including the much-criticized 'life adjustment' courses.

"Critics of life adjustment don't speak of the courses which help us understand great issues of the day—yet these are life adjustment too."

The final indictment, Dr. Brubacher said, is that many teachers are poorly trained. This is true, he agreed.

"Certainly they could be trained better, but deficiencies are not by cause or design," he said. "People attack poorly trained teachers as if we didn't care. Our critics forget that there always have been more school rooms than school teachers.

"Although we wouldn't consider lowering our standards to get more doctors, we would do it with teachers."

Dr. Brubacher asserted that the days of immoderate criticism of education are coming to an end.

"There is nothing wrong with the American system of education developed over the past 100 years that a general tightening of nuts and bolts all along the line wouldn't cure," he concluded.

A second example of a speech story illustrates how the reporter backs up his summary of the speaker's main point with direct quotations. It also illustrates the two-paragraph lead, with the name of the speaker opening the second paragraph.

Ministers or Bombs?—
Secretary Dulles Poses Issue

NEW YORK (AP)—Which of two types of plants is to survive—the kind that turns out ministers or the kind that turns out atom bombs?

This, John Foster Dulles said Tuesday night, is the issue of all time.

The Secretary of State addressed a dinner of the board of directors of Union Theological Seminary before he and Mrs. Dulles watched their daughter receive her bachelor of divinity degree from the institution.

"Out in Tennessee there is a plant which turns out bombs," Dulles said at the dinner.

"Here is a plant which turns out ministers of the gospel. The two seem remote and unrelated.

"Actually, the issue of our time, perhaps the issue of all our human time, is which of these two outputs will prevail. . . ."

Summary

Reporters need to handle their stories imaginatively, regardless of the forms their writing takes or how long or short the stories are. The basic story form is a pattern; using it, the reporter varies his approach to each story according to its peculiar characteristics. A constant question should be: "What is different about this story?"

Part Three

THE TECHNIQUES OF
REPORTING

Chapter 7

The Reporter in the City Room

The City Room at Work

The heart of a newspaper's operation is the city room. Here all the newsgathering facilities of the newspaper are centered, all the lines of communication with the local community and the world drawn together. Here the news content of the paper is organized, written, and edited; from it the copy moves to the composing room to be turned into type.

The city room is the reporter's home. His desk "on the floor" under the eye of the city editor is his base of operations, from which he goes out on assignments or covers his stories by telephone.

Every city room has its own personality, depending in part upon its size and the physical facilities of its building and in part upon the kind of men in charge of it. In some the furniture is old and battered; in others, it is new and efficient-looking, such as that in an insurance office. Some city rooms have an atmosphere of casual informality; others are more rigid and subdued. All have their moments of tension and bustle, when word of a big story breaking sends a shock wave of excitement through the room. But even in their most urgent moments, city rooms do not have the air of frantic chaos ascribed to them by the film producers.

A newcomer in the city room sees its inhabitants as a group of men in shirtsleeves sitting at typewriters, talking on the telephone with sets of earphones clamped to their heads, reading papers, scribbling with pencils, or possibly standing in little groups drinking coffee. There is an occasional call of "boy" or "copy," and a youth hurries from one desk to another with pieces of paper. The wire service teleprinters are off in one corner, clattering away in a monotone broken by the intermittent tinkle of bells.

Soon the new reporter learns that all this activity is a highly organized and disciplined operation, with lines of command as clearly drawn as in an army. His own job, he finds, has a well-defined place in the machinery.

The man in charge of the local newsgathering staff is the city editor. Each reporter takes his orders from him or one of his assistants and turns in his finished story to these men on the city desk. This is the nerve center of the big room, to which news leads flow by telephone, and from which assignments are handed out to the reporters.

The newcomer will discover, too, that not all the men in the room are under the city editor's supervision. Smaller groups work under the orders of the news editor and the copy desk chief. Their task is taking the stories written by the city staff, also the stories from the wire services, and giving them a mechanical polishing for publication.

The city editor is responsible for gathering and writing the local news. How the stories are played, the size headlines they carry, and the position they occupy in the newspaper is usually not his responsibility. Those decisions rest with the managing editor, to whom the city editor is responsible. Completed stories are passed from the city desk to the news editor and, under his control, to the copy desk. The news editor usually works directly under the managing editor's direction and carries out his policy instructions.

The news editor assigns each story a headline size and gives it a place on the page dummies he prepares for the composing room. He weighs the local stories against the wire service stories from out of town for their relative news value; also he selects the pictures that are to illustrate the stories. Large newspapers often have a picture editor who chooses the "art" and writes the captions for it under the news editor's supervision. On the copy desk the stories are processed for style, rechecked for errors of fact and grammar, given the headlines as ordered, and sent to the printers.

The managing editor has over-all responsibility for the day-to-day functioning of the editorial department. The heads of feature sections such as sports, women's, and entertainment report direct to him, just as the city editor does. The upper-echelon organization of newspapers varies considerably. Some are run by a combined editor and publisher, others have executive editors, and in some metropolitan newspapers there is an assistant editor who exercises full control over editorial policy and specialized departments. This division of authority may appear rigid. But in practice the chief editors hold frequent shirtsleeve consultations as the edition deadlines approach and fresh stories come in. The city editor's recommendations on how much prominence to give certain local stories carry much weight.

All this editing organization is beyond the immediate concern of the reporter. He takes his instructions from, and answers only to, the city editor. However, when one of his stories appears on the front page under a large or clever headline he should say a silent "thank you" to the men around the news and copy desks with whom he has little direct contact.

On small papers, where a few men do all the essential jobs, the city editor sometimes carries the news editor's responsibilities, too, and the reporter writes his own headlines. This is not a common procedure.

How the City Staff Is Organized

The city editor usually is a former reporter who has worked his way up through the ranks, a man (or occasionally a woman) who has wide knowledge of the city and has shown administrative ability. He is not necessarily the best writer on the staff, although he knows how to develop writing skill in others. Some of the best reporters in the world would fail as city editors and would refuse the job if offered. They hate the routine, the paperwork, and the constant pressures and responsibilities of directing an efficient staff. The city editor has an assistant, or on metropolitan newspapers several assistants, who directs the newsgathering and writing of specific stories on the daily assignment sheet.

The news staff is organized by beats. The reporter assigned to each beat is responsible for learning about and reporting all newsworthy events that occur in his field. A good reporter keeps informed on trends and potential developments and prepares background notes on them; when a story materializes on his beat, he is ready to cover it fully and quickly, not only the main facts but also its significance.

The purpose of beat assignments is to give the city desk automatic coverage on all the most frequent sources of news. The exact arrangement of beats differs with every city, depending upon local circumstances, but some basic ones are used everywhere. The police department is a fundamental beat; much news originates here and at all hours. Metropolitan newspapers have 24-hour coverage on the police beat, one reporter relieving another every eight hours. Smaller papers arrange their staff hours to fit their edition times, with arrangements for off-hour "protection" on big stories; that is, for someone within the police department to notify the city editor or police reporter at home if a major disaster or similar banner headline story breaks.

The main government offices in the city form another essential beat. This includes the city hall, city council, mayor's office, and county offices. In very large cities coverage of county affairs is sometimes put into a beat of its own, and in state capitals a special man is assigned to state affairs, including the governor's office. Coverage of the courts and district attorney's office often forms a full-time beat in major cities, while in smaller ones the courts are included in the county beat or sometimes in the police beat. Metropolitan newspapers often have radio cruise cars to supplement their police coverage. These have two-way radio contact with the city desk, plus facilities for monitoring police broadcasts. If the reporter and photographer cruising in the car pick up a police report of a disaster or crime, they rush to the scene. They also take assignments direct from the city desk on the two-way radio circuit. Use of these cars greatly accelerates the coverage of fast-breaking stories.

Every city editor arranges his beats in relation to the amount of news coming from them and the number of men he has on his staff (no city editor ever admits that he has enough).

Other news sources usually covered by beat men include the hotels, schools, chamber of commerce, federal offices (if there are any), and labor headquarters. Many city desks consider hospitals part of the police beat; others make them a special assignment. Not all of these secondary beats require full-time staffing. The reporter assigned to them works on other stories as well.

The city staff also has general assignment reporters; these men have no beat responsibilities but are sent out on day-by-day assignments from the city desk. Sometimes a man covers several stories a day, going from one to another, everything from a tree-planting ceremony to a bank robbery. The city desk draws upon this manpower pool of general assignment reporters for emergency coverage. When a train wreck occurs, for example, the man on the police beat calls in a flash and continues to cover police headquarters for late facts as the story develops. Meanwhile general assignment men are rushed out from the office for on-the-spot coverage. Beginning reporters are normally put on general assignment until they learn their way around and the city editor has had an opportunity to judge their ability. Most girl reporters get general assignment work, although many have distinguished themselves with detailed special knowledge of court and government beats.

Big city police reporters call the police press rooms their offices; they may go months without coming into the city room except to collect their pay checks. Their work is done almost entirely by phone. Major government buildings like the city hall and state capitol usually have press rooms, too, in which the beat men maintain headquarters.

Rewrite Men

The pace of newsgathering is so fast and editions are so frequent, especially on larger afternoon newspapers, that it is often impossible for a reporter to cover a story and get back into the office to write it before his deadline. He must telephone the facts to a man in the office who takes down the reporter's notes and then writes the story. This is the rewrite man.

Although he rarely gets a by-line, the rewrite man is among the most important members of the city staff, one of the most experienced and best paid. He must be a fast writer. He must also be quick to catch the significance of a story, accurate, calm, and a first-rate organizer. On major stories several reporters are phoning in notes; a single rewrite man assembles all these and weaves them into a coherent, smoothly flowing story. Many a sloppy reporter has been made to look good by a rewrite man who, in taking the reporter's notes on the phone, detects errors and omissions or tips the reporter on an angle to check.

On running stories which continue for several days, the same rewrite man usually handles the assignment from start to finish. Thus he knows the story almost as well as the reporter handling it. The young reporter can get much help and guidance from the old hands on rewrite. Rewrite men develop specialties; some excel at putting together complex stories, others at giving the daily weather article a bright twist or putting a heart tug into an otherwise routine police blotter story.

The role of the rewrite man is greater on an afternoon paper than on a morning paper. The pace of the A.M.'s (as the trade jargon goes) is more leisurely than the P.M.'s. Reporters generally have time to cover stories during the day; then they come back in and write them for the first early evening deadline. Sometimes an office boy picks up the stories after a reporter has written them in press headquarters. But most stories from established sources like city hall and the courts occur close to the afternoon paper deadlines. Thus, far more stories must be telephoned in by the P.M. reporters. Metropolitan afternoon newspapers have a battery of four or five highly experienced rewrite men, lined up close to the city desk, who do nothing but handle telephoned stories. Usually these are the top local stories on page one.

The City Desk in Operation

Control of all this bustling activity is kept through the city editor's assignment sheet. On this he lists at the start of the day all the scheduled or anticipated stories and the name of the reporter assigned to each; where a photographer has also been put on the story, his name is listed, too. Frequently on large papers a reporter and photographer are dispatched together, known in some cities as sending a crew on the story. As each story is completed and clears the city desk, it is checked off the sheet. New stories are added as they develop. At all times the city editor knows what each staff member is working on.

The city editor over the years has developed contacts of his own. Often he has come up through the reporting ranks simultaneously with police officers who are now captains or higher. Even though he no longer goes out to cover a story, the city editor tries to retain these contacts. Often he gets tips on impending developments through them. Not infrequently the city editor will give a beat man the lead on a story in his own territory because an old friend called to tip him.

Once the reporter's story is written, either by himself or a rewrite man, it is handed in to the city desk. There it is read closely, double-checked for facts, edited to eliminate loose writing or libel, and trimmed if too long. Frequently the city editor or his assistant sees something in the story that can be improved; if he can't make the repairs with a copy pencil he turns it back to the writer for revision or even complete rewriting. He may request a different lead, more colorful detail, or inclusion of direct quotations from the news source to support statements in the lead; conversely, he may say, "This is too long, cut it to 150 words." Usually, however, the desk man tells the reporter approximately how long the story should be before he starts to write. The editing done while the story is on the city desk is essentially creative; editing on the copy desk is largely mechanical, for style, punctuation, and spelling. A good copyreader challenges a doubtful fact and carries the story back to the city desk for confirmation. His is the final editing responsibility.

Once he has turned in his story, the beginning reporter usually returns to his desk and, while trying to appear nonchalant, watches surreptitiously to see how his writing fares. Will it be chopped to pieces on the desk, flung back for a rewrite, or, even worse, given to someone else to rehandle? Or will it sail gloriously through? There is almost as much thrill in getting a first story past the editor's hands as later seeing it in print. Don't be discouraged if a story is turned back for polishing. This happens to veterans, too.

A second pair of eyes, the city editor's, looking at a story with more objectivity than the writer can possess, and weighing it in relation to other stories that cross the desk, can see things that the writer misses. The old proverb about being too close to the trees to see the forest applies to the reporter immersed in a mass of fact and trying to blend it into a smooth story under deadline pressure.

Using the Editorial Library

Reference will be made in later chapters on reporting techniques to use of the newspaper's library. To use the library efficiently, the reporter should know what he can find there. A good library is a quick source of valuable information for both spot news and feature stories. It can be used to check the spelling of names, for background about people in the news, and for historical information.

The most important portion of the library to the reporter is its file of clippings. Each day's paper has been clipped, the stories suitably labeled and filed in envelopes. Usually there is a cross-filing system, with the clippings filed both by name and subject matter. If a major fire in the downtown area ten years ago killed a prominent banker, the clipping can probably be found under his name and under the heading of fires, as well. In larger libraries, at least, the librarians prefer to pull out the clippings themselves upon the reporter's request.

A reporter assigned to do a feature story involving an aspect of the city's history will find a wealth of material right in his own newspaper's library.

Files of the complete paper, all the way back to its first issue if possible, also are kept. These are in bound volumes or, a recent development, in microfilm form. Either way, they are available for immediate reference.

Photographs by staff photographers and the picture services

are filed similarly but on a more selective basis. Sometimes the attached captions will contain the elusive fact a reporter has been pursuing. The negatives of staff photographs are retained for a period of years, too.

In addition to all this, the library normally contains such reference books as an encyclopedia, almanacs, who's who books, books on local history, maps, and pamphlets on a wide range of subjects. The reporter who uses this abundant material properly will find his own job made easier, faster, and more accurate. It is one of his finest news sources.

Chapter 8

The Reporter, His Editor, and the Public

The Reporter Represents the Public

The reporter in pursuit of a news story is much more than a young man chasing facts for a salary. He is the representative of his newspaper, and through it he represents the public's right to know. His efforts are supported by a heavy accumulation of law and tradition, including the First Amendment to the Constitution. This states that Congress "shall make no law . . . abridging the freedom of speech, or of the press. . . ."

When carrying the proper credentials, the reporter is admitted inside the police and fire lines at disasters. Mention of his newspaper's name gives him an audience with virtually all public officials and celebrities. He mingles on a business-social basis with the most prominent people of his community. His ears pick up all sorts of gossip and scandal, much of it unprovable. Some people play up to him with blatant efforts to win personal publicity, but most Americans accept the reporter of an established news medium as the embodiment of something they have been taught to respect—the right of newspapers and other news media to report freely what is happening. In fact, many people are secretly impressed by his presence.

In this respect the reporter is a privileged person. Even though the people from whom he seeks news have never heard of him personally, most of them welcome him and cooperate with his requests. How he conducts himself personally and professionally once the doors have been opened determines how effective a reporter he is.

The freedom to report carries a corresponding responsibility for fairness. This is much less defined by law than is the freedom, but it is essential nonetheless. It is generally held in this country that a free press must also be an honest press, that it must give both sides in its news stories. Every American is entitled to a fair hearing in court, and he also deserves a fair hearing in a newspaper's stories. An accusation in print deserves a reply from the accused. It is not a reporter's function to pass moral or legal judgment on the people he is covering when he writes his story. His job is to find out all he can about the situation to which he has been assigned. Whatever personal views he may have about the individuals and issues involved should not color his coverage. A large part of a newspaper's reputation for objective coverage rests upon the reporter, since he is the man who deals directly with the news sources.

The Canons of Journalism drawn up by the American Society of Newspaper Editors cover this question under a point headed Fair Play. It states:

> A newspaper should not publish unofficial charges affecting reputation or moral character without opportunity given to the accused to be heard; right practice demands the giving of such opportunity in all cases of serious accusation outside judicial proceedings.
>
> 1. A newspaper should not invade private rights or feeling without sure warrant of public right as distinguished from public curiosity.
>
> 2. It is the privilege, as it is the duty, of a newspaper to make prompt and complete correction of its own serious mistakes of fact or opinion, whatever their origin.

If the accused man refuses to comment, the story should say so, to show that he has been given an opportunity to reply. There may be times when deadlines make it impossible to reach the accused in time for his comment on the charges. Nevertheless, the matter should be pursued and his rebuttal published at the first opportunity.

What the City Editor Expects of a Reporter

Reliability and accuracy in reporting facts come before all other considerations. The readers of a newspaper expect its stories to be correct; if a reader finds sloppy and inaccurate reports on stories about which he has personal knowledge, his faith in the newspaper slips. It is essential that basic matters of fact like the spelling of names, addresses, and dates be free of error. Nothing lowers a reporter's standing in the editor's eyes faster than repeated mistakes of this sort. Editors can and do challenge a reporter's facts, but even the sharpest eye cannot detect all inaccuracies.

Names are especially tricky. The reporter who asks a man's name, and then assumes that he knows how to spell it, will be in trouble and might find himself and his paper threatened with a libel suit. Always ask the man to spell it for you, if there is the slightest doubt. As every city editor knows to his sorrow, there frequently is only the slightest difference in spelling between the city's leading banker and a notorious burglar. Careless mixing of them causes embarrassment all around. Mistaken identity is a constant danger in newspaper reporting.

It is surprising how many different spellings there are of common-sounding names. A glance in the telephone book will prove this. Addresses contain perils, too. For example, you are interviewing the eyewitness of an accident and ask his name and address. He replies hurriedly, "Ed MacNeil, 642 Grand." Those simple words are full of traps for the careless reporter. Does Ed stand for Edward, Edwin, or Edgar? Which of the six frequent spellings of his last name does he use—MacNeil, McNeil, McNeill, McNiel, McNeal, or Macneil? Is that 642 address on South, North, East, or West Grand? And is it a street, avenue, place, or boulevard?

Or perhaps the name he gives sounds like Meyer. It might also be Myer, Meier, or Mayer, and it may possibly have an "s" at the end. The optional "O" and "E" in Scandinavian names is a source of trouble. Is it Peterson or Petersen? Other typical and rather common name difficulties include Stuart or Stewart, Philip or Phillip, Francis or Frances, Marian or Marion. There are many others. Every city desk has its own danger list of unusual spellings of local names frequently in the news.

Another Kind of Reliability

Being alert on the job at all times is as much a part of reliability as correct handling of detail. News stories break at any hour and without warning. A reporter out on an assignment or on his beat is expected to keep in frequent touch with the city desk by phone. Since news is relative and ever changing, the editor may want to take a reporter off one story at any moment and assign him to something bigger and more urgent. If the editor can't reach a reporter he is no good to him. Whenever possible, a reporter should leave the phone number where he will be available, even during his off-work hours. He may be summoned to work on very short notice in emergencies. The five-day, forty-hour week is in general use in newspapers, with time-and-a-half pay for overtime work. Nevertheless, there is an unwritten rule among newspaper men that the big story must be covered, no matter what the hour. A reporter may be summoned out of bed or called into the office on his day off to lend a hand. He gets his overtime pay in most cases, but many newsmen find almost more satisfaction in the knowledge that they have had a part in a major story. The simile about being as eager to answer the bell as an old fire horse may be trite, but it is widely accepted in the newspaper business as an apt description for reporters. Usually it is true.

Like all good employers, editors are interested in their staff members and are willing to help with personal problems. But a reporter should not expect his city editor to play nursemaid to him. His personal affairs are no concern of his editor unless they interfere with his work or make him appear to the public as an unfit representative of the newspaper. City editors will put up with more than most employers, especially if the reporter is unusually valuable for his specialized knowledge or writing. The camaraderie of newspapermen is considerable. But the reporter who abuses it will find himself without a job.

Give the Editor Your Full Confidence

The reporter must share all his information with his city editor. Don't try to hoard exciting facts until you have them all tied together for a sensational surprise exclusive, so you can look like a Hollywood movie hero playing reporter. Newsgathering is a team operation. If you run across some information that indicates the germ of a big story, inform the city editor right away. He is the one who must decide when the story is ready to break. Perhaps he will want to put another man on the assignment with you to check on certain angles. Perhaps he has reason to believe that the opposition paper is "on to" the story too, and wants to print it first, even if all the loose ends haven't been tied up.

Beyond certain obvious limits that grow out of experience, a reporter should not try to make decisions on what his editor wants from him. When in doubt, query the city desk. The editor will tell you whether to handle the story immediately, work on it further, or pass it up. Always be ready to tell your editor the sources of your information. He is entitled to know; frequently that knowledge helps him to weigh the validity and importance of the information you report.

Many city desks have a system of memos. The reporter submits background notes and tips on future news stories as they come to his attention. The city editor takes mental note of them, possibly correlates them with those submitted by other staff members, and files them for reference. Scraps of information from several sources, each too small to make a story, can add up to the outlines of an important news situation.

A typical reporter's memo to the desk might read:

2/18/59

Memo from Joe Baker, City Hall

A group of residents from the Glenview district had a private session with Mayor Wilson about a rezoning deal that may come up in the city council next month. Some developers want to put up a group of apartment buildings and stores. The residential owners don't want it and are trying to talk them out of filing for a zone variance. Don't know yet what the council's attitude will be, but one crowd of councilmen is pretty quick to approve such deals. The residents wanted to know whether the mayor will veto the variance if the council passes it. Their spokesman, Donald Creighton, 2453 Madison Blvd., told me Wilson promised to veto it unless somebody comes up with a lot better reason for the project than he has heard yet.

The material in the memo is too thin for a story at present. There are too many uncertainties at this stage, not even a definite decision by the developers to push their project. But it will be important news for that neighborhood if they do.

The memo is placed in the city editor's future book. This is a calendar of future events, a reminder of stories scheduled or likely to arise on certain dates. Memos like the above are put in the book for approximately the date the story may be expected to develop. If the story materializes, and the council is about ready to act, the note on what the mayor told his visitors becomes valuable. The reporter reminds the mayor of what he said previously and asks if he still intends to veto the measure. If the mayor says yes, there is a strong story: Mayor Threatens to Veto Glenview Apartments. If the mayor says he will sign the measure, there is a story in why he changed his mind.

Reporters on beats should keep their own future books, too, as a protective backstop if their memory slips or the city desk memo goes astray.

The Editor Expects Loyalty

Reporting is a highly competitive business. A reporter assigned to developing a story is supposed to keep the information he uncovers confidential until his paper has published it, and he should especially avoid discussing it with men from competing papers. Even on general stories being covered by all news media, the good reporter is nosing around for an exclusive angle. At press conferences and on police beats the basic information is made available to all reporters present and is willingly shared. But anything beyond what is obviously community property should be kept quiet until it is in print. Many exclusive stories have been deflated by a reporter's inability to avoid talking about what he has uncovered.

Journalistic loyalty goes deeper than not tipping off stories to the opposition. On a beat the reporter develops news sources, many of whom become his friends. His newsgathering duties may bring to light unfavorable facts, possibly illegal ones, about these men. It is not easy sometimes, but the good reporter will refrain from covering up such information. He will pass it on to his editor. If there are extenuating circumstances, he is free to plead them. But he should not block the flow of news either for friendship or to win personal favor. The reporter works for his newspaper, not for his news sources, a fact that men who have been on the same beat for a long time sometimes fail to remember.

Honesty Is Essential

This statement may seem so obvious as to be unnecessary. But it is one that a reporter should never forget. People will try to buy him off, either to get stories about themselves and their projects into the paper, or to keep out unfavorable ones. Rarely are such offers in cash. When they are, the reporter becomes indignant that such a bribery offer should be attempted on him. The buying-off process usually is more subtle, taking the form of flattery, gifts, and privileges. One device is "free loading," as the trade calls it. A reporter or editor is invited to a hotel or restaurant and given its finest service without charge. He may be invited on free trips by a travel organization or taken to parties by the representative of a business concern. Sometimes these invitations are directly connected with legitimate news stories. Frequently they are intended to build long-term good will for the sponsoring organization, to influence the reporter in its favor when some embarrassing news situation involving it arises.

When you are invited on such "junkets," file a memo in the back of your mind that many of these people care little about you personally but only want to influence your work.

Drawing the line between the legitimate privileges and perquisites of a reporter's job and the unethical payoffs is not easy. By the nature of his work the reporter receives minor privileges that don't come to an ordinary office worker. In many cities that includes movie passes and other free tickets to entertainments. These forms of press courtesy are long established and accepted. It is pointless and almost discourteous to reject them. Many individuals and organizations give press parties, hoping to establish a personal tie with newsmen. Attendance at these is regarded as quite in order, as is the acceptance of small token Christmas gifts, although such gestures frequently have much less influence on newspapermen than their donors seem to believe.

A good operating rule is this: accept ordinary courtesies and the minor privileges that are assumed to go with the job. Don't solicit gifts, no matter how small. When an offer troubles your conscience, check with your editor.

Such a case occurred in Cleveland one Christmas. A television station sent console color TV sets as gifts to the homes of the television editors of the three daily newspapers. The sets, worth several hundred dollars each, were installed in the homes before the arrival of letters disclosing the gifts. After checking with their employers, all three television editors returned the sets.

Louis B. Seltzer, editor of the Cleveland *Press*, in commenting on the case enunciated a working rule that is accepted generally in newspapers today: "We at the Press feel that any such gift of this amount or proportion or significance should not be accepted by our paper. Certainly such a gift as a necktie, a bottle of liquor or some other modest offering, which cannot be interpreted as anything other than an act of consideration or friendship, is acceptable. But we feel that we cannot go any further."

Mr. Seltzer might have added that any reporter who can be bought off by a necktie or a bottle of liquor is hardly worthy of the name.

The Editor Expects Enterprise

He wants his reporters to go beyond the "must" aspects of their jobs. Checking out the routine aspects of the stories he assigns is not enough. Any reasonably intelligent person with a little experience can turn in the obvious facts of a story; a successful reporter does this, but he also looks constantly for the extra angle, the additional bit of information, that makes the story stand out so the reader will remember it. The editor expects his reporters, especially those on the beats, to "hunch" stories. Initiative makes news.

The Legal Basis for Reporting

Within the bounds of the free press principle, there are certain legal ground rules about what official records the reporter may see and what information he can print without risking lawsuits against himself and his newspaper.

Generally a newsman has access to official reports concerning the actions of persons involving violations of the law, such as police arrest reports and court documents. He is not allowed to see official documents covering their purely personal affairs, such as the individual records in welfare department files, selective service files, and income tax returns. The theory involved here is the difference between the public's right to know and mere public curiosity. Many of the laws governing access to official information are state legislation, and thus vary in detail.

In recent years there has been sharp debate between editors and federal officials over the availability of information about our national government's activities for inspection by the press. The editors contend that government departments conceal legitimate news source material under classified secrecy regulations—a set of rules intended to prevent the leakage of defense information to potential enemy powers. A "secret" label on a document undoubtedly is a convenient way for a public official to hide from the public review and controversy material which might be embarrassing to him or his political party. The editors believe that constant vigilance is necessary to prevent drying up

Above: the huge city room of the Chicago *Sun-Times* with city desk in foreground; endless belt conveyor carries copy along. Below: an equally modern city room of a 22,000 circulation paper, the Winona (Minn.) *Daily News.*

Above: copy desk of the San Francisco *Chronicle;* here stories are edited, headlines written. Below: a Milwaukee *Journal* linotyper and copy cutter handle a fast-breaking story, piling up type slugs and copy for proofreaders. Type then goes into page forms so printing plates can be cast.

of news sources. The field of nuclear and other scientific development is especially susceptible to such governmental secrecy, since it is a question of judgment as to where the technical developments for defense, justifiably secret, end and where the attendant questions of fiscal and nondefense policy begin.

Although no such defense secrecy classifications exist in the states and cities, aggressive action by reporters and editors frequently is necessary there, too, for protection of the public's right to know.

There is nothing comparable to the *Congressional Record* on most public affairs. Unless the press covers them, they go unreported. The same is true of public documents; few citizens go to the trouble of searching through governmental files unless they have a strong personal stake in a particular action. Thus the reporter carries a heavy responsibility to keep close watch on all such material that comes under his eyes.

If a public official refuses to let a reporter see a document, and the reporter is confident of his legal right to examine it, he should not give up the fight easily. Perhaps the official is bluffing; perhaps he believes he is right. The reporter should discuss the matter with his editor, get expert legal advice, and continue the fight. Frequently the threat of publicity will cause the official to yield, and sometimes the paper has to publish a story about the refusal to open public files.

Newspaper editors generally operate on the principle that the public ought to know, and has a right to know, what is done by its appointed and elected officials, since they are acting as the public's agents in the conduct of its governmental affairs.

The Problem of Libel

Our legal system imposes definite restrictions upon what one person may say about another in print. These are governed by the law of a libel and create a problem that hangs over the heads of reporters and editors at all times. An adverse verdict in a civil suit for libel can lead to a court judgment involving tens of thousands of dollars, as well as to much legal expense and embarrassment to the newspaper. It is also possible, but far

THE TECHNIQUES OF REPORTING

less common, for an individual to be tried, convicted, and sentenced for the crime of committing a libel. Yet occasions arise when a newspaper must intentionally risk a libel charge to carry out its duty as defender of the right to know.

The laws of libel are so extensive and complex that some attorneys build a specialized practice in this field. However, the intricacies need not concern the reporter. There are a few basic rules which, if followed carefully, will carry him through virtually all situations he will encounter. Whenever he is in doubt, he should consult his city editor.

Libel is defamation of character in published form. A person has been defamed whenever statements about him tend to lessen his reputation in the eyes of others who identify him as the person defamed. The first rule for the reporter, then, is this: Any published defamatory material concerning a person or persons who may be identified by others reading the publication constitutes a potential libel peril.

This does not necessarily mean that the material is not to be published; obviously newspapers print many defamatory stories each day. It does mean that the defamatory material should be double-checked for accuracy and that the reason why the paper is running the material, despite its defamatory character, should be clearly known. Is the defamatory statement true, and if so, can the truth be proved in a courtroom (along with, in many states, a satisfactory argument that the story was printed for good motives and justifiable ends)? Is the defamatory material being used because it is part of a fair and accurate report of a public legislative or judicial proceeding? Is the defamatory material justified as "fair comment"—expression of opinion on a matter open to public criticism? If the story checks out for accuracy, and if the answer to any one of these three questions is "yes," the peril of a successful libel suit disappears.

Many citizens, however, do not have such a clear knowledge of what libel means, a circumstance that causes headaches for the men who put out newspapers. The first reaction of many irate persons involved in news stories unfavorable to them is to call the newspaper and threaten, "I'll sue you for libel unless you retract that story." In most cases the story is valid and legally sound, and the editor can shrug off the threat as meaningless. While it is necessary to guard against violations of the law, there is also a danger that the reporters and editors will be gun-shy and avoid publication of legitimate news stories because they fear such threats. Lawyers sometimes file suits to discourage papers from publishing further unfavorable stories.

Most editors work on the basis that if you are sure of the facts in your story, and its publication will serve the public interest, then go ahead and print it. Newspapers regularly take "calculated risks" in order to tell stories while they are news; the important thing is to know what sort of a risk you are taking and to weigh the reason for taking it. If the editor senses real danger, he puts the matter up to the newspaper's publisher, who will pay the judgment in a successful suit for damages.

Another basic rule for the reporter is to know and understand the laws governing libel in the state in which he works. Libel is governed by state laws. In civil actions for libel, these laws permit suits arising from claims of personal injuries (to reputations). In criminal actions, brought by the state, the charge is one of disturbing the peace. The laws vary in wording from state to state, but the wording of the New York definition of libel is typical:

"A malicious publication, by writing, printing, picture, effigy, sign or otherwise than by mere speech, which exposes any living person, or the memory of any person deceased, to hatred, contempt, ridicule, or obloquy, or which causes or tends to cause any person to be shunned or avoided, or which has a tendency to injure any person, corporation, or association of persons, in his or their business or occupation, is a libel."

It should be noted that the word "malicious" has a legal meaning different from ordinary usage. The question of malice must be settled in court. When a man has been falsely identified with an obviously defamatory phrase or word, malice is usually assumed by the court. Some of these words held to be libelous on their face through court decisions are: crook, swindler, confidence man, cheat, hoodlum, racketeer, coward, slacker, thief, seducer, kept woman, anti-Semite, Communist. Injuring a person in his particular calling or trade by imputing lack of knowledge or integrity is likewise considered to be malicious, if the imputations cannot be proved true. In such cases, specific damages need not be proved; in this respect libel cases differ from many other types of civil suits. Punitive damages may be assessed in the court verdict, in addition to compensatory damages for actual loss specifically shown. For example, a newspaper which falsely calls a college professor a Communist may well pay $100,000 in punitive damages because of the grave damage to his reputation; similarly, to imply that a doctor bungled an operation is to invite a large-sized suit.

In many cases, however, a specific showing of how the defamatory words injured the person bringing the suit is needed. In these cases the newspaper ordinarily may show absence of malice by demonstrating that the story was published with good motives, in exercising the newspaper's duty to keep the public informed, or for justifiable ends, such as the revelation of criminal actions by a public official.

Statutes in some states provide that publication of a prompt and complete retraction, expressing regret for the libel, shows good faith and curtails the awarding of punitive damages. Since the person bringing the suit must then prove the extent of the damages, publication of properly worded retractions is most important. In any situation in which the newspaper finds itself in error, of course, a prompt correction and apology is in order.

Here are some additional cautions concerning libel.

A newspaper is responsible for everything it prints—stories, pictures, headlines, advertisements, letters to the editor, syndicated columns, and press association stories supplied to it by others.

Every person on the staff who knew or should have known of the defamatory statement may be sued for libel—the reporter, rewrite man, copy reader, news editor, city editor, managing editor, publisher. Ordinarily the suit is brought against the publisher.

The newspaper cannot shift blame to the source of any defamatory material. Quoting the source carefully does enable the paper to plead good faith and lack of malice, in the hope of reducing damages.

Use of the word "alleged" is valueless in warding off a suit.

Identification of a person can be proved in court even though the newspaper did not print the name of the defamed individual. Use of an address, a picture, a description, or a set of details fitting a particular person may result in identification in the minds of others.

Fortunately for newspapers, some persons have such poor reputations that they are not likely to collect damages for defamation—but even persons with criminal records may in some circumstances find themselves able to bring successful suits.

An honest mistake, such as a mixup in pictures, a typographical error, or a mistaken identity of persons with similar names, can be libelous if the court holds it has injured a person's reputation. In most cases of such unintentional error, the person affected is sufficiently broad-minded to excuse the mishap if the newspaper willingly admits its blunder and offers to apologize in print.

Typical of the accidental libel are these two actual instances. In a page-one fire story, the hero was a truck driver. When the paper came out, he was described as John Smith, *drunk* driver. The society columnist of another newspaper, giving the list of guests at a party, included the name of a prominent bachelor with the whimsical comment "(stagging, of course)." It showed up in print "(staggering, of course)"—a clear implication of drunkenness. Neither man wanted legal satisfaction, however.

Mistakes caused by the stupidity or negligence of a reporter—such as copying down the wrong name of an arrested person or failing to check the city directory to make certain of a name and address—make the defamed person more likely to want compensation for damages. The only way a newspaper can defend itself in such circumstances is to plead that necessary pressures of speed cause unintentional blunders. This is a weak excuse for the paper, and an even weaker one for any reporter to use with his city editor.

When a newspaper has defamed someone and is being sued, it may seek to mitigate the damages in one of these several ways: running a correction, or a retraction and apology, to show good faith and absence of malice; pleading that the defamation was an honest and innocent mistake; pleading that it repeated a libel (as in running a press association story) in good faith; showing that it quoted usually reliable sources correctly and in good faith; arguing that the person defamed already had lost his good reputation. But mitigation will not absolve a newspaper from all damages. It is only a substitute for the valid defenses to actions in libel.

Truth, Privilege, and Fair Comment

It is vitally important for the reporter to know the ramifications of the three major defenses to actions in libel. These defenses are (1) truth, (2) qualified privilege, and (3) fair comment.

In some states truth is a complete defense in a libel action; in others, good motives and justifiable ends also must be shown. The major caution here is that the newspaper be able to prove under the rules of law the truth of any defamatory statement it makes. If you call a man a thief, you must prove the actual crime of theft; testimony regarding his general reputation as a light-fingered person will not hold up in court. If a speaker at a political meeting calls someone a Communist, and a newspaper reports the charge, the newspaper must be able to prove the person actually is a Communist. Merely proving that the statement was made gets the defense nowhere.

Sometimes, however, proving the truth of a statement does not prevent recovery for damages. For example, a libel settlement of $100,000 was awarded an admitted victim of a rapist because she claimed injury to her reputation through identification in the news story. Similarly, publication of the facts of a crime committed twenty years ago by a man who has lived a respectable life since, for no justifiable motive, would be considered malicious.

Privilege is a key word for the reporter. The press has been granted the qualified privilege of exemption from liability for defamatory statements appearing in published reports of legislative and judicial proceedings. This is because we believe the public has a right to know what has happened in legislatures and courts, which are in themselves privileged places (suits for slander may not be filed against persons orally defaming other persons on the floor of a legislature or in a courtroom). The qualified privilege extends to the newspaper account, however, only if it is a fair, accurate, and impartial report of the actual proceedings. In any action for libel involving such a report, this is all the newspaper has to show; it need not prove the truth of the defamatory statements quoted.

When a reporter is dealing with news material that is printable only because it is privileged, he must exercise extreme care against adding unprivileged material or destroying the privilege. It is essential to remember that any interpretive sentences added by the reporter to the actual privileged material in his story are not protected. Nor are headlines which go beyond the statements or allegations in the privileged material. Only statements made during the actual course of the legislative meeting or the court session are privileged; what a reporter hears in the hallway, or after adjournment, is not privileged. Neither is material which is ordered stricken from the official record.

Qualified privilege extends to reports of proceedings of the national Congress, state legislatures and, usually, city councils and other lesser bodies. Testimony before committees of legislative bodies is also privileged. State laws vary widely on extension of privilege to reports of proceedings of administrative bodies. Sessions of courts of record are privileged, as are those of such quasi-judicial bodies as utilities commissions and parole boards. Findings of a grand jury are privileged after they are returned to court. Warrants and affidavits are privileged when they have been issued or filed by a judicial officer.

The rule of thumb on determining the existence of privilege in judicial proceedings is this: Has a judge been in the case? If he has been, privilege may be assumed. If he has not yet entered the case, caution should be observed. For example, sensational news stories frequently are obtained when divorce actions are filed in court. A wife may charge her husband with misconduct and may name another woman. In some states these pleadings are privileged from the moment they are filed with the clerk of the court; in others they are not privileged until the judge has called the case to trial. The reporter must know where privilege extends in such situations, for he is on shaky ground using the material in advance filings unless he is protected. Many times law suits are dropped or the charges made earlier are altered when the case is actually heard.

Police records of crimes and arrests are not privileged material, except in a few states. As a matter of practice, newspapers generally use them whether or not privilege exists, provided the reporter is convinced that the facts are correct and that the use of the story is justified. This is a case of taking a "calculated risk." Statements gathered from police officers or district attorneys about a suspect, or from others involved in a case, are not privileged. If they are defamatory, the newspaper will be obliged to prove the truth of the charges made, in event of a libel suit.

Qualified privilege does not extend to reports of political meetings, public mass meetings, and other similar gatherings. Actually great latitude is permitted newspapers in reporting political campaigns; candidates make highly personal and seemingly libelous speeches about their opponents, and newspapers print them with little fear of libel action. But this is merely a disposition of the courts to protect the right of free comment and discussion about those seeking public office; it is not a certain protection.

Fair comment is the third defense in libel actions. Its use is restricted to printed material expressing opinions. The newspaper's right to criticize and comment upon persons who offer themselves for public approval is the same as the general public right. It extends over acts of public officials, candidates for public office, and those who offer artistic works or performances to the public.

Newspapers may comment freely on public affairs and may criticize men's conduct of their offices in severest terms. So long as the statement of opinion concerns itself with the skill of the official's acts, it is safe. If a crime is alleged against him, however, the paper must be ready to prove its charge. There is a sharp difference between ineptitude and illegality. If the newspaper discusses the official's private life in an unpleasant way, a suit may result.

Opinions may be expressed about a candidate's character, reputation, and ability when he offers himself for public office. These expressions of opinion may be quite severe, provided they are drawn from true statements of fact, or from what the editor believes to be true facts, and are offered for justifiable reasons.

The right of fair comment by a newspaper extends to its reports on public performances by musicians, stage performers, artists, and writers. The principle is that anyone who offers his talents for public approval, especially for pay, exposes himself to criticism in print. This criticism must be limited to the performer's work and not be of his or her personal life.

Invasion of Privacy

Closely affiliated with the question of libel is that of privacy. Under what circumstances does an individual have the right to keep his activities and his picture out of print? While not new, that legal issue has been debated with increasing intensity by editors and the courts in recent years, and a body of law is growing in some states. It is far less clearly defined than libel, however.

Generally, the name and picture of an individual may be used in a news situation without his consent, so long as the story is of timely interest to readers. No right of privacy exists in the case of news. However, a person's name may not be used for advertising or other commercial purposes in most states without his consent, usually obtained in writing. Limitations also exist upon the use of a person's picture and material about his life for dramatic and other entertainment purposes. The invasion of privacy is a greater worry for radio, television, and magazines than it is for the daily newspaper.

Protecting Your News Sources

General practice gives the reporter the right to protect the sources from which he obtains his news. Sometimes the name of the source must be kept secret to guard him against personal retaliation—physical, legal or economic. The reporter also wants to keep his lines of information open for later use, and public revelation of them might prevent this. However, irate prosecutors and courts sometimes demand that the reporter reveal his sources.

Most newsmen refuse to do so, unless they believe that public safety or welfare is clearly involved. Some have been sent to jail by angry judges for their refusal, but public indignation usually forces reduction of the penalty to a token form.

The conflict between maintenance of reporter confidence and demand for disclosure of sources of news has not been resolved. Approximately one-fourth of the states have enacted statutes which protect reporters and editors, similar to this Alabama law:

"Newspaper Employees—No person engaged in, connected with or employed on any newspaper, while engaged in a news gathering capacity, shall be compelled to disclose in any legal proceeding or trial, before any court or before a grand jury of any court, or before a presiding officer of any tribunal or his agent or agents, or before any committee of the legislature, or elsewhere, the source of any information procured or obtained by him and published in the newspaper on which he is engaged, connected with or employed."

In such states, contempt proceedings cannot be brought against reporters. But elsewhere reporters must depend upon the general protection of the First Amendment to the Constitution, and they do not always win their cases. The federal courts held in the 1957–58 case of Marie Torre, New York *Herald Tribune* television columnist, that she was obliged to name the source of a news item as a witness in a civil suit for slander. The duty to testify in the interest of fair administration of justice transcends the consequent impairment of press freedom, the courts said. Much depends, however, upon the nature of the demand for a reporter's disclosure of his news source. In other circumstances, the reporter has been upheld in his general right to decide the issue of confidence, even in a courtroom. No persons, including reporters, can be forced to testify before an administrative officer, and court decisions have upheld the right of newsmen to refuse to disclose sources of news under questioning by a legislative group.

Chapter 9

Interviewing–Foundation for All Reporting

Conducting the Interview

The basic step in all reporting is the interview; that is, talking with people to obtain from them information that will interest the newspaper's readers.

Interviewing consists of far more than putting a series of questions to a person and writing down his answers. It is an exercise in human relations. The reporter seeks to build an atmosphere of trust and respect that will enable him to draw the maximum amount of information from the person being interviewed. If he succeeds in getting his subject to volunteer facts, and not merely give minimum answers to the reporter's questions, he is on his way to a much better news story than he might otherwise obtain.

There are two kinds of interviewing. One is the spot news interview, either by telephone or in person, to obtain the facts for a story; several persons may be questioned in the course of preparing a single story, each contributing a small portion or merely confirming what another source has said. The second type, more leisurely and formal, is the news feature interview. In this the reporter is assigned to talk at length with a prominent personality to obtain his views on current affairs or to a person whose achievements or role in life make him interesting to others in his community.

We will discuss the techniques of these two types in turn. First there are some general comments that apply to all interviewing.

Many beginning reporters in search of information are hesitant to approach people for fear of appearing ignorant or bothering the person being interviewed. Although such an attitude of uncertainty is quite understandable, and the reluctance to impose upon other people is commendable, there is no real reason to be shy about seeking and conducting an interview. News comes from people, and a reporter's work involves talking with dozens of them every day. Therefore it is important to establish a suitable frame of mind when dealing with news sources.

Almost everyone respects a newspaper and the force it represents. As its representative the reporter also commands respect; asking for information is his duty and people expect it of him. When he identifies himself as from a newspaper, the other person automatically is on the alert. Some men and women will go to great lengths to get their names into the paper, others just as far to keep theirs out. The reporter represents that power to them; even though the final authority of deciding what is printed may not rest in his hands, many people believe it does. The reporter is a man of stature in their eyes.

There is no need for a reporter to try to impress people with show-off heroics, playing the big man. This may be covering up for his own uneasiness and uncertainty, but it doesn't work. Many people react negatively to this kind of approach and are more likely to "dry up" than to talk freely. The reporter who approaches a news source with quiet confidence in his ability to do his job and carries out a sensible, sympathetic questioning is far more likely to come away with a good story.

Most people are cooperative. Sometimes they will go to surprising lengths to help the reporter. Frequently on crime and disaster stories the reporter is getting news from people whose life has been shaken by the events being covered. They react in different ways, and the reporter must learn to judge the influence of their emotional condition on the statements they give him. Men and women who have just lived through a tragedy, or witnessed it from close range, will in good faith give conflicting reports on what they have just seen. Even under relaxed circumstances the untrained human brain is a poor eyewitness recorder of events; under emotional and physical stress people say they saw things that never happened. Whenever possible the reporter should get several versions of an episode. He must reconcile the conflicts as much as possible through further questioning, and where contradictions remain he must choose the version that seems most plausible.

Treat the average person with respect, and he will do the same to you. Persuading news sources usually gets better results than browbeating them. Be persistent but avoid becoming argumentative. There are times, however, when a reporter must get tough. If he believes that the man being interviewed is holding back vital information the public should have, especially if the man is a public official, he may have to bore in with a series of hard, extremely frank questions and try to catch the interviewee contradicting himself.

The trouble arises when the news source has a vested interest in a situation, something he is trying to hide or put into the best possible light. This does not necessarily involve illegal activity. It may be social position, job security, family relations, or official power. If the reluctant public figure refuses to answer legitimate questions, it may be necessary to remind him that he has frequently asked the newspaper for favorable publicity, and now it is his turn to repay.

Most personalities who depend upon publicity are willing to talk with reporters. Many of them try to cover up unfavorable situations not by silence but by glib double-talk. That is where the reporter's acute ear is important. Often men who are trying to conceal something will tip off the fact under direct and skillful questioning, when a reporter puts one statement against an earlier one and detects contradictions. When the questioner is able to challenge with, "But a few minutes ago you said so-and-so," he puts the evasive witness on the defensive and may obtain the facts he needs. So don't shrug your shoulders and give up when a news source refuses to cooperate. Keep talking and asking questions as long as you can keep him on the phone or in your presence. He may be goaded into admitting something he never intended to let out.

In everyday reporting such cases are rare. A straightforward inquiry usually gets the information desired, if the person being questioned knows the answers. The success of most interviews depends upon the reporter's ability to ask the right questions. This is certain: The newsman who has prepared himself and looked up the background of the man he is talking to will produce a better interview than the one who just gets on the phone and starts talking.

The Spot News Interview

The reporter's approach to his sources while checking a news lead should be direct and forthright. Establish your identity immediately in a firm manner and state your business. If the story you are checking is involved and confused, summarize it quickly, so the person on the other end of the phone knows immediately what you are talking about and doesn't become impatient while listening to a long description. The more business-like your voice sounds to him, the better are your chances of getting information. There is time enough to develop the details as your conversation continues. Breaking the ice is a major step.

Here is the approach experienced reporters normally use on a telephone inquiry:

"Hello, is this Walter Powell? Mr. Powell, this is George Thompson at the Courier. We have a report from the police that an automobile jumped the curb and smashed into your house. Is that correct?"

Thus within the first few seconds the reporter has told who he is and what he wants, and he has established the point that his paper is striving for accuracy by checking a police report right at the source. From this point the reporter can ask questions about the details: Was anyone injured? What room of the house did the car strike? What damage was done? Did Mr. Powell or anyone else in the house happen to see the car coming? What did the driver say to Mr. Powell? Is the driver still at the house so the reporter can talk to him? Other questions will suggest themselves as the conversation continues.

The story may end up in print as a two-paragraph item among the routine traffic reports. But if Mr. Powell says that his family was just starting dinner and the car came through the dining room window, spilling the soup in his lap, the reporter has a human interest angle that could put the story on page one. That is the sort of eye-catching little story that readers will talk about at their own dinner tables.

Some reporters on routine telephone checks just say, "This is the Courier calling" without using their own names, on the assumption that they as individuals have no meaning for the news source. This practice is acceptable when the reporter is dealing quickly with someone he may never be in contact with again. Where follow-up conversations are likely, however, the extra link of a personal name is a psychological advantage; it helps to personalize the newspaper for that news source. He may like to brag to his friends that he knows George Thompson of the Courier.

This same approach should be used for in-person interviews. Seeing the news source gives the reporter advantages over talking to him on the telephone. In the example of the runaway car, if Reporter Thompson had gone to the scene of the accident and interviewed Householder Powell, he might have seen a bandage on his cheek. "Is that from the accident?" "Oh, yes, when the car came through the wall, it knocked a souvenir beer mug off the shelf and it hit me in the face."

Here is an extra colorful detail to go along with the spilled soup. The victim might not have thought to mention it on the telephone, but the on-the-spot interview developed it. However, it is physically impossible for a city editor to send his reporters out on every minor story, so a large percentage of the day's news leads must be checked by telephone. The decision of when to "send" on a news tip is one the city editor must make several times a day.

On a spot news interview the reporter should always try to obtain more detailed information than he thinks his story may need. Accuracy cannot be emphasized too heavily. Be sure that names and addresses are correct and complete. Get enough detail so that the story will be chronologically smooth and the contradictions reconciled.

Making assumptions is a very dangerous business. Never guess in a news story. If you are not sure of a fact, don't use it, because once a statement is in print there is no way to call it back. Humans frequently behave illogically under stress. Don't assume that because you would have done a certain thing under the circumstances, the person actually involved in the episode would behave in the same manner.

Frequently an editor calls back to a reporter for clarification on some point. Unless the additional information is available in the reporter's notes, he may be in difficulty; the news source may have disappeared or at least be unavailable for further checking. Sometimes a fact that seems insignificant may be just the thing an editor wants to give the story an unusual twist or "lift." The reporter's rule should be: Get it right and complete the first time. But whenever possible he should protect himself by obtaining the address and telephone number at which the source will be available, for later reference.

Checking back on incoming telephone calls is another wise precaution. Hoaxers who try to trick newspapers with fake stories are a constant concern. The callback is the soundest protection against the man who telephones to report falsely a prominent person's death or to represent himself as an important man with a statement for the paper. The reporter should take down the information the voice gives him, ask for the informant's telephone number, wait a few minutes, then call back for confirmation. On death tips a confirming call should be made to the family, business associates, mortuary, or some other authoritative source. Printing a news story on the basis of one incoming phone call is always risky.

Even the largest and most cautious newspapers sometimes are victimized. Late in 1956 the New York *Times* was fooled by a hoaxer with a false death report. It sought to explain away its error in a whimsical editorial:

> Mme. Hedwig Rosenthal, a sprightly woman whose reminiscences are sprinkled with stories of eminent people, had difficulty yesterday morning in getting regular delivery of The New York Times. And no wonder. It contained her own obituary notice.
>
> The Times had unwittingly printed the story. A woman

who said she was the niece of Mme. Rosenthal, had offered
the information to this newspaper and it had been accepted
in good faith. The truth is that she has no niece in this country.

All of this was most disconcerting to Mme. Rosenthal who
said she created something of a sensation when she walked
down the corridor of the Great Northern Hotel yesterday in
search of her missing paper . . . she did not know who
might be posing as her niece.

A device that is sometimes useful in interviewing a man whom
the reporter suspects of holding back information is to imply
that you know more about the situation than you actually do.
If he believes that you are informed about the basic situation, he
may let the barriers down and talk rather freely about details,
thus providing confirmation on a story that the reporter only
suspected. By skillful backtracking in his questioning, the reporter then can pin down the complete story from his reluctant
source. Keeping a secret is not easy for many people; sometimes
they actually welcome the opportunity to discuss their big news
with a caller, once they believe the story has been made public.
Obviously this technique can be used only by an experienced
and quick-witted reporter who knows how to "fish" for information. A beginner might find himself deeply embarrassed if the
news source realized through clumsy questioning that the reporter has misled him. But properly used, this method has
produced many news beats.

One example occurred in Los Angeles a number of years
ago in the heyday of the flamboyant evangelist, Aimee Semple
McPherson, whose antics made headlines all over the country. A
rumor circulated that she planned to be married but none of
the reporters in town could obtain confirmation. Finally a newsman who had covered her activities in the past called her and
started the conversation by saying, "My, you sound happy today!"
Aimee replied that she did indeed. "You sound exactly like a
bride, the way I thought you would," the reporter went on. "Oh,
you've heard about it!" Aimee said. "Come on over, I want to
talk to you."

The reporter went to her home and she told him about her

plans to be married on Monday. Thinking quickly, he saw the opportunity for an exclusive story. He proposed that instead of waiting until Monday, she should fly to Arizona secretly on Sunday morning, to be married there, fly back, and announce the news to her congregation at the Sunday afternoon service. The dramatic evangelist liked the idea. The reporter then called an airline operator and said, "Will you loan me an airplane Sunday if I promise to get the name of your airline on front pages all over the country Monday morning? I can't tell you why."

The executive agreed. The reporter then put the evangelist and her bridegroom and a photographer on the plane. They flew to Yuma, Arizona, and were married at the steps of the airplane, so the company's name showed in the photographs. Enroute back to Los Angeles the reporter wrote his story with the short, sharp lead: "Behold the bride—Aimee Semple McPherson!" His paper rushed out an extra edition to catch the crowds at a mammoth Sunday afternoon air show, simultaneous with Aimee's presentation of her husband at her afternoon service.

All of this developed out of clever questioning on the telephone, plus ingenuity on the reporter's part (in close cooperation with his city editor, who helped make the arrangements). Sometimes a reporter must be a salesman, too.

Taking Notes at Interviews

There are no rules about taking notes during telephone or in-person interviews. Every reporter develops his own technique. Unfortunately few American newsmen know shorthand, a fact that most of them regret but few do anything about. An elementary course in shorthand is an excellent tool for any young reporter. Most English newsmen have such training, and they have a definite advantage when taking down the statements of a news source.

In place of shorthand reporters develop their own systems of abbreviation. A few common examples are "trou" for trousers, "pox" for police, "tt" for that. Put quotation marks around the sentences you set down verbatim, not around those you paraphrase. The chief principle of note taking is elimination of unnecessary words and phrases. Omit the articles and prepositions from sentences. If you get the key words and phrases down on paper, these can be expanded into full sentences a little later while the notes are still fresh in mind. Don't try to write down so much that your handwriting degenerates into a scrawl that cannot be read later.

Take this statement by Senator John L. McClellan at the opening of a Senate labor investigation:

"In the near future we expect to hold public hearings with particular attention to the problem of labor-underworld alliances in the area of New York. At that time some nationally known hoodlums will be called before the committee to explain their connection with labor and management groups."

A reporter's notes on the statement might read about like this:

"Near fut we expect hold pub hearings with partic attn to problem labor unworld alliances in area NY. At tt time some nat known hoods will called before comm explain connxn with lab manage groups."

The words omitted or abbreviated are all easily filled in by the reporter when he writes or phones in the story, since they are in context and help to explain each other. It is more important to get two or three key sentences complete, and paraphrase the essential thoughts of secondary statements, than to scrawl down parts of every sentence. If the speaker is talking rapidly and starts to say something very important while you are still trying to get down a previous statement, jump ahead in your notes to the more vital comment. Then concentrate until you have that down in firm, usable manner. The only sure road to successful note taking is practice. One good method is to take notes on speeches you attend, even though you are not assigned to report them. After you get home, read the notes and try to expand them on paper into a form usable in a news story.

On matters of fact the reporter should never trust his memory. Write them down. If you are not sure what the man said, ask him to repeat it. If he is hazy about a statement and there is a way to cross check it, do so. The memory plays odd tricks, especially with numbers. Another reason for careful note taking is to bolster the reporter's position if an argument with the news source develops after the story is in print, as sometimes happens. A reporter's notes are valuable supporting evidence for his accuracy.

Politicians especially have a trick of denying statements they made to a reporter, if the story in print embarrasses them. "I was misquoted" is one of the oldest and cheapest ways for a public figure to squirm out of a predicament. In most cases he was quoted exactly as he spoke. He knows it and the reporter knows it. But once the denial is issued, it becomes for the reading public a matter of the prominent personality's integrity against the reporter's.

If the editor is convinced that the reporter's story is accurate (here is where those notes help so much), he will usually give his staff member full and vigorous support, in and out of print. But the politician has built a backfire to ease his embarrassment.

However, if the public figure *was* misquoted by an inaccurate reporter, the paper is obligated to apologize, its reputation for accuracy and fairness is injured, and the reporter's own position is weakened in the eyes of his city editor. All reporters, copy readers, and editors make occasional mistakes. That cannot be avoided and is generally accepted in the profession as inevitable. But a good reporter rarely makes such a misstep. When the same man makes similar errors frequently, he is tagged as a sloppy workman.

Why do public figures make statements if they deny them later? Sometimes they speak in anger; they are thoughtless about how their words will look in print or they are putting up trial balloons, testing an idea on the public through the news columns. If the reaction is strongly unfavorable, they try to get out from under by shifting the blame to the man who wrote the story.

A smart reporter protects himself whenever possible against such a denial by asking the public figure to repeat any controversial or unexpected statement. If the mayor of a city says the state governor should resign because he is too old and incompetent, the reporter wisely rephrases the statement back to him something like this: "Then you are saying, Mr. Mayor, that the governor should quit immediately because he is no longer capable of holding the job?" Or "Why do you think he is incompetent?"

Usually the news source will restate his views, often elaborating them with more colorful quotes as he warms to his subject. If a later quarrel develops in which he denies the statement, the reporter can recall his effort to obtain confirmation. Such a confirmation question also guards against unintentional misstatements by the man being interviewed. Maybe he said it and didn't mean to; the sound reporter will not take advantage of a slip of the tongue to get a sensational story. Occasionally such a double-check will deprive the reporter of an exciting quote, but more frequently it helps to build acceptance for himself with his news sources. A public figure who is treated fairly by the press usually reciprocates. Those who do not soon become known among newsmen for their untrustworthy ways and tend to get a bad press.

Such precautions are less necessary when a group of reporters are present. They can check each other's notes, and frequently do, on parts that are in doubt. It is much more difficult for a public figure to pit his word against that of several reporters. But the exclusive story every newspaper seeks does not come from such mass gatherings.

The Press Conference

Many public figures prefer to give out their news to all reporters at the same time, so they hold press conferences. These are simply mass interviews in which the assembled newsmen take turns asking questions, and the information is available to all on an equal basis. There are several advantages for the public figure in using the press conference technique. He saves time by seeing all newsmen simultaneously; he is able to reach a maximum audience; and he avoids charges of favoritism.

The most famous news conferences in the world are those held by the President of the United States. The country's chief executive stands up before a hundred or more newsmen, answering or parrying their inquiries in rapid-fire order with the knowledge that what he says will be flashed around the world within a few minutes. White House reporters are trained to ask leading, blunt questions. As a whole our recent Presidents have been adept at handling these questions, although there have been times when a correction or clarification has been issued by the presidential news staff a few hours later to clear up misunderstandings or errors. The rule is that the President cannot be quoted directly unless he specifically authorizes the quotations. No other public figure receives such protection. The Presidents, like lesser officials, usually make advance preparation for these conferences with their news secretaries, working up answers for the questions most likely to be asked. When a matter of unusual importance or complexity is certain to come up, the President sometimes reads a brief prepared statement on the subject. After that he either declines to answer more questions on this topic or agrees to expand upon his views. The questioning at such high-level official conferences is always polite, if sharp.

When a controversial or notorious figure calls a press conference, the give-and-take sometimes becomes rough. It is assumed that if a man calls a press conference, he has something newsworthy to say. Reporters are too independent to be pushed around or handed evasive answers by men whom they do not respect. If they believe that the man holding the conference is trying to deceive them, their questioning becomes aggressive and intense. Sometimes a "no comment" reply under such questioning is very revealing.

Competition between rival reporters is put aside in a press conference; the assembled newsmen are united in their effort to obtain news. Information developed in the meeting is common property, and, when necessary, reporters compare their notes to check their accuracy. If two newspapers carry conflicting reports of the same conference, the accuracy of both is brought into doubt.

From a reporter's standpoint the press conference has both advantages and disadvantages. He gets access to public figures who might otherwise avoid being questioned. On the other hand, nobody ever obtains an exclusive story in such a gathering. If a newsman is working to develop a special story of his own in that particular field, he may refrain from asking a question on which he badly needs an answer, for fear that it will tip off the story to all his competitors. Instead he will try to see the news source privately for a moment immediately after the conference and ask it, or even wait until he can reach the man alone in his office.

Some reporters develop a bad habit of arguing with the news source or making a speech instead of asking a question. This irritates both the source and fellow newsmen and rarely produces information. The reporter should always remember that he came to hear what the news source has to say, not to show off his own knowledge.

A recent development at press conferences is the presence of television cameramen. When TV was a novelty these cameramen had a tendency to monopolize the meetings, ordering the news source around to meet their technical needs and asking him to repeat statements for their benefit. This caused severe irritation among reporters who feared, rightly at times, that the disturbance was preventing them from developing the news. Gradually the TV men and reporters have evolved a working arrangement. This varies from one community to another, but most frequently there is mutual agreement that the news source will take a few extra minutes after the close of his news conference and go through his paces for the TV cameras.

Many commercial organizations use the press conference as a device to get news of their activities into print. The company's public relations director calls the conference for newsmen to hear the firm's president or other high official. When the reporters enter the room they are given prepared kits of material, often including the text of the host's remarks in advance, his biography, picture, and elaborately printed brochures about the company's work. All of this is intended to show the host in the best possible light (and also to demonstrate the publicity man's efficiency to his employer). Much of this printed material ends in the reporter's wastebasket after receiving a casual glance. But experienced publicity workers know that a concise, straightforward biography of the host is appreciated by reporters.

The Off-the-Record Menace

The news source who gives out newsworthy information but demands that it not be printed presents one of the most vexing problems a reporter has to face. Making a hard and fast rule to cover this situation is almost impossible because circumstances vary so greatly. Sometimes the request is a form of evasion by the news source, by which he tries to keep embarrassing information out of print by a shoddy play on the reporter's honor. After pledging the newsman to secrecy he gives him a piece of legitimate news. If the story appears, he accuses the reporter of a betrayal; if it doesn't appear, the reporter finds himself in the compromised position of withholding a story the public deserves to have.

To avoid this situation some editors announce that their reporters will not listen to off-the-record material. Thus if they are able to develop the story from other sources, there can be no question of a betrayed confidence. Nothing is more exasperating than to be "sitting on" a story obtained off the record and to find the same facts in print in a rival newspaper.

The difficulty here is that there are circumstances in which the news source legitimately can request that certain information be kept off the record, at least temporarily. In solving a crime the police at times ask the newspapers to withhold certain facts until arrests are made, so the suspects will not be alerted. If the reporter and his city editor are satisfied that this request is for a sound purpose they usually will comply. Generally it is held that the public's right to know overrules the discomfiture or harm to any individual involved in a legitimate news story. The reporter should remember this in weighing off-the-record requests. National defense material is sometimes made available to reporters for their background on the understanding that they will not print it without official security clearance.

A good reporter develops news sources who trust him sufficiently to confide their plans. If he betrays this confidence by rushing into print with everything he is told, his sources soon dry up. So it comes down to a question of judgment: Is the off-the-record request legitimate and in the public interest, or is it a cover-up device?

As a rule it is impossible to keep off the record anything significant said in a press conference. Too many people are involved. The story is sure to leak in one form or another, so the reporters should tell the source flatly that they cannot respect his secrecy request. Most experienced officials realize this and do not attempt such tactics. The most ridiculous of all requests for off-the-record treatment is by the speaker who stands before an audience of a hundred or more and blandly informs any reporters present that what he has to say is not for publication. Such requests should be ignored; anything he chooses to say before an audience certainly will not remain secret, and to curtail the freedom of the press in this manner is improper.

The News Feature Interview

When the city editor tells a reporter to go out and interview somebody, he usually has in mind a more leisurely and comprehensive discussion than arises in the preparation of a spot news story. Most newsmen speak of checking a source when they are working on a breaking story, reserving the term "interview" for the more formal discussion with a celebrity or unusual personality. It is from such talks that news feature interviews develop.

The formal interview demands and deserves advance preparation by the reporter. The meeting is an interplay of the celebrity's personality and his own; how they react to each other and the reporter's knowledge of the man he is interviewing have a strong bearing on the kind of story he obtains. He is endeavoring not only to elicit some newsworthy comments but to get the essence of the celebrity's personality down on paper. Some of the best interviews actually contain little "hard" news. They do give the reader a portrait of an interesting man or woman and at least a glimpse of his philosophy and ideas.

The reporter given such an assignment should remember that the first principle of any interview is to report what the news source has to say. The essential thoughts the interviewee seeks to communicate to your readers should not be buried in the story under the trimmings of personality quirks and the circumstances of the meeting, if they happen to be unusual. These supplementary details lift an interview out of the routine but rarely should they be permitted to dominate it. Details of the interviewee's personality should be woven into the story without becoming conspicuous.

Think in headlines. When preparing questions for an interview say to yourself, "What can I ask him that will produce a lead angle?" If you think in advance of what you would like the source to say, perhaps you can get him to say it. This does not mean putting words into his mouth; rather, it means getting him to talk on a question that has news value. Knowing what makes news is the reporter's business, not the celebrity's, and so the reporter should be the one to shape and direct the interview within the bounds of good conversational manners. Unless he holds the discussion to a fairly firm course, it can meander from one green conversational pasture to another without many results worth printing.

Since many personalities who make news are extroverts and are frequently self-centered, keeping them on the track isn't always easy. With some it is almost impossible. They are accustomed to dominating conversations while their admirers listen. The interviewer faces the task of breaking in tactfully with specific questions. If he doesn't, he may suddenly find his allotted time gone and little accomplished. Many prominent men and women have an instinctive news sense and give the reporter what he wants with a minimum of prodding. Others have no idea at all of what makes news; they may be charming and anxious to cooperate but very unproductive unless the interviewer steers the conversation toward his goals.

It is poor technique for the reporter to restrict his interview to a set of questions submitted in advance. On rare occasions the celebrity will talk only on this basis. If he insists upon this condition there is nothing to do but accept his demand; however, once the conversation has started on this limited basis most men will tend to forget their own rules and become more expansive. Limitations of this sort are usually imposed by celebrities who are afraid of the press, a fear that can be at least partially erased if the reporter makes the interviewee feel at ease. A skillful interviewer tries to convince the man he is questioning that he is really interested in the answers and wants to learn more about the man's special field. The best way to communicate this feeling of sincere interest is to *be* sincere.

The interviewer should go to his assignment with a set of basic, newsy questions formulated either in his mind or on paper to provide the framework for the discussion. They need not be asked in sequence, depending upon the flow of the conversation.

An interview might be described as a conversation directed toward a goal. Its pace will depend upon the attitude of the person being interviewed. If he is obviously in a hurry and has squeezed this appointment in between others, get down to business as quickly as possible. If he is in a relaxed mood and indicates that he has plenty of time, some preliminary conversation is usually advisable before the reporter plunges into his questioning. This enables the two parties to get the mental range of each other and creates a more informal atmosphere for the serious discussion. The interviewer should not let this go on too long, however, lest the other person become restless.

A veteran Associated Press reporter, Saul Pett, tells in a descriptive dispatch about a controversial labor leader, James Hoffa, how he tried almost in vain to establish an informal level of understanding when he interviewed Hoffa in Detroit. At that time the labor leader was under Congressional investigation and had been receiving much unfavorable publicity.

The interviewer sensed a hostile tone when he entered Hoffa's office. So he tried to break down the barriers with an unexpected and trivial personal question. Sometimes this technique will put the news source at ease. Here is how Pett describes what happened:

> It was an unusual interview. In tone, it ran the gamut from frigidity to mere coldness.
>
> Hoffa greeted the reporter with a handshake which, while it unfolded from a big square fist and a huge forearm, was surprisingly limp. His blue-grey eyes were cold and skeptical, his manner reluctant and on guard. He said he had only a few minutes for the interview.
>
> Seeking some kind of rapport, the reporter began, "First a crucial question. My wife wants to know why you always wear white socks?"
>
> "Because my feet sweat less in them," Hoffa said. No smile. Period.
>
> End foothold. Hoffa, wearing a white, short-sleeved shirt,

blue tie, shiny grey trousers, moved impatiently in his chair. He shifted his taut, powerful frame (height 5 feet 5 inches; weight 170), but the chip on his shoulder remained obvious.

. . . The phones rang repeatedly and men frequently poked their heads in the door for whispered conferences. On the phone, Hoffa seemed to settle things quickly, concisely.

By including these descriptive paragraphs, interspersed with a report on what Hoffa said in reply to the news questions, the interviewer deepened his reader's understanding of the labor leader's personality. Also he added a narrative touch which helped to tie together the long dispatch.

The worst mistake a beginning interviewer can make in talking with a prominent man or an expert in some field is to show his ignorance of the man's work. Before going to see him look up his biography in *Who's Who*. Check your newspaper's clipping files for references to him and see what he has said in print previously.

Let us say that he is an authority on earthquakes, a subject about which you knew nothing. Fifteen minutes spent reading an encyclopedia article on earthquakes and their causes will enable you to talk more intelligently with him, and the knowledge you show through your questions will encourage him to talk more freely. Scientists and other specialists are often reluctant to discuss their fields with newspapermen because they fear that through ignorance a reporter will twist what they say and embarrass them in print. The interviewer cannot be expected to have expert knowledge in every field, but he should have at least a basic comprehension of the subject under discussion. Nothing will ruin an interview faster than a question that the news source considers stupid.

An unprepared interviewer might ask the expert how the intensity of earthquakes is measured, thus showing total ignorance in the field. The reporter who has looked in the encyclopedia will know that the temblors are recorded on a seismograph. He may refer in his conversation to the Richter scale. He will be aware that scientists have identified certain geological faults in the earth's surface along which earthquakes are most likely to occur. He will have at least slight knowledge of some great quakes such as the San Francisco earthquake and fire of 1906. And he will know that there has been much discussion over many years about the possibility of forecasting earthquakes. Does Mr. Expert accept the theory sometimes put forward that the upheavals come in cycles? Does he have a theory of his own, and if so what does he foresee? Mr. Expert explains his beliefs and says that he anticipates a large earthquake in the western United States within ten years. Right there the interviewer has an idea for a news lead: Expert predicts major American earthquake within ten years. He can focus his questioning on this angle and develop the expert's supporting evidence for his prediction.

None of the material just mentioned is technical. Any reporter can brief himself on it from clippings and reference books in a few minutes. If he fails to do so, he is not doing his job as he should.

As the interviewer talks with the celebrity and records what he is saying, he also should be absorbing something of the man's personality to be included in the story. Close your eyes momentarily and think of descriptive words to fit the man sitting before you. Is he tall or short, pudgy, unusually thin, round faced? How is he dressed? What distinctive mannerisms has he? Does he put his glasses on and off as he talks, or twirl them? Does he pull his ear or run his hands through his hair? Details of this sort spiced into the interview will help to turn him from a news source into a personality for the reader.

Cartoonists emphasize some notable feature of a celebrity's appearance, like Franklin D. Roosevelt's long cigarette holder or Dwight Eisenhower's grin. The interviewer likewise should reach for identifying details in his story but he should avoid resorting to harsh caricature. This makes his report too editorial in tone.

Here is an example of the close-up physical description by a noted foreign correspondent, Homer Bigart of the New York *Times.* The following sentences were scattered through his interview with King Iman Ahmed of Yemen: "His large protuberant eyes were never still and his fleshy lips made chewing movements as the Chief Minister translated his greeting. . . . He spoke quickly in a low, hoarse voice. . . . He shot disturbed, sidelong glances at a tape recorder that a Swiss newsman thrust on his table. Beneath the table his hands played with amber beads. Sometimes he raised a hand to tug at his black-dyed beard. . . . Several small Yemenis described as children of his servants clung to his robes during the interview."

See what life these touches give the story! They help to put the King in his setting and to show that, like any other man, he was subject to the reactions of uneasiness and vanity.

How much note taking should the reporter do in an interview of this sort? Less than he does while checking facts on a spot story, seems to be the general practice. He is dealing here with ideas more than detailed facts, and ideas are easier to remember. Each interviewer develops his own methods in this respect and may vary them according to the person being questioned. Some men and women "freeze up" at the sight of an interviewer busily scribbling down everything they say. The conversation turns into an ordeal for them. If the interviewer detects such a reaction, he should concentrate on the person and reduce his note taking to a few essential phrases.

Always write down statistics and matters of fact that the news source gives you. Get his key direct quotations onto paper, too, but don't scramble to jot down everything he says. Train yourself to remember his conversation on the basis of a limited number of essential but fragmentary phrases. It is highly important for the reporter to expand his notes as soon as possible after concluding the interview. Even though the story may be for future release, such as a Sunday feature, you should write up your notes in detailed form while the discussion is fresh in your mind. The story itself can be handled later. Cold notes are journalistic poison.

Now let us put all these principles and techniques to work in a hypothetical interview—imaginary, but one that you might very well have to handle while working on the college paper.

A famous explorer has come to the campus for a lecture and the city editor has assigned you to interview him. The first step is to make an appointment. Where is he staying and when will he arrive? If he is coming under the auspices of the college administration, the appropriate office should be able to give you these facts; otherwise get them from the head of the sponsoring group. Call the explorer and arrange a time and place for your conversation. This should be fixed to suit his convenience, although it is quite in order for you to indicate any deadline problems you may have. Most prominent men are cooperative on such matters.

The time and place are arranged, but there is more to be done before you meet him. His name is a household word. But how much do you really know about him? Probably less than you think, as you will soon realize when you ask yourself a few basic questions. What part of the country does he come from? He is just back from the Antarctic: How many previous expeditions to polar regions has he made? What books has he written? Those are just a few of the biographical facts that you should know, both to save time in the interview itself and to make you better prepared for talking with him. All these answers and many others are to be found in *Who's Who in America* in the college library. Probably the library has one or more of his books, too; at least a quick look through them would be helpful. If newspaper clippings about him are available, read them.

Now you know something about the man you are to see. Next, what should you ask him? It would be wise to write down five or six questions, to crystallize them in your mind, even if you never refer to the notes during your conversation. The main facts of his adventures are fairly well known, but he may have one or two concise, colorful anecdotes to relate that would fit well in your story, giving the campus readers the flavor of the man they are to hear lecture. So ask him for them.

Undoubtedly he has some strong opinions about the future of Antarctica, based on personal knowledge of a type that few men in the world possess. The interviewer might ask whether he foresees a day when mankind can break through the heavy ice cap and reach the south polar continent's mineral wealth. Politically, does he anticipate an international struggle for domination of Antarctica? What is some of the knowledge we have gained about world weather conditions through observations near the South Pole?

Since you have only a few hundred words for the story, try

to make your questions provocative and of a type that can be answered concisely. Don't waste his time and your own with such inane questions as how does he like State College campus, and does he think that your football team will defeat the Aggies next Saturday?

Thus prepared, the interviewer goes to his appointment in the explorer's hotel room. He finds him in his shirtsleeves, with an open newspaper dropped on the floor beside his chair. The atmosphere is relaxed and leisurely. So relax a bit yourself. There is nothing to be tense about, even though he is famous. Chat about whatever comes naturally for a few minutes; then start your questioning. Perhaps one of the basic questions you have prepared in advance will start him talking in such an interesting and newsy manner that you won't have time to ask everything you had written down. But never mind; you probably have more material than you can use anyway. As you take notes, think about which of his statements sounds like the most likely lead for your story. If necessary, question him further on the point until you have it well developed. It is good technique to have strong direct quotes to support the statement in the lead paragraph.

Although you may be having a wonderful time conversing with the celebrity and want to remain a long time, don't overstay your welcome; a date for an interview isn't a social invitation for the entire afternoon. When you have all the material you need, excuse yourself with thanks and leave. Then go home, to the newspaper office, or somewhere else where you can sit down for a few minutes and develop your notes. The reporting half of your job is finished; all that's left is writing the story!

Our explorer friend probably is too wise to do such a thing, but some interviewees might ask to see your story before it is published, in effect to censor it. Only under rare circumstances should the interviewer agree to such a request, which is contrary to normal newspaper practice. Just reply politely that your paper has a policy against submitting its stories for approval. If the material covered is of a technical nature, the interviewer might want to have the story checked for accuracy; that is about the only reason for letting the person interviewed get an advance look at what you have written.

Six Pulitzer Prize reporters: top, James B. Reston, New York *Times*, and Relman Morin, Associated Press (see chapter 17); center, Russell Jones, United Press International, and Clark Mollenhoff, Des Moines *Register* and *Tribune* and Minneapolis *Star* and *Tribune;* bottom, Homer Bigart, New York *Times*, and George Thiem, Chicago *Daily News* (see chapter 12).

There is infinite variety in reporting assignments. Above: William C. Payette, United Press International correspondent, stands in cathedral in Ecuador destroyed by earthquake as workmen search for bodies. Center: UPI's Claire Cox interviews actress Lauren Bacall in a New York hotel suite. Below: sports writers cover a Big Ten football game from the glass-enclosed press box at Minnesota's stadium, while operators transmit their copy to their home offices.

Next let us look at an actual newspaper interview developed very much along the lines described above. It was written by one of the authors of this textbook and published in the Los Angeles *Mirror-News*. We quote it in full, not because it is any better than hundreds of others published each year in newspapers all over the country, but because it illustrates many of the points detailed in the preceding pages. The news peg was simple, the publication of a new book by the popular philosopher, Will Durant. Note however that this fact played a secondary role in the story as finally written.

Philosopher Durant Finds
Too Much Liberty in U.S.

By Phil Ault
Mirror-News Staff Writer

Philosopher Will Durant, busily writing the history of civilization on a smog-bound Hollywood hilltop, thinks that the United States is suffering from too much liberty.

Our morals are going to pieces, and we're headed for a big war around 1975.

You can cheer up, however, the war will not wipe out civilization.

So said the white-haired little man with the long view in a Mirror-News interview. Being a philosopher, he is less upset about these dire things than ordinary folk.

They've all happened before, somewhere in history. Yet we still are here.

The fifth volume of Durant's monumental seven volume story of civilization, "The Renaissance," will be published Friday. More than 300,-000 words of it, all scrawled in longhand with a ball point pen. (Simon and Schuster: $7.50.)

The occasion provided a good excuse for Durant to emerge from the late 1400's, where he is now probing around for volume six, and take a philosopher-historian's look at present-day America.

500 Years Forward

Jerking himself 500 years forward in his rocking chair, Durant proclaimed: "Probably we have had too much liberty in the United States. We're especially overdoing moral liberty."

Biting off his words precisely, he expounded, "Liberty is a trial and demands a lot of intelligence. We made ourselves sovereign without making ourselves intelligent."

Then, more cheerfully, "However, the various challenges will probably save us.

When a Hitler comes along, we forget our night clubs and brothels and submit to discipline."

On Kinsey

As for American morals, there is nothing in the Kinsey report that hasn't been accepted as perfectly normal somewhere in the past.

But that doesn't make it right, as far as Durant personally is concerned. He is a conservative on the subject. Once a man weds a maid, he says, they should fight it out together the rest of their days.

American women are so busy enjoying their freedom, he maintains, that they aren't providing much cultural grace.

"The industrial revolution has broken down our moral code, which was designed for an agricultural society," he said. "Morals change according to economic conditions. We are moving from the village to the city, from early to late economic maturity and marriage.

"For a time this is breeding moral disorder but a new moral stability may come when the old code becomes adjusted to urban life."

As for war, it is inevitable. Not next year, or five years hence, but about 1975. That is to give the United States and Russia time to grow a new crop of fighting men who can't remember the horrors of the last war.

"Will the war wipe out civilization?"

The little man in the short-sleeved shirt, now 67, rocked a bit on that one. He peered through his shell-rimmed glasses, then replied:

"No, I don't think so. The destruction probably will be no greater than in past wars, in comparison with the growth of population and property."

Men always have had wars, and from what Durant can see they will keep right on doing so. Wars are a form of natural selection and give men virility and pride.

In the second-floor workroom of his big home the philosopher has 3000 years of history jotted down on small paper notes, all neatly numbered and tucked away in cardboard boxes. Around him the walls are ceiling-high with reference books.

Each volume in his gigantic life work goes through three complete drafts before he is satisfied.

Forty Years' Pleasure

"The Renaissance" is one of his favorites because of its colorful characters. He has been gathering material for 40 years and "the book just wrote itself"—all 750 pages.

For a final bit of prediction, what countries does Durant see as the major powers when the year 2000 rolls around?

"United States, Russia, China, India and Brazil."

The British won't like that.

This interview had to be written to meet the space limitations of a tabloid section and was weakened by that fact. The writer's decision was to cram as much information as possible into the restricted space, although the result was a slightly choppy effect. Another 200 words would have made it substantially stronger. A comparison drawn by Dr. Durant between Renaissance days, about which he was writing, and contemporary times would have been significant. Also, he should have been allowed to develop his reasons for selecting the five countries he named as world leaders in the year 2000.

Dr. Durant's comments about current morals, the position of American women, and the prospects for another global war were in response to questions prepared in advance. But his provocative forecast of the year 2000 was a spontaneous contribution to the discussion. To give the interview a smoother flow in print, this thought was presented in question-and-answer form, although he volunteered the comment. Such treatment, judiciously done, is a small exercise of literary license.

Eight Guides to Good Interviewing

The following suggestions will help the reporter obtain lively, newsworthy interviews:

1. Find out as much as possible about your news source in advance.
2. Prepare a set of basic questions to ask him.
3. Approach the source with confidence, remembering that you represent the public's right to know.
4. Add power to the interview by using direct quotations to explain his major points.
5. Ask direct, searching questions but do so without arousing antagonism.
6. Take ample notes on important facts.
7. Watch for news lead angles while you talk.
8. Seek to catch the interviewee's personality and physical characteristics.

Chapter 10

Getting the News

Many Kinds of Assignments

The general assignment reporter is the all-around man of a newspaper staff. No two days of his life are the same. His job is an editorial grab bag, from which he pulls a constantly changing succession of stories to whet his curiosity and tax his skill. Within a few hours of an average day he may interview the mayor, cover a strike, write a feature about a woman's 100th birthday, handle an accident report phoned in by a source in the sheriff's office, work up a story on a speech from a publicity handout, and listen sympathetically to a feminine subscriber who is angry because her name was accidentally omitted from a list of hostesses in yesterday's paper.

To be successful the general assignment reporter must have a flexible mind, good general knowledge of affairs both in his community and beyond the city limits, and a never wavering curiosity. Many reporters prefer this kind of job to the more specialized but restrictive work on a full-time beat.

Depending upon the size of his paper, the general reporter may have a specific beat to cover as part of his daily routine, in addition to being on call from the city editor for unexpected assignments. The metropolitan papers have a pool of reporters with no regularly assigned duties who stand by for orders from the city editor. Such a reporter may spend his working hours inside the office one day, checking stories by telephone, and the next day be out on the street constantly, rushing from one assignment to another, as directed from the city desk by telephone. The smaller the staff, the more "must" beat assignments a reporter has.

No matter how the details of the general reporter's tasks may vary, all of the reporters encounter identical problems. The purpose of this chapter is to examine the most important of these and explain how a good reporter meets them.

The reporter's most important task is to present his story to the readers in a clear, straightforward, and accurate way. This involves more than good writing; beneath that must be a full understanding by the reporter of what the story means. If he doesn't have a comprehensive understanding of the facts, motives, and circumstances involved, he cannot expect his readers to have it after reading his story. The traditional requirements of who, what, when, where, why, and how are basic. Of these "five" "W's" and "H," modern journalism places increasing emphasis on "why." The best reporter puts meaning into his stories by digging beneath the surface facts for the reasons why the story is happening. This does not mean editorializing in the news columns; what it does mean is adding perspective. There is a resemblance here to the ancient legend about six blind men who touched different parts of an elephant. One touched the animal's tail and thought it was a rope, another the side and thought it a wall, the third mistook the tusk for a spear, the fourth the knee for a tree, the fifth the trunk for a snake, and the sixth the ears for a fan. A reporter who merely quoted what each of the blind men said would produce a false, misleading story. He must add the extra fact that brings it all into focus—they were all touching an elephant.

Humans being what they are, it is necessary for the reporter to be cautious about motives. Not *too* dubious, because a great many people are forthright and scrupulously honest in their dealings with newsmen. But even the most honorable and best intentioned men instinctively put themselves in the best light possible, rationalizing their actions even without realizing what they are doing. Far too many others consciously attempt to deceive reporters with half-truths and concealed facts.

A shrewd editor once said, after watching human behavior

from close range for half a century, that a man always has two reasons for doing something—a good reason and the real one. So look for the motive, not only what a man says, but why he says it.

Covering the Municipal Beat

A major source of stories for every newspaper is the city hall. If the city is also the county seat, as is frequently the case, the county offices are usually included on the same beat. The reporter covers the public meetings held by the city council and other municipal bodies. He must become acquainted with the mayor and drop into his office frequently for a chat. He must also make frequent rounds of the various city departments, commissions, and clerical offices, from which many of the best stories can be obtained if the reporter knows how to dig them out. Whenever possible, have a specific question to ask, because the news source approached in this firm manner has a stronger feeling that you know what is going on. Frequently the mayor is at odds with the council, or there is a feud running between the heads of two city departments. By asking one for comment about the statements or actions of the other, lively and controversial stories can be developed. Through spite or political maneuvering, one source will frequently tip off the reporter about something suspicious going on in his rival's department. The good reporter stays neutral in these city hall quarrels, listening to the claims and woes of both sides without becoming involved personally. The more friendly he is with secretaries, clerks, and minor officials, the greater his prospects for picking up bits of gossip that may contain important news leads. Information comes from people. Get out and talk with them!

Another thing a city hall reporter learns is that the political front men aren't always the best sources for stories. The mayor or city manager is responsible for presenting the municipal budget to the city council, for example, but the budget itself probably has been prepared by a financial expert on his staff. He works on it for weeks before the formal presentation by the mayor, and frequently can provide good tips and explanations on what is to come. Similar leads can be developed in such fields as city planning, health, zoning, and traffic. Many experts receive little public credit for their work and enjoy the opportunity to describe the problems they face. Find out who is the real source of expert knowledge in governmental matters, and go straight to him.

The same technique should be applied on the broader fronts in reporting from state capitols and from Washington.

A reporter on the local government beat can develop good follow-up stories by keeping a close watch on dispatches from the state and national capitals. If Congress enacts a law changing social security benefits, how does that affect payments from the local office? How many local post-office employees will benefit by the congressional bill raising postal workers' salaries? Interviews with the wives of a dozen such men on how they will spend the extra money might provide revealing human interest material. A cutback in the state highway building budget may mean delay in constructing a much-needed railroad underpass in your city. These stories are not handed out on a platter or disclosed in public meetings. But they are there for the asking if an enterprising reporter seeks them out. Visitors from other cities and countries who have come to see how your city does things often provide excellent interview material.

Getting Access to News

There is a tendency among many officials, both elected and appointed, to conduct public business in secret. Since their work is the public's business, this practice cannot be justified except in special cases such as the discussion of personnel. Reporters and their editors must carry on a constant fight for free access to information. Some public officials simply don't want to be bothered by what they consider the "nuisance" of press coverage; a smaller number have something embarrassing or even illegal to conceal. By reacting vigorously whenever a roadblock is erected to keep them from obtaining stories, reporters on the government beat can contribute to the growing fight by the press for freedom of information.

The closed meeting is a device often used to keep news from reporters. The executive session is a variation of this in which the official body will discuss a matter without press or public present, then convene publicly to take formal action along the lines agreed in advance. This is an abridgment of the public's right to know, since the board's reasons for its actions and the attitude of every member are pertinent to a full understanding of the story.

The legal requirements about open meetings vary from state to state. California, for example, has a law requiring all public boards to hold open meetings, except when considering a few specialized categories of business, and ordering the boards to give advance notice of special meetings to newspapers which request it. A recent study by the Legislative Research Council of Massachusetts showed that in 38 cities surveyed, the prevailing policy, practice, and statutory requirements about open meetings varied sharply not only from city to city, but also from one board to another within the city. Of the 455 assorted boards checked, 248 held open meetings, 132 held closed meetings, and 75 provided incomplete information.

Frequently there are stories about reporters who have been evicted from official meetings because the members wanted to conduct their business in secret. The reporter caught in such a situation should protest vigorously, remembering that he is the public's eyes and ears. Even if he loses the dispute he may still be able to obtain word of what occurred. By questioning the various members in turn after the session adjourns he frequently can pick up bits of information which, when pieced together, will give a broad outline of what happened. Also he may find a board member who objected to the secrecy and is willing to give him a detailed report. Sometimes, too, the story of the reporter's eviction makes better news than what actually happened in the meeting.

Actual Operation of a Small City Beat

Here is a description by a reporter in a midwestern city of 25,000 of the way he covers the city beat for his afternoon

newspaper. This is an assignment frequently given to a young reporter on a small daily.

The city man leaves the office about 8:55 a.m. First stop
is the municipal building where the city water and light
board is located. I check with the secretary of the board
and also the superintendent of utilities. Superintendent is
a very good source and able to inform on progress of the
city's latest well. Lots of feature material here since they've
been having one tough break after another, cave-ins, etc.

I check both secretary and superintendent by phone in
the afternoon for advance information—that way I don't
spend too much time in the morning.

Next stop in the municipal building is city recorder and
the city engineer. Certain seasons I get a lot from recorder
but usually fairly quiet. He handles dog licenses, issues various other licenses. A good source for news on city council
and their battles with the mayor.

Engineer is usually a little busier—work on streets in
spring, snow removal in winter, also dope on a new sewage
disposal plant recently passed in a bond election. Also information on project for changing names of all city streets in
a better plan for cities of this size.

The big union in the city (4,000 members) is against
changing names of streets.

From the municipal building I stop off at the labor center
to see the president of the local. I am on exceptionally good
terms with him and he is a very good source of news on
union and company matters. The big company in town and
the union are arguing about a $14,000,000 trust fund which
the company discontinued. Lately there have been many
front page stories on this, all on tips from the union president.

The union has a weekly paper and has often blasted my
paper for its various activities and Republican political stand.
On several occasions the president has barred my paper's
reporter from the labor center. (Being a Democrat is of ut-
most importance for good coverage here.) Also contact him
in the afternoon for advance information.

Next stop is ambulance service, for their runs in the previous 24 hours. Being on good terms with the switchboard operator is important. Some house calls look routine but might be news, such as a polio case tip from the girl on the switchboard. The hospital gives us dope on accidents but wouldn't mention this kind of case unless we asked or knew from another source.

Since this city is a county seat, the sheriff's office is part of the beat. Accidents in the county are covered through him. He's very good on calling when a traffic fatality occurs. We have another man who checks all other county offices.

From sheriff to fire station, also get weather report there. They want new trucks badly and are good source of news —little items that make sidebar stories.

From fire station to police, juvenile bureau and municipal court. With police I check the blotter and traffic accidents. Many crimes are by juveniles and not on the regular police blotter. I check on this at the juvenile bureau and can often talk them into letting me use these items.

I only cover municipal court trials if they are important. The rest I get from the clerk of court. A good contact, she supplies details about court scenes that make good feature stuff.

The police and fire stations are directly across from the courthouse, which is one block from the ambulance service. From court I go back to the paper, arriving about 10:45 a.m. The deadline is noon.

If I encounter big news along the way, I phone the paper to let them know. As an example, one day a check at the police station showed the report of a break-in at the city clinic with some narcotics stolen. That was our main story of the day.

After getting my copy in before the noon deadline, I monitor the radio for a complete check of all local news at 12:15 p.m. Then I have a 45 minute lunch period.

In the afternoon I work on tips for both news and feature stories and go out to take pictures for the next day's paper. By phone I check the airport, railroad and mayor's office.

The railroad is a source of good feature stuff on old timers when they retire. The mayor's office is a good source, since he is always in a squabble with the council. He gives plenty information, most of which can be worked on ahead of time.

I arrive in the office at 8 a.m. and am able to work on stories for about an hour before going out on the beat. During this time I write stories on meetings covered the previous night or any fire or police story on which I have been called out during the night. Also I write the cutlines for pictures.

I cover all meetings of the utilities board, safety council, union, special events, banquets, political rallies and important speakers. On the average I count on being out two nights a week—not counting the police and fire calls.

This memo on actual beat operation underscores several of the points made in preceding pages. The time problem—even on a small paper with only one deadline, it is important for the reporter to keep his office informed when a major story breaks. Development of sources—the personal link between the reporter and the men who can supply him news is essential. In this case, even the circumstance of the reporter's political beliefs helps with one key source. (Generally it is wise to keep your personal beliefs on such matters as politics and religion to yourself, unless you see that they will help cultivate a source. The reverse might be true.) Cross-checking of sources—notice that one of the reporter's best places for information about the fight between the mayor and the city council is the city recorder, who is not directly involved but has access to much information.

Sources for Stories

Drawing up a list of sources for news stories is almost a pointless effort; they are everywhere, waiting to be developed by the alert reporter. Few of them come ready-made. Once a story idea is plucked from a casual conversation, a book, or another newspaper, the reporter must nurse it and mold it until a hard, printable article emerges.

One story which won first prize in a state contest came about because an editor's curiosity was whetted by a sentence in a book review. Writing about a juvenile book on aviation, the columnist remarked that the author had checked her facts about pioneer aviation with Charles Taylor, the man who had built the engine for the first Wright Brothers plane. Taylor was living in the same city. The editor had never heard of Taylor and was surprised that such a man was still alive. So he assigned a reporter to interview him.

The reporter eventually found Taylor in the county hospital, a destitute charity patient. The facts checked out; he really had built the first successful airplane engine. The press associations picked up the story and it received wide national attention. The aircraft industry, in gratitude, provided money on which Taylor lived the few remaining months of his life.

There are some standard starting points for stories which an enterprising reporter should keep in mind. Anniversaries make a good news peg. When something unusual happens in your community, make a note to check it a year later and see what has happened to the people involved. A press association reporter in Boston made page one nationally by going back to see how a man who won $100,000 in a lottery had spent it. His lead: "So he took the $100,000. . . ."

In another city a reporter made a similar checkup on a Negro football player who had become a minister and was appointed to an interracial church. With all the furor over integration, what had happened to this man during his first year of ministering to a mixed congregation? The result was a deeply moving story of good faith and cooperation.

Much as they have been worked over, holidays still offer possibilities for fresh approaches on stories. Watch the papers; sometimes several small items in your own paper and the wire services will indicate a trend that can be developed into a major story. Listen to conversations. During an idle chat may come a little inner voice which says. "I wonder what ever happened to so-and-so" or "There's a situation that might be worth investigating."

Making your sources news conscious is a part of a reporter's

job. Encourage them to pass on tips, even if most of the suggestions are useless; one in a hundred may prove very valuable.
A reporter should never discourage a volunteer tipster by a brusk,
"That's no good." Say that the idea may have possibilities and
you will check into it, or give a valid reason why a story isn't
likely to develop. Not only is this good manners, but you are
training the source to your needs.

Reporting Meetings and Conventions

The general assignment reporter's work involves attending
innumerable meetings, all the way from small committees to
large and complex conventions. He knows from long hours of
bored sitting that most speakers talk too long, that officers' reports are usually devoid of news, and that committee meetings
have an unpleasant habit of degenerating into trivialities. If he
is on a metropolitan paper and assigned to the so-called "rubber
chicken" circuit, he can predict almost down to the color of the
ice cream what the banquet menu will be in each hotel. Yet
despite their time-consuming aspects, such public meetings do
produce many news stories, sometimes of banner headline caliber.

Prominent speakers at business and political meetings often
have their speeches mimeographed in advance for reporters. This
is very helpful in getting precise quotations, of course, although
it tends to deaden the reporter's story if he is not careful because
the job has been made too easy. Even though an advance copy
of the text is in hand, whenever possible the reporter should attend the actual speech. Frequently the speaker will depart from
his prepared text and insert remarks of much more interest; also,
a personal hearing gives the reporter a stronger feeling of what
the speaker considers important. If a statement is included in the
advance text but not actually uttered, the general practice is to
assume that statement is on the record anyway unless the speaker
requests that it be deleted.

Covering speeches, either as they are delivered or from prepared texts, is largely an exercise in watching for newsworthy
angles. Each of the speaker's major statements should be submitted to a quick mental scrutiny by the reporter; is it a new

proposal, a controversial position, a simplified explanation of a complex issue? Does it contain a distinctive phrase that will stick in the reader's mind? If so, it provides a peg upon which the entire story can be built and an eye-catching headline written.

Some of the best speeches are devoid of sensational aspects, but are effective because the speaker brings an involved situation into focus and explains the background in language easy to understand. Since the reporter cannot record everything the speaker says, he must exercise skill in selecting the key quotations and paraphrasing other portions in such a way as to give a clear flow of narrative.

Speakers of national prominence frequently put a specific hour of publication at the start of their texts. The purpose is to assure uniform release of controversial matter through all news media. Although there is no legal reason for them to honor such embargoes, newspapers and radio and TV stations normally do so for their mutual benefit. If violations were widespread, some sources might stop putting out advances, and this would delay early publication of important news contained in the speeches. Publicity-wise speakers who know that their remarks will be carried nationwide by the wire services sometimes make a release date two or three hours before they actually speak. This is to enable the newspapers to be on the street with the story at the same time it is broadcast or telecast. This practice is widespread during national political campaigns.

If a speaker leaves a question half-answered or suggests a provocative point in his address, the reporter should see him after the meeting to obtain clarification. In his story he should make clear what was said by the speaker from the platform and what was given later in supplementary information.

A reporter should try to capture the "feel" of a meeting as well as what is said. The fact that the group is angry, hot, or amused, or interrupts the speech with frequent spontaneous applause, helps the reader to understand what took place. He wants to know what were the main things said or accomplished and the atmosphere in which they were done. He cares little or nothing about the committee reports and other parliamentary routine.

A sprinkling of pertinent or humorous dialogue brings a story to life. Sharp exchanges between a speaker and his audience, or the chairman and other members of a board, should be quoted verbatim whenever possible. Sometimes a single direct quote will give a story the extra punch that helps the reader remember it. An actual example: a small city restaurant owner was charged with violating the health ordinances by operating an unsanitary establishment. He pleaded not guilty and denied the specific charge that there were rodents in his restaurant. "They weren't rodents, only very small mice," he testified. That punch line gave the routine item appeal because it revealed so much about the man and his business.

Here is another example of how a reporter with a sharp ear for conversation turned a routine report of a state legislature committee meeting into front page material. The United Press reporter at the New Mexico capitol could merely have listed what the committee decided about the minor bills before it. His story would have been buried far inside, or not used at all. Instead he caught the mood of the meeting thus:

'Put It on the Pile'

How House Committee Acted
On Some On Last-Minute Bills

SANTA FE, March 7 (UPI)—Work hit a feverish pace during the last week of the State Legislature.

Bills died right and left, mostly by inaction, to save time for the most important issues.

The following discussion took place in a House committee meeting around 11 p.m., one of the last nights of the session. Members, their ties loosened, were grouped around the chairman as he read the numbers and subject matter of the bills.

"Senate Bill No. 450 . . . about highway access."

"Looks O.K. Move to pass."

"All in favor aye, so ordered."

"House Bill 443 . . . something about adoption."

"I think they lost interest . . . put it on the pile."

The "pile" was a stack of some dozen bills, stacked to face down, doomed to be locked in the chairman's desk until the janitor finds them after the session is over.

"Senate Bill 456 . . . investment of . . . what. . . ."

"Move do not pass."
"Why?"
"It's too long."
"All in favor aye, so ordered."

The committee's action was hurried, but the members knew what they were doing.

They had studied the bills at earlier meetings and had postponed action.

Many of the bills duplicated legislation already passed, and others were sponsored by legislators whose interest had cooled off.

The convention is a unique feature of contemporary American life, a mixture of business, conviviality and sometimes raucous horseplay. When a state or national convention comes to his city, the general assignment reporter has a strenuous task. He must cover the major speeches, frequently given by men of national stature, the discussions in sectional meetings, the activities of the convention leaders, and the social events. These gatherings frequently are the source of human interest features, too. The discussions in sectional meetings offer lively material for the reporter who takes the time to attend them.

Most large conventions have a press headquarters at which reporters are provided with typewriters and working space. Programs and advance copies of speeches and similar materials are distributed here. With the press room as his home base, the newsman roams the convention area in search of stories. At such meetings he often has access to many excellently informed men and women in a specialized field, such as medicine or engineering, and can talk with them in a relaxed atmosphere. He can acquire background information of great value in this manner. This gives the ingenious reporter the opportunity to think up story angles that aren't to be found in the prepared speeches. Good interviews can be obtained easily. One device is to poll the delegates on a controversial issue in their own field; the division of opinion makes good reading. If a vote is scheduled on a disputed resolution or candidate, the informal poll is good here too. The British have an expression "stirring up the animals" when they try to put life into a dull situation. A reporter with an eye to a newsworthy angle sometimes can do this at a convention. Always look for the "fun" stories, too. Convention delegates away from home are prone to act in an uninhibited manner. The reporter cannot expect the convention publicity man to put him into contact with all the interesting delegates. He must mingle with them and keep a close watch on the identification tags which are a standard part of a delegate's equipment.

The presence of television cameras for live telecasts from public hearings and conventions has caused a new problem for the newspaper reporter. Much of his audience has already seen and heard the speakers whose speeches he writes about. Television's advantage is immediacy, but only a story of high dramatic merit (a controversial Senate hearing or critical United Nations debate, for example) will hold an audience. Viewers find that the nuggets of big news and colorful testimony are almost buried in the mass of byplay and petty comment.

The newspaper reporter's challenge is to present highlights of the actual testimony at hearings, plus finding off-camera news angles that will add significance and meaning. Who will testify next, what additional comments the witnesses had to make after they left the stand (careful, these aren't privileged!), the background of the witnesses, the purposes of the investigating committee—those are the things to seek. The presence of a TV camera should put the newspaper reporter on his toes. It has been well established that viewers who watch a televised convention or hearing still want to read about it, just as a baseball fan who attended yesterday's game is an ardent reader of the sports writer's account in the next morning's paper.

The presence of live cameras at the national presidential nominating conventions has changed the conduct of these meetings. Their managers try to make them move faster and have more entertainment value. Yet the amount of newspaper wordage filed from the convention halls remains as high as ever, although this coverage now puts a greater emphasis on the "why" than in the pretelevision days.

Television men are working hard to bring their cameras into courtrooms, legislative chambers, and other areas previously forbidden to them, but they still face strong opposition. When a newsworthy event is televised, the newspaper can backstop its men on the scene by having a reporter take notes from a TV set in the office. Usually these are turned over to the rewrite man who consolidates them with the notes being phoned in by the reporter on the scene.

Working with Publicity Representatives

Many of the stories a general assignment reporter handles are brought to the newspaper by publicity representatives of civic organizations and commercial firms. Men and women handling publicity for their clubs and community groups usually do so free of charge, receiving nothing except a thank you and a title such as press chairman. As a group they are not especially skilled in publicity techniques and the needs of a newspaper; while their information is valuable to the reporter, he often has to coach them in providing the kind of facts he needs. The volunteer work done by these men and women in presenting the facts about their organizations' work is of great value to their groups and to the newspapers as well.

The other kind of publicity representative with whom the reporter deals is the paid agent of a business, trade organization, or institution of some kind. These men and women are wise in the ways of newspapers, many of them having been former reporters, and clever at thinking up "angles." They know what makes news, although frequently they try to coax newspapers to publish stories about their clients which have very little reader interest. In dealing with them, charming and helpful as they may be, the reporter should always remember that they are being paid to represent their clients or companies. Some are conscientious information men who understand the principles of public relations and who strive to do honest jobs in working with news media; others are merely opportunistic press agents who are interested only in getting their clients into print for commercial gain. It is with the latter group that most trouble comes.

The most commonplace form of commercial approach is the publicity release, or handout. Typed or mimeographed, and bearing the sender's name at the top, it announces some item which the publicity man believes to have a possibility of publication. Frequently the city editor does consider the contents newsworthy and gives the handout to a reporter or rewrite man to be prepared as a news story. Many editors, especially on papers with larger staffs, pride themselves on never publishing a handout exactly as it has been received. Even though the item has been well prepared, these editors have it redone as a matter of principle. Others lack either the time or the care to do this. Whenever possible copy from a commercial source should be edited since inevitably it has been slanted to the advantage of the contributor.

Many handouts of no apparent value come to a newspaper every day. They must be scanned, however, because sometimes they suggest an idea for a news story quite different from the one proposed by the press agent. One metropolitan newspaper made a check of the handouts received in a single day by all its editorial departments—city desk, sports, women's, business, entertainment, and other specialized sections. The total came to more than a thousand!

The reporter who is given a handout by the city desk for handling should read it carefully and then ask himself, "What other facts about this situation would our readers like to have? What significant background is not included here?" Usually the actual facts in a press release put out by a reliable publicity man are accurate. If they aren't, he won't be trusted again in the city room, and he knows it. But he isn't going to include material detrimental or unflattering to his client. If such facts exist, and are pertinent to a well-rounded news story, it is up to the reporter to find them by checking the library files, calling other news sources to cross-check the story, and asking the publicity man for further information.

Sometimes a city editor will go along with a publicity man's stunt idea just for the fun of it, especially when news is dull and he thinks it will give his readers a chuckle. A clever example of such a promotion story in which the newspapers and politicians cooperated occurred in the state of Washington. On the Fourth of July 3000 persons, including the governor, gathered on a 40-acre tract of sagebrush out in the wasteland and formally dedicated a town that didn't exist except on the real estate promoter's planning boards. What brought them out? The fact that the new town was named George, Washington. The promoter had planted cherry trees along the main street and put a hatchet at the top of the flagpole. Everybody involved knew that the stunt was just an effort to get free publicity for a real estate promotion. But the holiday was a slack news day, and a wire service account of the dedication was published from coast to coast.

A reporter on such an assignment should "go along with the gag" but write his story with a tongue-in-cheek approach to show his readers that he hasn't been taken in by the promoter, but just wants to share the fun.

Handling of commercial publicity stories may involve the newspaper's business office policy. Because a newspaper is a commercial organization and can continue to publish only if it succeeds financially, it must maintain good relations with the companies which buy advertising space in its pages. These companies sometimes bring pressure to get coverage in the news columns; the business office and managing editor decide what must be used to satisfy the advertiser and what can be ignored. Some of these stories are newsworthy by any objective standard although others are just an effort to obtain free advertising. The situation is different in every city, according to local practice that has been built up through the years. Often the biggest space users ask for the least publicity, while small aggressive firms become obnoxious in their demands.

So when a reporter or rewrite man is given a handout with a "must" label on it which he considers to be a waste of space, he should handle it without grumbling and to the best of his ability. In an ideal world he wouldn't be forced to demean himself, perhaps, but in this practical one the advertisers help to pay his salary. He can be sure that his managing editor won't let any more "puff" copy into the paper than necessary; he doesn't like it any better than the reporter who handles the material. This is a lesson that some reporters have difficulty in learning, but they must learn it.

On the other hand, interesting publicity releases sometimes are discarded because the commercial source which submits them spends all of its advertising dollars in another newspaper or other types of media.

Astute publicity men and women come into the newspaper offices and establish personal acquaintances with the editors and reporters. Frequently the really wise ones pass on tips for feature and news stories in fields outside their own to ingratiate themselves with the staff. This relationship can be mutually advantageous, if the reporter always keeps in mind what the publicity man's true function is and does not let personal friendship unduly influence his handling of a story.

Printed publicity handouts are available to everyone and thus cannot provide any newspaper with an exclusive angle—unless the man handling the story thinks of one that he can develop by asking questions. When a publicity man brings a story idea to an editor, however, general practice is to consider it as exclusive to that paper if the editor likes the idea sufficiently to assign a reporter to develop it. Among publicity men this is known as "planting" a story. If the publicist commits the sin of giving the same story idea to rival editors, he is guilty of "double planting."

Here is an example of looking for the newsworthy angle in a handout. During World War II many thousands of American soldiers were stationed on an isolated island under severe censorship. The wire service correspondents stationed with them had heavy limitations on what they could report, lest the enemy obtain information about the condition, number, and exact positions of the soldiers. The result was an almost total news vacuum about the activities of some 35,000 American men in a strategic area.

When Christmas approached, the commanding general issued season's greetings to his troops, a statement about 200 words long, full of routine holiday wishes. In it he remarked in passing that he was glad to see his men in such good health and fine spirits despite their rigorous post. One reporter cabled home a brief dispatch stating that the general had issued a Christmas message to his men. Another reporter, working from the same handout, wrote a lead stating that the general reported that the American soldiers on the island were in good health and fine spirits. His story was played in newspapers all over the United States, while the other drew little attention—all because he had shifted the emphasis in the available facts and found an angle, answering a question that editors and their readers had been asking.

Dealing with Threats

The reverse of the publicity seeker is the man who tries to keep a story out of print and uses threats in an effort to do so. Many reporters have been told at one time or another, "I'll get your job if you print that!" Such threats are made out of ignorance of the newspaper business. It is the editor who decides what is printed, and he almost certainly will print the story once he hears about the threat. Report any such efforts at intimidation to your editor; you can count on his backing. Another version is, "I'll see the publisher and withdraw all my advertising if that story is printed." The reporter's responsibility in this case is to assemble the facts for his story and to pass along the threat to his superiors. They can make the decision on the basis of over-all information which the reporter lacks.

There are instances in which companies actually have canceled their advertising in protest against a newspaper's treatment of a news situation. A large department store in a major city withdrew all its linage from one newspaper because the editors put a secondary front page banner on a wire service dispatch about a wild outbreak of cut-rate competition among New York department stores. The local store had asked the newspaper to minimize the story, because it feared that the publicity would start popular pressure for similar price cutting in its area. The editors, realizing the news interest for their readers in the ridiculous bargains offered and the huge crowds these drew, gave the story the play they believed it deserved, despite the store's warning. The action cost the paper several thousand dollars in revenue, but strengthened its prestige in the eyes of readers and other advertisers.

A major automobile manufacturer once took similar punitive action against a nationally circulated newspaper because it printed an enterprise story about the company's new models before the firm was ready to make the information public.

Difficult as the decision is at the time, the newspaper which resists such pressure from advertisers emerges stronger because it stood its ground. Eventually the advertiser returns to the newspaper's pages, too, because his advertisements draw people to his store and earn him a profit. Actually, very few cases arise in which the advertiser takes such drastic steps, or even threatens to do so. In turn, newspapers frequently make minor concessions to advertisers in news coverage when they believe they can do so without dangerously compromising their principles. A news story about a waitress who slapped a patron and was arrested might carry only the restaurant's address, not its name, if the owner protested that publicity would injure his establishment's reputation through no fault of his. If the same restaurant were convicted of violating city health ordinances, the editors would feel obligated to publish its name, no matter how much the owner protested.

Another form of pressure comes from readers who cancel their subscriptions because they disagree with a publication's news treatment or editorial position on a controversial issue. Frequently when a newspaper endorses a political candidate, it receives a few cancellations from supporters of his opponent. Similar organized pressure sometimes comes from fraternal, social, or religious groups. If the editor is satisfied that his news columns are treating the issue objectively, and he is only exercising his rightful editorial opinion, he usually stands firm.

If deep emotions have been aroused in a community, it requires courage for the editor to support a minority viewpoint. When Harry S. Ashmore, executive editor of the Little Rock *Arkansas Gazette*, took a position on racial integration in schools contrary to that held by many of his readers, the newspaper lost 10 per cent of its circulation—a severe financial blow. But later, as their need for the paper came to outweigh their temporary emotional upsurge, the readers began to return. Ashmore reported no loss of advertising because of this editorial stand, however.

Working with Photographers

Pictures are as much a part of a newspaper's coverage as words, although a much smaller part. Some stories can be told adequately with a picture and caption. In others, such as a fire or a wreck story, the pictures supplement the story and help the reader visualize what is happening, or what the people in the news look like. The question, "How about art?" is always in the back of the city editor's mind as he makes his coverage arrangements on big stories.

On smaller newspapers the reporters frequently take their own pictures. Even on metropolitan papers some men who cover large outlying districts are both reporters and photographers, usually known as combination men. Most medium-sized and large dailies have staffs of news photographers, sometimes consisting of 20 or more men. Usually the city desk sends a reporter and photographer out on a spot or feature story together. The pair are known as a crew, and on really big breaking stories such as a disaster there may be several crews from the same paper, working on different aspects simultaneously.

Efficient teamwork between reporter and photographer can be important. News photographers are proud of their highly technical craft, which at times involves considerable danger and always requires instant readiness for "grab" shots. Beginning reporters who are fortunate enough to draw assignments with veteran photographers can learn many tricks of the business from them. It is considered a cardinal sin for overambitious young reporters to order photographers what pictures to take. The reporter's job is to get the facts, the photographer's to get the pictures. The two men can help each other greatly with suggestions, but this must be done on the basis of mutual respect. It is the reporter's responsibility to brief the photographer on the facts and purpose of their assignment. The photographer must submit proper identification of the people in his pictures for caption material. Always make sure that the names, ages, and other facts turned in by the photographer correspond with those used by the reporter when writing about the same people in his story.

Chasing Pictures

The reporter is sometimes assigned by his city desk to obtain photographs of people suddenly thrust into the news, usually through tragedy. This is an unpleasant task at times, because the relatives he must approach are frequently grief-stricken. A sympathetic explanation of why the paper wants to run a picture of the victim will usually bring about cooperation. This is one of those moments when the reporter's sincerity and deep-seated interest in his fellow humans is important. Few editors today condone outright picture stealing from bereaved and uncooperative families, an undesirable practice that some reporters have used at times in the past.

Handling Rewrite

The term "rewrite" in its common newspaper usage means taking facts from a printed source, such as another newspaper, or from another reporter by telephone and working them up into a story. Sometimes this involves additional reporting by the rewrite man and sometimes merely a rearranging of the available facts into a smooth-reading story which is phrased differently from the source material.

Metropolitan newspapers, especially those published in the afternoon, have several men whose sole function is rewrite. While they rarely have by-lines in print, they are key members of the staff. Most reporters spend part of their day in some phase of rewrite work.

The rewrite man must always treat the facts with even more caution than does the reporter who gathers them. The reporter has talked directly to the news sources and hears all the material in context, with the qualifying phrases and details. Out of this he distills the most important facts for relay to the rewrite man. The latter must be careful not to go beyond the information given to him; if he strains too hard with them to make an exciting story, or drops important qualifying phrases in his desire for simplicity of writing, the story can easily be twisted out of its true form.

Each time a set of facts is passed on from one person to another, there is additional opportunity for error and misinterpretation.

Typical of a rewrite man's errors are these actual examples. In one, a man checking a story by telephone sought a woman whose first name he didn't know. His first call was to the wrong woman. His second reached the person he wanted. When he wrote the story he used the right woman's name and the wrong woman's address. The story was printed that way and led to a legal demand for a retraction from one woman, which his paper had to make. In the other, a long obituary story was published Wednesday about the death of a prominent civic figure, with announcement of plans for the funeral on Friday. The next morning the same rewrite man, rehandling the story in briefer form for the Thursday paper, stated that the funeral "will be held today" —a day ahead of schedule. To make matters worse, the deceased happened to be the publisher's father!

Both of these errors were made by experienced big city rewrite men who suffered mental lapses. They momentarily forgot the basic rule of rechecking a story before turning it in.

It is common practice for the staffs of afternoon papers to rewrite secondary stories from clippings taken out of the morning papers, and morning staffs do the same with material from the "P.M.'s." Whenever possible the man doing such a rewrite job should look for a fresh angle to make his story appear different. When a continuing situation is involved, he should always check for late developments. If a prominent merchant has been stricken with a heart attack during a civic banquet, for example, the afternoon man rewriting the morning clip should unfailingly call the hospital for a late report on his condition. The rewrite man should never forget that his stories will be read several hours after he has written them and therefore should be cast in the most up-to-the-minute terms possible. When the reader receives his afternoon paper at 4:30 p.m., he probably has already read or heard about the merchant's attack, which occurred 18 hours earlier. His primary interest is in the man's condition. That should be the lead of the afternoon paper story, to be followed by a report on the circumstances of his seizure for the benefit of those who had not heard them. Since the morning newspaper is essentially a report on the previous day's happenings, the late angle is of somewhat less importance in organizing an A.M. story.

This leads to the question of the "today" angle. Some editors of afternoon papers are hypersensitive about "old" news and will not permit a lead which states that something happened last night. This rule can lead to absurdities as the rewrite men strain for a "today" angle. A better practice is to seek the today approach, but if it cannot be developed without sounding forced, state that the event happened last night, or develop a lead in which the time element can be avoided. This problem is especially difficult for the overnight rewrite men of the wire services, who must find ways at 3 a.m. to make last night's news sound fresh for publication in scores of papers across the country to be read at 3 p.m. or later.

Here is an actual example of the today lead absurdity, printed under pressure from the advertising department in a large city daily:

> Employees of Jones Brothers' mortuaries were still in a carnival spirit today, two weeks after a picnic celebrating the firm's 50th anniversary in business.

Another metropolitan rewrite man, bored with hunting the today approach on last night's news, wrote this sacrilegious lead which was killed by his city desk but was much quoted by his fellow rewrite men:

> God today was considering the prayers offered up last night at the Congress of Peace in Civic Auditorium.

These extreme examples above should not distract us from the fundamental importance of seeking a strong second-day lead on a running story. This calls for ingenuity and planning ahead. Trick phraseology to make "last night" sound like "today" isn't enough. Whenever possible a new idea should be incorporated. Let's say that the mayor at that civic banquet last night attacked the operators of parking lots in the city for charging excessive fees. That is the spot story for the morning papers. The lazy rewrite man for the next afternoon's paper, working from the morning clip, might write a lead like this:

The city's parking lot operators stood accused by Mayor Johnson today of charging too much for the use of their space.

A more enterprising man would call two or three of the prominent parking lot operators, also the manager of their trade association, if they had one, and ask for comment about the mayor's assertion. Almost certainly they would disagree with him and cite reasons for their position, such as the high price of the land they used. This serves the double purpose of giving the accused an opportunity to answer and creating a controversy in print. This is what is meant by developing a second-day angle.

His lead might read like this:

Spokesmen for the city's parking lot operators today accused Mayor Johnson of misleading the public with his charge that parking rates are exorbitant.

The earlier lead merely rehashes old news; the second carries the story forward and gives the copy desk man something firm on which to base a headline.

Similar approaches can be made in running stories of trials or investigations. What witnesses will be called today? What new approach does the prosecution intend to make? Sometimes in nonjudicial proceedings, like a legislative hearing, a fresh angle can be obtained by asking the man in charge to summarize what he believes he has achieved to date. The rewrite man should remember that to almost every political action, there is a reaction.

Follow-up stories need not always be built around somebody's views or plans. The newsman himself can develop factual leads, such as the number of witnesses heard to date and a tabulation of the major facts they have brought out. This round-up approach can be very helpful to the reader; in effect it pauses for breath with him part way through a complex situation and puts the developments into focus. Such an interpretive lead must be handled with care lest the writer let his own opinions creep into the story.

On newspapers with more than one edition a day, and on the wire services, the rewrite man has to rehandle a story between editions, incorporating late developments and eliminating errors or outdated information.

First he (or a copy boy) clips the entire story from the paper and pastes it together on a sheet of paper (a "pasteup"). If he rewrites the first part of the story completely, he has written a new lead. He indicates at the end of his new lead where it picks up in the earlier story. If the story is rewritten completely, it has been subbed. Sometimes only two or three paragraphs down in the body of the story are rewritten; the original paragraphs are killed and a substitution made. If new material is to be placed in the middle of the story, it is an insert; if at the end, it is add matter. Typesetting is expensive and time-consuming, so no more of a story is reset between editions than absolutely necessary. The rewrite man is responsible for seeing that all the changes he makes in a story are properly marked. If they aren't, the type may be assembled in the wrong sequence and the story in print will not read correctly.

In taking a running story from a reporter at the scene of the news action, the rewrite man must keep his eye open for good descriptive phrases and words which help the reader visualize the action. The rewrite man must get the situation clearly fixed in his own mind before he writes the story and therefore should interview the reporter and go back over the reporter's statements until everything is certain.

When a reporter phones in a story to a rewrite man, he should begin with a concise summary to give the rewrite man an overall picture. After that, he should give the details. This eliminates confusion and delay. Thus, it would be good form to start by saying, "This is a fire in a furniture warehouse on Center Street in which two men have been killed and five firemen overcome by smoke. It's still out of control." Then the reporter can proceed with the address, names of the victims, and other details. If the deadline for an edition is near, the rewrite man may keep the reporter waiting while he writes a quick lead and turns it in to the city desk; he then gets back onto the telephone for further details.

On spot news breaks, the reporter normally does not try to

dictate his lead and story in final form. But an experienced leg-man, working just from his notes, frequently dictates his material so smoothly that the rewrite man needs to give it only a final polishing as he runs it through his typewriter. On large news-papers, a reporter in the field who has the time and facilities may write his own story, then telephone it into a dictation machine at the office for transcription and delivery to the city desk. Reporters on out-of-town assignments also send in their stories by telegraph, using the special low press rates. This is called "overheading" a story by many newsmen.

These lead paragraphs from a reporter's eyewitness account of a southern California brush fire, phoned in to a rewrite man shortly before deadline, are a good example of how the man on the spot and the man in the office cooperate to present a pic-ture easily visualized by the reader. All the facts and impressions came from the reporter, but they were rearranged and pointed up by the rewrite man's brisk, punchy handling.

> The Malibu-Zuma area looked like a huge glowing barbe-cue pit when I arrived on the scene before dawn today.
>
> I could see the cherry red reflection of the flames in the sky when I left my home in Venice. But I was unprepared for the flaming ferocity I found when I topped the hill in Pacific Palisades.
>
> Whipped into a frenzy by the screaming winds, the flames raced across the tinder-dry canyons faster than anything I have ever seen.
>
> Rocks bigger than a man's fist and charred by the intense heat exploded like bullets. They whistled like shrapnel as they tore through the air.
>
> The roar of the flames and the wind was terrifying as I groped through the smoke along Pacific Coast Highway to Zuma Canyon.

The by-line, of course, went to the reporter. But the success of the story was due almost as much to the rewrite man, who ex-tracted from the field man's copious notes the visual images and the sounds which, when packed into 130 words, made the scene intensely realistic for the reader.

Guides for Good Reporting

The following eight rules, if followed sensibly, will help to make you a better reporter and rewrite man:

1. Look for the motive behind the story you are covering.
2. Get excited about a good story, but don't be so carried away by it that you fail to get the important information.
3. Talk to as many people as possible on your beat. News tips come from unexpected sources.
4. Keep your own feelings about the situation out of your story. Leave the editorializing where it belongs, on the editorial page.
5. Never write your story until you have all the circumstances clearly in mind.
6. Make a final recheck of the facts before turning in your story.
7. Tell your story in terms that everyone can understand, and watch for the human emotions involved.
8. Always look for a fresh angle that will give your story more power than your competitor's.

Chapter **11**

Covering Police and Court News

Police News Is Essential

Stories that originate in the law enforcement functions of government—the investigation, arrest, and trial of citizens for offenses against the common good—bulk large in the daily news report. Covering police activities and the courts is a basic part of reporting the news; also, it is a type of reporting to which many newcomers are assigned early in their careers. Editors know that the experience gained in covering this kind of news will be helpful to a reporter all his working life, not only for the training it gives in accuracy and enterprise, but in the understanding of human emotions that it brings him. On the police beat and in the courts a news reporter sees life in all its most unpleasant stages. There is very little of what the glamorous magazines call gracious living around a police station. Most of the people who pass through its doors are in trouble, either as the perpetrators or victims of misdeeds. Grief is more frequent than humor, and sad endings far outnumber happy ones.

The purpose of this chapter is to explain for the beginning reporter the basic functions of the law agencies he will be covering, to describe the operating methods of police beats in metropolitan and small cities, and to set forth some of the problems and principles involved in covering the administration of justice through our courts.

It might be said that the law catches a criminal quickly but convicts him slowly. Although there are many exceptions to both halves of that statement, broadly speaking it is true. A man who robs a store may be arrested within a few minutes after he leaves the premises, but his sentence will not be pronounced for weeks or months. If he chooses to appeal it to a higher court, the matter may drag on for years. During all this time, from the moment he commits the crime until his case is finally settled and his allotted term in prison begins, his actions may make news.

Functions of Law Agencies

The task of protecting the people against law violators and making the country safe for law-abiding citizens is primarily in the hands of municipal police departments. Every incorporated community has one as part of its city government. The department is headed by a chief, appointed by the city council either on a political basis or as the result of competitive examination. The chief is an administrative officer, not a policymaker; his job is to enforce the laws of his city, county, and state—not to make arbitrary policy rulings of his own. When a police chief tries to exceed his authority, an occurrence that has been all too frequent, the press has an important role to rally public opinion against his abuse of power.

The police department is organized along semimilitary lines with captains, lieutenants, sergeants, and patrolmen. In small cities the force may consist of only a chief and three or four other men, ranging up to a force of thousands in metropolitan centers. Most appointments and promotions are on the basis of competitive examinations and service records. The functions of the departments are the same, no matter how large or small.

In larger cities the police force is divided into uniformed and detective divisions, the former being much the larger. Its tasks include patrolling by foot and by automobile, traffic control, answering complaints and alarms, and similar routine duties. The detective division, whose men work in civilian clothes, is concerned with the investigation of complaints and crimes. Sometimes there is a special section for juvenile work. Detective divisions frequently are subdivided into sections for handling homo-

cide, narcotics, burglary, robbery, auto theft, and other specialized types of crime. The men assigned to these details become
highly proficient in understanding the operating methods of
criminals and have a large knowledge of habitual offenders.

In larger cities there are neighborhood substations, usually
called precincts or divisions, which answer to central police
headquarters. Both uniformed men and detectives operate from
these substations, usually under different commanders.

A reporter covering a police department must develop acquaintances and friendships in as many of these divisions and
bureaus as possible. They are the sources from which many of
his best stories come. He needs to know the exact allocation of
authority so that he can turn to the right man in a hurry for the
information he needs.

Police work in unincorporated territory is in the hands of the
county sheriff. His duties and responsibilities are roughly comparable to those of the city police chief, although he usually is
an elective official and is thus much more active politically. Except in a few metropolitan counties the sheriff's routine police
duties are less arduous than those of a police chief. The sheriff's
territory is larger but the concentration of crime is less. He does,
however, usually have certain additional duties such as running
the county jail and policing the courts. Cooperation between
sheriff and the police chiefs in his county is important to proper
law enforcement. Some states have variations of this policing
arrangement, or call the officials by different names, but the basic
separation of authority between incorporated and unincorporated regions of a county is generally practiced.

State police forces are usually concerned primarily with traffic
control in rural areas, although they have additional duties of
investigation and enforcement in some states. City and county
fire departments are organized on lines similar to police and
sheriff's offices. The reporter covering police normally has the
fire department on his beat; most fire department calls, however,
are so minor as to be of negligible news value. When a major
fire does occur it is an exciting event in a community because
the action is so readily visible. Fire and police departments work
closely together; police patrolling is necessary in fire areas to

keep the crowds out of the firefighters' way and to direct the heavy traffic that always is attracted.

A major national police organization is the Federal Bureau of Investigation. To regard it as a nationwide police force similar in duties and authority to local police departments is erroneous. Actually it is no more than its name states: a bureau of investigation with authority in cases involving violations of federal laws. Safeguarding our national security is also an FBI function. Since most of the statutes governing crimes are state or local in nature, there are many fields of criminal activity which the FBI does not enter. It has no authority to patrol, regulate traffic, and carry out similar routine police functions. The organization of our country by states and the inherent distrust of a powerful national police force, influenced by the experience of dictator-dominated European countries, makes the creation of such a force in this country not only undesirable but virtually impossible. The FBI does serve as a national clearinghouse of police information. Its master file of fingerprints is the source to which all police departments turn, and its annual reports prepared with the cooperation of local officials are a major source of crime statistics. The FBI has offices in numerous cities, and police reporters in those cities include the federal agency on their beat. Few stories emanate from the FBI, however, because of the nature of its work. When they do occur, they are usually in the form of an announcement after conclusion of a case. On bank robberies it is a major news source. The Treasury Department also has a police organization for protection against counterfeiting.

Prosecuting the Offenders

The authority of the police in a criminal case virtually ends with the arrest of a suspect, except to hold him for trial and offer evidence in court. The formal filing of charges against him in the courts is carried out by the prosecuting attorney, an elected county official, also known as the district attorney or state's attorney. The city attorney sometimes has jurisdiction over violations of the municipal code, and the federal district attorney handles cases involving federal offenses. The state attorney general, or whatever term is applied to the chief law officer of the various state governments, rarely has a hand in criminal proceedings.

The prosecuting attorney is one of the most powerful officials in any county. A vigorous man in the office can force many illegal situations into the light and bring powerfully entrenched criminals to justice. A weak official can let these things slide, and a crooked prosecutor, a breed of man too well known in American history, can subvert the most brilliant police work by failing to prosecute the case properly. Thus it follows that the prosecutor's office is one of the most important and active news sources. In his office the decisions are made as to whether sufficient evidence exists for prosecution to be carried out, whether the charge should be reduced from a felony to a misdemeanor (a favorite device to get prominent people out of trouble with a minimum sentence), and how the prosecution should be conducted. Here "deals" are sometimes made with defense attorneys to obtain pleas of guilty in return for small penalties or for an accused man to turn state's evidence against another defendant. The prosecuting attorney usually controls an investigative staff.

Closely connected with the prosecutor's office is the county grand jury, a group of citizens impaneled under court supervision to investigate accusations against individuals and determine whether sufficient evidence exists for the accused to be brought to trial. If the jury believes this to be so, it returns an indictment against the accused, specifying the charges on which he is to be tried. Evidence is presented to the grand jury by the prosecutor, and if an indictment is returned it is his duty to conduct the prosecution. In most cases grand jury sessions are closed to the press, although transcripts are sometimes made public after an indictment has been returned. Once a transcript has been filed it becomes a court record and is privileged for publication. Some states give county grand juries authority to investigate and report with recommendations for action upon situations in which no criminal offenses are involved. Some criminal cases in state courts are brought to trial through a complaint issued by the prosecuting attorney's office, rather than by grand jury indictment. There are also federal grand juries.

Another noncourt jury with which the police reporter is concerned is the coroner's jury. This is a panel of citizens called to witness a coroner's inquest into the cause of a suspicious death and to return an opinion as to the cause. Frequently its verdict is nothing more specific than "at the hands of person or persons unknown." Inquests rarely have much importance in the prosecution of a murder case, since only minimum evidence is presented, but frequently they provide emotionally charged news stories because they are held shortly after the crime occurs with members of the victim's family present, as well as the accused.

Organization of the Courts

There are two basic types of court proceedings, criminal and civil. The government is the accuser in criminal actions and the defendant is charged with commission of a specific offense against the law. In civil cases one individual or organization sues another to determine damages, ownership rights, and similar points of property that they have been unable to settle between themselves. Divorce cases and injunction petitions are civil actions, too. The government prosecutor is involved only in criminal cases. Although both civil and criminal cases sometimes arise out of the same set of events, they are tried separately.

Both kinds of court action provide important and exciting news stories. Generally criminal trials have more emotional interest because the physical fate of an individual is at stake. Civil trials tend to last longer and become more technical, but they too have moments of drama. Some trials, both civil and criminal, are conducted before a judge alone, and in some a jury participates, depending in part upon the desires of the defendant and in part upon the point of law involved.

Background for Police Reporting

One of the first things a police reporter must learn is the basic terminology. An elaborate jargon is used around police stations, a kind of trade talk in which slang words, abbreviations, and code numbers describe offenses and practices. The beginner

will learn soon enough that when a policeman refers to the
"M.O." he means a criminal's method of operating, and that
"bunco" means fraud. Don't worry; you'll feel a bit lost and naïve
when you first enter the police world, but you will soon be trad-
ing the jargon with the old-timers. If you don't know what an
expression means, ask someone. Every force has a set of terms
and code numbers all its own that can be learned only by listening to others talk.

What is more important, and can be learned from a book, is
the basic list of offenses with which police forces deal. These are
the violations that you will be writing about, and it is essential
that you have them correct in your stories. The FBI annual crime
report lists eight categories considered of major importance in
police work. In order of the number of offenses reported nationally, these are: larceny-theft, burglary—breaking and entering,
auto theft, aggravated assault, robbery, rape, murder and non-
negligent manslaughter, and manslaughter by negligence.

Many types of law violations, other than these, are handled
every day by police departments, everything from parking violations to sale of narcotics. Much of the business that goes onto
the police blotter is so petty and routine that it is devoid of news
value. Especially in the larger cities, where the volume of daily
police complaints is very heavy, reporters "pass" many more reports than they even offer to the city desk. But everything should
be given a quick check; occasionally an insignificant report will
contain the germ of a human interest story—a new version of
the "meanest thief" or a person who has had an unusual item of
some sort stolen. The reporter should scan the police report with
an eye to the unusual. Becoming cynical and careless of human
values is an occupational hazard of the police beat; often it is a
pose by younger reporters, but one rarely indulged in by the
old-timers around headquarters.

At the end of this chapter there is a list of important police
and court terms that every reporter should know.

The FBI crime report for 1956 comments, "Crimes against
the person, as a group, reach a high during the warmer months,
while crimes with property as their object occur more frequently
in the cooler period of the year. More killings due to negligence

occur at the end of the year than at other times. These negligent manslaughters, mostly traffic deaths, differ from other crimes against the person in that their curve seems to follow closely the rise in traffic hazards due, in part, to increasing darkness at the onset of winter."

These federal statistics show that eight times as many men as women are arrested every year.

How a Metropolitan Police Beat Operates

The press room in central police headquarters of a major city is covered by the newspapers 24 hours a day. Even during their off-publication hours the metropolitan papers need immediate coverage on big news developments so that they may be ready with stories and pictures for their first editions, with exclusive angles if possible.

Each paper covers its main hours of operation with its most experienced police reporter; cubs are broken in mostly on the night and early morning beats when deadlines are less frequent. In one typical metropolitan police room, the junior man of the four daytime regulars has 20 years' experience. Here is the daily routine as practiced by one of these veterans:

Arrive at headquarters about 5:30 a.m., approximately an hour and a half before his afternoon paper's first edition deadline. He isn't due on the job until 6:00 but wants to check the nightwatch men before they go off duty. He reads the log of stories handled during the night. Reporters in this headquarters are responsible for coverage of 14 division stations. Each must be checked by telephone at least every two hours, both the uniformed and detective watch commanders. The reporters divide this task. Also they must make frequent checks of the coroner's office, receiving hospital, and the headquarters complaint board, to which the public's incoming calls are channeled. Usually the operators on the complaint board call the press room on an important lead, however. Also the incoming teletyped reports from division station houses are open for inspection.

The press room is manned constantly; at least one of the reporters always listens to the loud speakers that pipe the two-way conversations on the police radios into the room. Periodically, one of the reporters makes the rounds of the chief's office, the detective bureau, burglary, narcotics, and other specialized offices. He asks a routine question, "What's doing?" or "anything I ought to know?" and then raises any specific item on which he needs an answer. This might involve a development in a murder investigation or an inquiry from his city desk. It is usually agreed among press room reporters that they share all information gathered on these trips, except for answers to inquiries originating from their offices. The man who makes the rounds knows that one of the others will call his office if a hot story breaks while he is out of the room. This is called "syndicating" a beat. City editors dislike the practice because it tends to eliminate exclusive news breaks, but they accept it because it protects them against being beaten. One danger of syndication is that the reporters will band together and fail to report a news development for some reason of their own, perhaps as a punishment to a police official with whom they are feuding. However, most responsible reporters do not indulge in such petty conspiracies. The city editor sometimes tries to get around the syndicate by sending out a reporter direct from the office on a tip.

The announcer on the police radio reports a bank robbery at a certain address, dispatching cruise cars to the scene. One reporter reaches for that indispensible tool, the reverse telephone directory. This is a book issued by the telephone companies of larger cities, and made available for purchase at a rather high price, in which telephones are listed by address first and then the individual's name. If the bank's address is 2850 Jackson Street, the reporter quickly jots down the telephone number at that address, and those at the addresses next door and across the street. The reporters in the room divide the numbers and call them as quickly as possible, asking for information about the robbery. With luck they may reach an eyewitness of the holdup or the getaway. Each of the numbers checked may yield, or can confirm, a few facts. Once the basic information is confirmed, each reporter telephones his city desk with the news. The city editor rushes a team of a reporter and a photographer from the office to the scene, or perhaps dispatches a radio cruise car if one is moderately near. If the paper happens to be on deadline, a rewrite man writes the sketchy information into a bulletin-type story that will stand until further information arrives.

Incidentally, experienced police reporters know that about 90 per cent of bank robbery calls are false alarms because somebody in the bank has accidentally stepped on the alarm button. A bank robbery alarm turned in before 9:30 a.m. in a city with a 10 a.m. bank opening is almost always meaningless; it is standard bank practice to set the time locks on vaults for 20 minutes before the start of business. Police check every early call, nevertheless, on the possibility that somebody has been locked in the vault.

After the first bulletins have been phoned in, the beat reporter telephones to the scene and obtains as much detail as possible. He keeps a close check with the robbery division in headquarters for an official estimate on the amount of money stolen, reports on police efforts to pursue the robbers, and, later, word on suspects arrested. The reporter on the scene also phones in to the city room the information he obtains from the victims and eyewitnesses. A rewrite man puts together the facts flowing in from headquarters and field reporters, and the result of their joint efforts is the story that goes into the paper.

One of the best sources of news tips to headquarters reporters is the police ambulance dispatcher. A cooperative dispatcher (and the reporters try to cultivate his friendship) phones the press room whenever he dispatches ambulances on an important call. It was such a call that started the reporting machinery rolling in the following actual story of a big city streetcar accident, which we shall follow from the moment the first tip came to headquarters until the detailed story appeared in a street edition two hours later.

Shortly after 8 a.m. a telephone rang in the police press room. It was the police ambulance dispatcher, reporting that he had just sent three ambulances to the scene of a streetcar accident at a specified intersection. Moments later the operator in the central headquarters microphone room, from which police calls are transmitted, phoned with the same information. The reporters immediately checked the reverse directory for telephone numbers at that corner and put in calls to several of them. One call reached a woman clerk at the bakery into which the streetcar had plunged after jumping the tracks. (Even in the midst of a catastrophe people usually answer the insistent summons of the telephone bell.) Under questioning she gave the reporter an eyewitness story of what had happened, including numerous colorful details. The reporter shared his information with others in the room, and each then phoned his city desk. The city editor quickly dispatched a general assignment reporter and photographer to the scene. Meanwhile one of the police reporters reached the transit lines public relations official, who obtained the motorman's name and number from the transit emergency squad and also the company's report on the cause of the accident.

The office reporter arrived at the scene within a few minutes and set about getting eyewitness descriptions from the group crowded around the wreckage. He sought the extra touches of detail that would help readers visualize the scene. As he worked, the ambulances were carrying away the injured to a nearby hospital. When he had a substantial amount of information assembled, he telephoned the city desk and outlined to an assistant city editor what he had. He was transferred to the rewrite man assigned to the story, who took notes on the typewriter (for speed and clarity). Only a few minutes remained before the next deadline, but the rewrite man already had the story fairly well organized in his mind from his talks with the police beat man. Working from the notes provided by both reporters, he wrote this story:

30 Hurt as Loaded Streetcar Smashes into Grocery

A loaded streetcar jumped the tracks at Vernon Ave. and Hoover St. at 8:04 a.m. today, leaped a curb after hitting an automobile, and demolished the front of a corner grocery and bakery.

About 30 persons were hurt, none of them critically. Eighteen were taken to the Receiving Hospital.

R. D. Mann, special agent for the Transit Lines, said a similar accident occurred a year ago at the same intersection, but that nobody was hurt then. He said a switch at the corner "flipped," causing the trolley to make a sudden turn. There was no explanation of the defective switch.

The front of the Quality Bakery, 800 W. Vernon, was crushed by the streetcar.

Grace Johnson, 61, wife of the proprietor of the bakery, was trapped for 15 minutes between a counter and the wall. She received back injuries.

Motorman J. R. Harrison, 38, who was not hurt, said there were about 60 persons on the trolley.

He said about half the passengers were children on their way to school.

"It was all a jumble of arms and legs," Marian Jones, 16, of 138 W. 61st St. reported.

The Jones girl was standing behind the motorman.

"I heard him shout," she said.

"Then I heard a grinding noise. That must have been when the wheels were going over the pavement. Then I was thrown, and everybody came tumbling down on top of me."

A fire hydrant was knocked over by the streetcar and water shot 50 feet into the air. Rolls and pastry from the bakery window were strewn over the sidewalk and street, some floating down the gutter.

An unidentified woman standing near the rear door when the trolley jumped the curb, was thrown into the gutter.

"She was unconscious, and would have drowned in all the water running down the gutter if I had not pulled her up onto the sidewalk," said Joe Brandle, 45, of 4435 S. Avalon Blvd.

John Sims, 144 E. Ann St., said he saw a schoolgirl fall out of the door and into the gutter.

"I helped pull her out of the water," Sims said. "Her head seemed to be cut. Then I went back and got a woman out of the water."

Five persons in an auto hit by the streetcar when it made its sudden, left turn at the intersection received minor injuries.

George Johnson, 63, the baker, estimated damage to his shop and its wares at $20,000.

When a crane arrived and pulled the streetcar out of the store front the one-story stucco building creaked ominously and seemed in danger of collapse. Police ordered that no one enter it.

Harrison said he was westbound on Vernon at 15 miles an hour when he approached the switch-point. He suggested that automobiles passing over the switches had jarred them loose. The switches aren't used any more because busses have been substituted for trolleys on Hoover.

The descriptive touches and quotations add substantially to the reader's interest and help him to visualize what happened. There are eyewitness accounts from two angles—the accident as experienced inside the streetcar and from the outside. The teen-age girl's description of the sounds and the way other passengers fell on top of her make the action vivid. The extra touch of the bakery goods floating down the gutter adds a colorful, authentic detail, the sort of naturalistic glimpse that film directors seek.

One major gap in this well-rounded story was the exact number of persons injured and their names. While the rewrite man was pounding out the story, the police beat and office reporters both went in pursuit of these facts. The beat reporter called the hospital and obtained from a clerk the names and addresses of the injured, taken from their admittance cards. Just after these had been given by telephone, the office reporter arrived at the hospital in search of the same information.

From a reporting standpoint, the task was made easier by the fact that all the injured had been taken to the same hospital. Frequently in major disasters the casualties are treated at several hospitals, considerably complicating the problem of compiling an accurate list for publication. This is especially true when victims are given preliminary treatment at one place, then transferred to a less crowded or more convenient hospital for further care. Casualty lists should always be double-checked for duplication.

By the deadline for the second edition after the wreck, the original story had been fixed to clarify the casualties.

The second paragraph was changed to read: "Thirty-five persons were hurt, none of them critically. All were treated at the Receiving Hospital." At the end of the story was added the list of those admitted for treatment, with name, age, and address of each. Pictures taken at the scene were printed with the story in this edition.

This is an excellent example of a straightforward, fast-breaking news story originating on the police beat. The detailed story was on the street only two hours after the accident occurred, yet the reporting was so fast and accurate that the only change necessary in the later edition was addition of the casualty list. Two minor changes would have improved it, however. One involves reporting—the name of the unidentified woman who was saved from drowning. The other was a matter of writing organization—inclusion of a reference near the top of the story to the water geyser and the fact that one passenger almost drowned. Had this story been for a morning paper, the general assignment reporter who went out would have come back to the office and written it himself, with the help of notes from the police beat. On a smaller paper, the police reporter himself would probably have gone to the scene and covered the story.

Not all stories from the police beat need such urgent handling. Many are obtained from the written reports turned in by policemen sent out to answer an emergency call or to investigate a citizen's complaint. Traffic accidents are usually covered in this manner; in larger cities, at least, there are too many such mishaps for each to be covered in detail. While the police report may contain all the facts necessary for a routine story, frequently an extra telephone call or two will uncover additional sidelights that lift the story onto a higher plane of human interest. Here are two versions of the same story, printed in different newspapers. The first was taken directly from the police report, with the facts arranged in orthodox newspaper form:

Butane Blast Injures Man, Shatters Trailer Home

Exploding butane gas early yesterday shattered a Palms trailer, seriously injuring a 39-year-old roofer.

William Earl Cooper, the trailer occupant, was treated at Santa Monica Hospital for third-degree burns on the legs, arms and body. Doctors said his condition was fair.

Cooper told investigating officers that he went to bed about 10:20 p.m. Tuesday in his 16-foot trailer at 9942 Na-tional Blvd. He said he turned on a butane heater.

At 4:20 a.m., the heater exploded, demolishing the trailer and hurling pieces of metal which damaged six other trailers nearby.

Cooper said his dog also was in the trailer with him. Police said they were unable to find the animal, but the Chihuahua, burned and still frightened, later turned up at the home of Cooper's employer.

The reporter for another paper made an additional phone call to the address of the trailer park. From the manager he obtained details which gave the story an additional dimension:

Kitchen Blast Caps
Trail of Tragedy

Trouble has been going steady with William Earl Cooper. An explosion, which destroyed his trailer home early today and almost killed him, is only the latest in a series of stunning tragedies.

Here is the log on Cooper's recent buffeting by fate, detailed by Theodore N. Gagnath, manager of the trailer court:

Seven weeks ago a Santa Monica pedestrian was killed by Cooper's car. He was exonerated.

Five weeks ago, his brother-in-law shot and killed his sister in Phoenix, Ariz.

Ten days ago, his mother died.

A week ago, three cars Cooper uses in his roofing business were repossessed.

Early today, Cooper awoke and lit a cigarette. Butane gas, apparently leaking from his trailer kitchen stove, exploded with a roar that waked neighbors for two blocks around the trailer court at 9942 National Blvd., Palms. Cooper's trailer home was reduced to kindling.

As a final ironic note, Cooper was planning to trade the trailer on a larger model today, preparing for his forthcoming marriage.

Cooper is in Santa Monica Hospital with critical burns.

While the second version has far more human interest than the first, it omits an important fact, the victim's age; also, it lacks the detail about the dog. When putting a special twist on a story, the reporter should remember to include the basic facts as well.

Handling Casualty Reports

Almost the first question to enter the reader's mind when he sees a story about an accident, explosion, tornado, or other catastrophe is, "Was anybody killed or hurt?" A correct casualty figure is essential in every story of this sort, and frequently it is difficult to obtain. Meticulous checking of hospitals, doctors' offices, and mortuaries is the only sure method, and even that does not always produce a conclusive figure. Sometimes relatives or friends report a person as missing who is believed to have been near the scene of the accident; the supposed victim may turn up hours later quite safe, having been elsewhere all the time. A good rule of thumb to remember is that almost always the final toll of dead and injured is smaller than first reports indicate. Eyewitnesses are so overpowered by the emotional impact of what they have seen that their reports of "dozens dead" or "bodies scattered all over the place" must be sharply discounted. Since preliminary police reports are usually based on what witnesses tell the officers, these too must be treated very cautiously. Most city editors have unpleasant memories of incidents when too many victims have been "killed" in banner headlines and revived in subsequent editions. So in early stories of a disaster, unless the casualties are confirmed by actual count made by staff members or authorized sources, they insist on a qualifying phrase such as "an estimated 25 persons were hurt," "at least 10 persons were killed," or "a deputy sheriff reported counting five bodies." Another reason for caution in handling casualty figures is the false claims for damages that often result from people who assert that they have been injured. Beyond many an accident lies a damage suit and the reporter must be careful that his story does not imply guilt to any participant. State that two cars collided, not that one ran a red light and smashed into the other, unless the official police report says it that way. Legal responsibility for an accident should be determined in court, not in a newspaper story. It is general police practice for reporters to see the basic sheet of an accident report but not the follow-up sheets of investigations until the case has been closed. (This is to discourage feeding of information to attorneys handling damage claims.)

Where to Check Stories

The police reporter cannot develop stories only by asking questions of officers and witnesses. He must consult records and unofficial sources when seeking to establish the identification and background of people in the news. Significant and frequently surprising facts can be unearthed by probing through records. Here are some of the main sources to which the police reporter turns: the state motor vehicle department for information about ownership of automobiles and holders of driver's licenses, the state police records in criminal investigations, the registrar of voters, the telephone book (amazing how people overlook this most fundamental of all sources!), public utility offices for information about dates when their customers started and stopped service, the city health department for vital statistics, the marriage license bureau, the coroner's office for family deaths, city directories in those cities where they are issued, past employers, the penitentiaries, Dun and Bradstreet for credit information, the Retail Credit Bureau and similar organizations whose business is checking an individual's background, and the Better Business Bureau.

A diligent reporter, starting with only minimum information, can frequently develop an extensive knowledge of an individual's life and career by checking the sources listed above, even though the person involved may have no criminal record.

The police and sheriff's offices keep detailed records on persons who have been in their custody. These are a rich mine of information for the reporter, although his access to them is often restricted. In most metropolitan police departments, at least, he can't go wandering at will through the elaborate and highly organized records sections, although he can obtain information when he requests the records of specific persons. The file contains a "make" sheet on each person arrested by the department —when he was taken into custody, what charges were filed, and the disposition of his case.

Some official records are never open to the newspaper reporter on the theory that in certain fields the individual citizen's dealings with his government are entitled to full privacy and should not be made known to the public. The most important sources that cannot be inspected by reporters include files of the Internal Revenue Bureau, Social Security, Post Office Department, Draft Boards, and the FBI.

Devices Reporters Use

Newspaper editors are divided in their opinions about the use of subterfuges, falsehoods, and misrepresentations by reporters to obtain news. Some state that they will never knowingly publish a story obtained by misrepresentation, in the belief that the newspaper's reputation for honesty and fair dealing is more important than any news story, no matter how big. Others hold to the contrary, contending that the importance to the public of a major news story outweighs doubts about the way in which it was obtained. A poll of American editors would probably show the majority sharing this latter view. Some who publicly endorse the more conservative view of reporter's ethics might act otherwise when put to the test of having a staff member turn in a spectacular story obtained by dubious methods. The temptation to print the story overcomes the ethical theory. Many police reporters operate on the principle of "get that story, regardless." Others find that they just don't have it within themselves to lie. It is worth remembering that for every story obtained by falsehood, a hundred good ones get into print through straightforward checking and cultivation of news sources.

Generally speaking, unless a reporter's actions in getting his story involve a serious legal offense that will embarrass the paper or result in prosecution of him, or the newspaper, his paper will publish the story if it concerns news the public should know.

Every veteran newspaperman has a fund of stories about his own prowess and cunning in obtaining news, whether it be hiding in a closet to listen in on a private meeting, or pretending on the telephone to be a real estate agent to obtain information about a man who refuses to see reporters. A person who refuses to answer a reporter's questions will often give out the desired information if the questioner says he is taking a survey. Some reporters carry meaningless gilt badges marked special officer, or similar pseudo-official lettering; these sometimes will impress the gullible or frightened sufficiently for the newsman to gain admittance to a banned area. On occasion this type of police reporter will pretend to be anything from a window washer to an undertaker. His assumption is that if he gets into the scene of the news, he will obtain his story or suffer no greater indignity than being put out if discovered. Another device that has been used is putting a hearing aid against the panel of a closed door and turning up the volume to hear the discussion inside the room.

In defense of this kind of newsgathering, editors point out that these subterfuges are frequently used to pry news from public figures who are using devices of their own to conceal legitimate news from the public. They argue also that certain public figures, such as film stars, are virtually created as celebrities by the publicity given to them by newspapers. If they fail to cooperate with reporters when involved in a truly newsworthy situation, they are fair game for the wiles of an enterprising reporter.

Use of Juvenile Names

Another controversy in police reporting involves publication of the names of juveniles—youths under 18—who are involved in crimes. One group contends that such publication works an injustice on the youngster who may have been caught in a teen-age prank or led astray by older acquaintances. His reputation is tarnished and his future handicapped by the revelation of his crime. Another group opposes publication of names because it believes that it only gives the youth the notoriety he is seeking and will lure him into further illegal exploits so he can show off his press clippings to his gang. On the other side are experienced police officials and educators who contend that withholding of juvenile names only coddles the offenders and helps them to evade a sense of responsibility.

In many cities youthful offenders are handled by a juvenile division of the police department and a juvenile court, not open to newspaper coverage. In others there are no legal restrictions but the newspapers enforce their own standards. Broadly speaking, the practice is for newspapers to withhold the names of juvenile law violators unless the crime involved is a capital offense or of an otherwise unusual or serious nature. The reporter should turn in the names and addresses of juvenile offenders when available, just like any other names on a police report, and let his editors make the decision on publishing them.

Many newspapers also avoid using the names of women who have been the victims of sexual assaults, unless the victims indicate their willingness to be identified. In addition to the recognition of concern for human sensibilities, there remains the possibility of a libel suit by the victim.

Racial Identification

Racial identification of persons involved in stories has also been a subject of discussion. A growing sensitivity on matters of race in most parts of the country has been cause for removal of such labels from most stories. The majority of newspapers now identify a man involved in police action as Negro, Mexican, or Chinese only when he is wanted and this physical characteristic helps the public identify him. Racial identity sometimes is used in favorable stories when it is pertinent to a full understanding of the person's achievement. Newspapers in the South follow somewhat different practices.

Tips from Veteran Police Reporters

While preparing this chapter the authors gathered the advice and suggestions of long-experienced police reporters in several cities. Some of their comments are printed here.

"The first thing I tell a cub is that you get your stories from your friends, not your enemies," one explained. "If you violate a confidence to get a beat today you almost certainly will miss out on a bigger story later because the news source is mad at you. No story is worth breaking a confidence. The perfect story hasn't come along yet. There is always a bigger one in the future to think about."

Several of the veterans emphasized the quality of kindness, an attitude they have developed over many years of handling the most distasteful and violent stories in which they have seen human emotions laid bare thousands of times. One put it, "I don't think anyone should grow calloused. If you have to write about people in trouble, tell the facts, but be merciful. Don't make more trouble for people who are already weighed down with problems."

Another recommendation was, "Challenge everything! Assume nothing."

Sometimes a reporter encounters uncooperative police officers and detectives. If he believes he is being deprived of information to which he is entitled, he should by-pass the obstructionist and go to the top. The police chief is politically conscious and frequently will intervene if lower echelon men try to withhold facts; he doesn't want to face a press reprisal if he can avoid it.

Another suggestion: Never let a police source believe that you are the only one to know an important fact. If the police official thinks this is so, he may try to bind the reporter to secrecy. But if the reporter has already passed the fact on to other people, he can say that he cannot suppress it because the fact is already in general circulation and somebody else is sure to print it.

Always have plenty of change in your pocket, because you never know when you will need to use a pay telephone in a hurry. Some reporters carry a roll of dimes at all times.

When out on a fast-running story like a murder or fire, a wise reporter always looks around for an available telephone, especially if deadline time is approaching. On big stories in remote areas there are often many more reporters than telephones. This stimulates considerable ingenuity among the newsmen in tying up a phone for use when needed. One favorite method is paying a householder a fee for exclusive use of his telephone. When waiting for a major story to break in the field, a reporter will sometimes put through a call to his office on one of the available telephones and then chat on about anything he can think of, or even read the telephone book, to keep possession of the line until the crucial news breaks. An occasional reporter still resorts to the old ruse of hanging an "out of order" sign on a telephone he wants to keep for himself. The wire service maxim that no story is better than its transmission applies just as truly to local stories about tragedies and crimes.

Another tip from the veterans: Using the names of policemen in stories whenever this can be done legitimately builds friendships for the reporter on the police force and may be repaid with an important news lead later on. Policemen have their share of vanity.

Covering the Prosecuting Attorney's Office

Once a man has been arrested, the task of conducting the state's case against him falls to the prosecuting attorney's office. On metropolitan papers this office is usually included on the courts beat rather than police because its work is tied so closely to the courts. On smaller papers all three arms of the law may be included in a single beat.

The prosecutor's office provides news about the formal filing of criminal proceedings, plans for the conduct of trials, disposition of cases that are not considered strong enough to be brought to trial, and, at times, the pronouncement of certain legal opinions. Over and above these daily details, the prosecutor's office is the source of many investigations, cleanup drives, and much gossip about political and criminal activity in the area. It is an important listening post for a reporter. When a hard-driving man is in power, the office is one of the best news sources in a city. A metropolitan prosecutor's office may have a staff of 50 or more attorneys.

One of the chronic claims about politically minded prosecuting attorneys is that they refuse to push charges with sufficient vigor when the defendant is a prominent public figure or has political or economic influence. One of the authors asked a long-time and highly reputable district attorney of a metropolitan county about these charges.

"Even if the district attorney would like to hush up the case, it is very hard for him to avoid prosecuting it if the press is pushing him," he replied.

Thus he underlines one of the most important functions of the reporter covering the prosecutor's office: to watch for anything that looks like a cover-up. He should specify in his stories what the possible charges and penalties against the defendant might be, so that the public will be aware of the possibilities.

The district attorney also said, "The newspapermen often know as much about a case as the police do. I assure you that a district attorney as an elected public official is very much aware of a newspaper's power and accepts the need to cooperate with it. He always has to think of the next election."

Covering the Courts

A reporter cannot hope to cover a court beat adequately without the cooperation of the court clerks and other officials. Personal acquaintance with the judges is also helpful. Because legal proceedings are frequently prolonged, and in larger cities there are several actions in progress simultaneously, it is impossible for a reporter to "sit in on" all trials. His problem is to organize his time and sources so that he keeps posted on all important decisions and attends the most newsworthy trials in person.

In large county and municipal court systems there is a calendar court. Here the judge in charge assigns the various pending cases to specific judges. Close watch on the daily calendar is essential because it contains the leads to the day's potentially newsworthy trials. Some judges will hear several small actions or criminal cases a day. Others may preside over a single case that drags on for days or even weeks. Federal courts frequently have involved civil cases, antitrust actions, and the like that run for months.

The testimony and legal arguments in many cases are so technical, or the crimes involved so routine, that there is little of interest to readers. But frequently there are highlights even in the dullest trial, such as the testimony and cross-examination of a principal witness. A friendly court clerk will usually tip reporters when such moments are imminent.

With the rarest exceptions, civil and criminal trials are open to the public and press. Reporters sit at a table inside the rail that separates audience and participants, and here they are free to take all the notes they wish. However there are no telephones or teleprinters inside a courtroom for reporters. The reporter must leave the room to send his story into the office. On big stories such as sensational murder trials, a paper may have at least two reporters on the job so that one can relieve the other while he phones in his material.

On most secondary court stories, however, the verdict, any comments by the judge, and the essence of the testimony is all that is required. If the reporter isn't present, he can usually obtain a briefing from the judge himself or from the clerk or court reporter. If an unusual angle develops in an otherwise routine case, an obliging clerk frequently telephones the facts to the pressroom. Attorneys for the contesting parties are a good source for information and documents in their cases. Reporters usually include the names of cooperative attorneys in their stories. But be careful that the attorney doesn't try his case through your columns.

During all except minor actions, a court shorthand reporter takes down a verbatim report of what is said. However, because of the time and expense involved these notes are not always transcribed, and so a newspaper reporter cannot depend upon them as a news source. Even when transcripts are made, they are not available for several hours and thus are frequently too late for use by the reporter. When his paper wants to publish verbatim question-and-answer testimony, he must take it down himself. This is less difficult than it seems, because witnesses usually speak deliberately, selecting their words with care. Even so, it requires meticulous attention. In an unusually important trial a newspaper might send over a stenographer to assist the reporter.

Many touching, often comic human interest stories are to be found in the daily grist of minor cases by a reporter who has the time, the "feel," and an ear for dialogue. The actual outcome of the trial may be of no importance as news, but the actions and testimony of the principals, properly presented with a sympathetic understanding, make splendid vignettes of human behavior. Unfortunately most American court reporters have so much to cover that they cannot or do not give sufficient attention to this kind of story. The courts column of some London newspapers is one of their best-read features. The success of these stories depends upon the writing. Magazine editors search for stories that catch the real meat of life—its conflicts, disappointments, and odd twists. Newspapers need the same kind of stories. But in far too many American cities this raw material of the human drama in the courts is almost untouched. The beat reporter and photographer are too busy getting routine stories and pictures about the divorce suits of attractive young women whose husbands have been mentally cruel to them.

Good human interest stories can also be found in the probation reports which are sometimes made to a judge before he pronounces sentence upon an individual. Although made for the judge's guidance in fixing the penalty, these reports are part of the court record and thus privileged for publication.

Another important news source on this beat is the civil filings. To institute civil proceedings for damages, divorce, child custody, and other noncriminal issues to be settled in court, the plaintiff files his complaint in the office of the court clerk. This outlines his charges against the defendant and frequently gives some supporting detail. If damages are claimed, the complaint specifies the amount. A divorce action states the grounds for the divorce request. In some states the complaint becomes a part of the court record, once it is formally on file, and thus becomes a privileged document from which newspapers can quote freely. In other states the filed complaints are not privileged until the judge has called the case to trial. Reporters must know where privilege extends, since the allegations in civil suits are often sensational and angry, and also defamatory in their nature. Divorce complaints frequently contain spicy details of the defendant's alleged misbehavior. Many times a civil suit is settled before coming to trial, and its allegations are not subjected to a court test. Sometimes a defendant answers with a countersuit, thus getting into the record his complaints against the other party—a good source for a follow-up story.

Some persons file civil suits in a desire for publicity. Their lawyers tip off the city desks that a filing is about to occur, and publicity men are on hand to see that reporters get all the details and a picture of the plaintiff. Other complainants hope to avoid publicity, if possible. A favorite trick of lawyers handling such a case is to file the suit in the last few minutes before the clerk's office closes for the day, in the hope that the reporters will have made their last check of the filings and departed. In metropolitan counties where the county court has several suburban branch offices, potentially sensational suits are filed late in the day at an outlying branch, believed by some attorneys to be the most inconspicuous way possible to get an action started. Thus a reporter should make frequent checks of the clerk's office, including one at closing time.

The reporter who develops friendships among the clerical workers in the court offices, buys them an occasional cup of coffee, or does small favors for them, often is repaid by news tips when stories of unusual interest are breaking.

Watching for Libel

A reporter handling police and court news must keep an especially careful watch for libel. Through carelessness he may easily involve his newspaper and himself in an expensive lawsuit. Let us review some points made in chapter 8.

In criminal actions, a suspect is never legally accused of a misdeed until he has been formally booked by the police. Until then he is merely held for questioning. If the police suspect a man of a major crime but are short of evidence, they book him on a holding charge such as suspicion of burglary. He must be released after a specified number of hours on a suspicion booking, unless sufficient evidence is found for a formal complaint.

What the written police report says about a man is usually considered safe to use, provided the reporter is convinced of its reliability (in some places it is privileged material). Much less safety attaches to the use of any additional comments about the case by the investigating officer. The same is true of civil complaints. The plaintiff may say much more sensational things about the defendant in conversation than he states in his written filing, but these are not part of the formal record and so are in no way privileged.

In covering trials, conversations with the principals and their attorneys during recess periods are helpful in comprehending the course of the courtroom action, but are not privileged. A reporter who writes a story based on controversial matter an attorney says he plans to use in court or in a filing is taking a risk; the attorney or his client may change his mind at the last minute, leaving the reporter with an unreliable and legally dangerous story. Sometimes the risk may be worth taking, but that is a decision to be made by the editors, not the reporter.

Terms a Police Reporter Should Know

Felony—a major crime, usually punishable by imprisonment as well as by a fine.

Misdemeanor—a minor offense, punishable by fine or short term in jail, such as traffic violations or disturbing the peace.

Homicide—killing of one human being by another. Under this general heading are several degrees of murder and manslaughter offenses, punishment graduating from death downward.

Murder, First Degree—deliberate, premeditated killing.

Murder, Second Degree—killing without premeditation or deliberation.

Justifiable Homicide—a killing committed intentionally, but without evil design, as by a police officer on duty or in self-defense.

Manslaughter, First Degree—taking a life unintentionally, with a dangerous weapon or in a cruel or unusual manner.

Manslaughter, Second Degree—taking a life unintentionally, without a dangerous weapon or not in a cruel or unusual manner.

Robbery—stealing or taking anything of value from a person or in his immediate presence by force or violence or by putting him in fear.

Burglary—breaking and entering a premises to commit theft, also unlawful entry even though no force was used to gain entrance.

Larceny—unlawful taking of another person's property. *Grand* larceny involves thefts above a certain specified amount, *Petty* larceny below that amount, usually $50.00.

Rape—having sexual intercourse with a woman or girl forcibly and without her consent.

Statutory Rape—where no force is used, but victim is under the age of consent.

Accessory Before the Fact—one who helps another commit a crime, even though he is not present when the offense occurs.

Accessory After the Fact—one who harbors, protects, or aids another, although he knows that the other party has committed a crime.

Disorderly Conduct—violations of the public peace, safety, or order.

Extradition—the turning over of an alleged criminal by one state or country to another. Some offenses are not subject to extradition procedure.

Chapter 12

Investigative Reporting

The Need to Investigate

If a newspaper is to fulfill its role in a community, it must do more than report the surface, easy news from routine sources. As a force for civic good it must search for the concealed stories—those the public should know about, but which have been unwritten either through neglect or a calculated effort by someone to hide them. If the newspaper doesn't do this job for the public, who will? Development of such stories is called investigative reporting.

Articles disclosing conditions in slum areas, health hazards, insufficient school facilities, and other such civic ills fall within this category. Such "situation" stories can often be developed by an enterprising reporter without encountering any opposition more serious than lethargy, although the stories when published may create a strong reaction. When newsmen dig into unsavory situations involving possible criminal offenses, they face a more serious problem. Every year there are examples of editors and reporters, on large papers and small ones, whose tenacity and courage bring to light unethical conduct by public figures and sometimes outright criminal actions. Occasionally a newsman on such work suffers a physical beating at the hands of criminals whose path he crosses, and in rare instances, death. These episodes are so unusual that they attract much attention, but every day the investigative reporter must show moral courage in the face of social and economic threats of a type seldom encountered by men working on more orthodox stories.

Investigative reporting requires a special set of news talents, of which relentless tenacity is foremost. A reporter assigned to a difficult investigation may go weeks without seeing a line of his copy in print. He may have to fight off a feeling of frustration when his leads fail to develop and he cannot find printable evidence to support his suspicions. Yet if he is convinced that those suspicions are justified, he will keep plugging away, hoping for a break. When that break comes, as it often does, he may be on his way to a Pulitzer Prize.

He must have the instincts of a detective, and develop the ability to think as the suspect thinks. If he were in the position of the man he is trying to catch, how would he go about concealing his actions? Primarily, the investigating reporter must be a well-grounded newsman who knows where to go for information and has a knowledge of what information is printable evidence and what is merely rumor. He must be able to deal with all sorts of people, even the most undesirable, and if necessary take on some of their coloration. His own affairs must be above suspicion, because blackmail is a frequent tool for public figures in trouble. They try to protect themselves by "getting something on" the reporter, editors, or publishers or the paper which is trying to expose them.

Never overlook a news tip, no matter what the source! That is a cardinal rule. A newspaper attracts suggestions for stories by mail, by telephone, and by personal visit. Many of these can be tossed aside after a casual glance because they contradict facts that the newspaper has in its possession. Some are quickly shown to be the imaginings of mentally disturbed persons. Out of the daily chaff the city desk sifts a few grains of information and gossip worthy of further investigation. It does not matter that these have come in anonymously, or from men who have a personal motive of revenge or financial advantage; they may prove to be the basis for an extremely important news story no matter what reason the tipster had. A Chicago newspaper once suffered a severe trouncing from its competitor because a cynical reporter "brushed off" a telephone caller. A much-sought mass murderer called the paper, identified himself, and said he wanted to confess. The reporter, thinking that it was a prank, refused to believe him. So the man called a rival paper, which took the precaution to arrange a meeting and question him. He really was the wanted man, and the paper had a banner-line exclusive. The odds were all on the side of the blundering reporter, because frequently a sensational murder leads to false confessions from publicity-seekers. But his failure to "check it out" was disastrous.

Rarely does the tip itself provide a printable story. It is only the point of departure, and what emerges in print may be quite different from the story originally envisaged. When a reporter is assigned to an investigation his first thought should be, "How can I get factual and, if possible, privileged proof of the allegations made by the informant?" Second, "What other angles does this tip suggest?" He sets to work checking records, interviewing sources suggested by the tipster, and trying to separate fact from rumor. Does the wrongdoing involve only one man, or is there evidence of a conspiracy involving several?

If luck is with him, he will build a body of evidence that is almost good enough to print. He and his editors must make a decision: Should he go directly to the men involved and confront them with the evidence, hoping to jar the complete story loose? Should he talk with men known to be friendly with the suspect, who could give essential information but might tip off the entire investigation? The danger of "burning up" a story is ever present, and the reporter's tactics must be chosen to fit the individual situation. As a general rule, however, where a suspicion of wrongdoing exists the reporter should try to gather as much evidence as possible before tipping his hand.

Some newspaper investigations are done in cooperation with the police. A reporter following up a tip may discover that police investigators are already at work on the matter; usually an agreement for sharing information can be developed, with the understanding that the reporter's paper gets the story exclusively when it breaks. When the suspected wrongdoing involves the police department, as in the case of vice and gambling pay-offs, the reporter may have to exercise great care in avoiding a tipoff to police of his investigation. An unscrupulous police officer has many methods at his disposal to conceal evidence and create difficulties for the investigator.

Many of the best investigation stories published in American newspapers do not involve criminal activity but disclose unsavory and distressing conditions that are due to civic lethargy. This kind of reporting is among the most satisfying assignments a reporter can have and calls for much diligence, ingenuity, and breadth of vision. The reporter working on such a story is a social historian, yet he must have the writing skill to make his report interesting to a mass audience.

Assignment: Slum Cleanup

Here is an assignment that a city editor might give you with instructions to develop it into a series of stories.

Your city has an unsightly area of cheap rooming houses, bars, dubious hangouts, and rundown homes. Several murders and a number of teen-age hoodlum gang fights have occurred there. The city editor wants the story behind the headlines. Just how bad is the area, and why? The purpose of the stories is to point the finger at the basic causes and to propose some lines of civic action.

How would you go about developing the series from the start of the assignment until the stories are ready to print?

Here is the procedure that has been used on several metropolitan newspapers in preparing similar stories. The first step is to define the scope of your investigation. What is the exact geographical area to be investigated? Does it have a commonplace local name such as the West Side, the Valley, or Skid Row? Then comes a list of aspects to be covered. Some of the main ones are the health situation, crime records and police costs, property ownership, the schools and churches, racial problems, municipal and recreation facilities, housing, and juvenile delinquency.

With this list in hand, the reporter determines where he can go for information in each field. Official statistics will provide the foundation upon which he can develop his articles.

Health. The city health department has figures which may

be very revealing. A blighted area usually has an exceptionally high tuberculosis rate. Is that true here? Get figures comparing this area with other sections of the city. What about pest control? Does the department have a greater problem in this section? Check the coroner's death statistics. How do hospital facilities compare with the rest of the city? Talk with two or three doctors to get anecdotes and personal experiences that will personalize the statistics.

Property ownership. The neighborhood is conspicuous for its rundown buildings. Is this because the residents have little pride, or are they too poor to afford the upkeep? The reporter can go to the city building department for answers; he should find some of them in the inspectors' reports. How many of the buildings have records of fire, health, and building code violations? How much effort have these departments made to enforce the municipal ordinances, and how well have the courts backed them up? Have the departments instituted condemnation proceedings against the worst health and firetraps or merely filed their inspectors' reports with a shrug? The latter has happened in some cities until a newspaper has turned publicity upon the situation. The reporter goes to the worst buildings and interviews the residents and managers. He discovers that the owners don't live there. Who does own the property? Again he can get the answers from the records—this time in the county's land files where the deed for every piece of property is registered. Checking a dozen typical buildings, the reporter may find that in ten cases the owner lives in another, perhaps wealthy part of the city or in another city entirely. He may establish a pattern of absentee ownership which frequently leads to neglect. To put teeth into his stories, he can get in touch with the owners of the buildings most frequently cited for municipal code violations and print the list of offenses along with the owners' excuses.

Crime rate. Is there really more crime in the neighborhood than elsewhere, or is it, as some residents contend, that the papers just play up crimes in this area? Check the police statistics. How do offenses such as robbery, homicide, narcotics, and drunkenness compare with other neighborhoods? Many cities have a breakdown of police costs per individual resident by police precincts. How much more does it cost the taxpayer to police this blighted area than other parts of the city? Spend some time at the police station in the neighborhood, if there is one, to hear the officers' stories of what they are up against. Must they patrol the streets in pairs at night? Do they have enough plain-clothes detectives to check vice? Are they vigorous in trying to keep down petty crime, or do they blink their eyes at some of it? Do you detect any hints of police protection for gambling and vice? If possible, talk to the men who run the gambling games and to the prostitutes, questioning them about pay-offs. If they claim that they are "paying off," demand specific information of time, place, and amounts. This information should be cross-checked as carefully as possible before publication; few editors will accept the testimony of one or two petty criminals as con-clusive. But if you find a substantial pattern of reports, you have run across an important spot news story.

Racial problems. Frequently blight areas attract mixed racial strains, including nonwhite groups which have difficulty in find-ing housing in the better neighborhoods because of prejudice. The recent pattern in large cities is population movement toward the suburbs, leaving an area of once-attractive houses into which low income and transient groups move. Racial and other barriers go down. Sometimes this leads to serious stresses. Does that situ-ation exist here?

Education. How do school facilities compare with other parts of the city? Go to the board of education for statistics on average class size, teacher load, age of buildings, and other criteria to determine whether the pupils are receiving below-standard treatment because they live in a poor neighborhood. Talk to the principals and teachers in the neighborhood schools about truancy rates and pupil turnover. How does the transient nature of the school population affect discipline? What special steps have been taken to control teen-age delinquency? Talk to the district's ministers and the police juvenile division about the same problem.

Recreation facilities. Does the neighborhood have its share of playgrounds and other supervised facilities where youths can gather? What do recreation leaders say they need—more help,

The nerve centers of the United Press International (above) and of the Associated Press (below), the news rooms of their New York City headquarters. Here news flows ceaselessly from world-wide bureau networks onto leased wires for newspaper and radio-television clients.

Top: a U.S. president faces more than 200 reporters in the most important of all press conferences. Dwight D. Eisenhower has a smile for reporters. Center: Adlai E. Stevenson talks with radio and newspaper reporters at a campaign stop in the Twin Cities. Bottom: Nelson Rockefeller holds a press conference after his election as governor of New York.

equipment, places to meet? Does the city recreation department have any plans for providing these?

By the time the reporter has checked all these sources, and others that will come to mind as his notes develop, he probably will have more facts about the neighborhood and its problems than anybody in town. All the material is there for the asking, but nobody has ever had a reason to assemble it all before. From roaming the streets, listening to conversations in corner bars, and talking to residents of all sorts, he will have a "feel" for the area. If he shows a sympathetic attitude, he will have no difficulty in getting the residents to talk. And no matter how broken down and impoverished the section may be, he will find a strong strain of neighborhood pride among many of its residents—men and women who seem to be truly happy and content.

The facts are all in his notebook. He has finished his research. Now how does he get all this into news story form in such a way that people will want to read it? Newspaper readers do not want sociological textbooks. To hold their interest the stories must be factual and constructive but told in a way that makes them attractive to read.

The answer lies in human beings. The reporter who can translate all his statistics and official reports into terms of the men and women who live in the neighborhood has captured the art of the storyteller. For example the police records report 30 cases of auto hub caps thefts from the area in the past three weeks. Do any of the reports mention a witness? If so, look him up and get his story. Perhaps he is an old man who was sitting on his front steps when a gang of a half-dozen youths worked their way down his block one night, prying hub caps off one car after another. He called to them to stop, but two of the gang threatened him and forced him to stand in the dark corner of his porch until the thefts were finished. If the reporter starts his article about juvenile crime by describing the episode through the old man's eyes, he has captured his audience. Then he can work in the statistics to show how commonplace such incidents are and explanations by the police about their efforts to control the thefts. A lead paragraph loaded with statistics has a deadening effect upon any reader's interest.

The reporter must organize his stories. The editor, after hearing a verbal report on the material, suggests a series of six articles. A logical first step in organization is for the reporter to list his conclusions—the significant facts that his investigation has established, and the recommendations, partly his own and partly those of persons he interviewed, on steps that can be taken to improve the situation. These should form his concluding article. The first five articles should be arranged so that a factual background is laid for all the major conclusions to be reached in the last article. The opening installment must be sufficiently colorful and closely enough related to the general news situation to catch the reader's attention. It should give the reader an indication of the aspects to be covered in the subsequent articles. But it should not be overloaded with "teaser" material; on a major series of this type the reader expects information to get his teeth into from the start.

Occasionally news stories based on personal investigation by a reporter are written in the first person. More common is the report with a by-line in regular news story form, with perhaps an interjection of the "I" approach where the reporter's own experience adds substantially to his story's meaning.

Winning a Pulitzer Prize

Each year the Pulitzer Prize committee awards a gold medal to a newspaper for disinterested and meritorious public service. The basis for the award is courageous and skillful investigative reporting, which in most cases has led to the correction of an evil situation. There are several well-qualified entrants each year, demonstrating the vigor of enterprising newspapers in the task of guarding the public's interest.

One of the most notable reporting exploits to win this much-coveted medal was the exposure by the Chicago *Daily News* in 1956 of a $2,500,000 fraud in the office of the State Auditor of Illinois and the subsequent imprisonment of State Auditor Orville E. Hodge. George Thiem of the *Daily News* state capital office at Springfield did most of the investigative work, but the story developed so many ramifications that altogether the newspaper assigned 21 reporters, desk men, and rewrite men to it.

Since the Hodge scandal is an almost classic example of how an investigative story can grow from a casual tip, through the diligence and courage of a newspaper, it is recounted here in step-by-step detail. The beginning reporter will find in it both technical guidance and realistic evidence of the persistence, ingenuity, knowledge, and luck which go into this kind of reporting.

The story was born on a Saturday when Michael J. Hewlett, the Democratic candidate against the Republican Hodge for auditor in the election scheduled several months hence, came to see the *Daily News* executive editor, Basil Walters. He wanted to pass along some facts and gossip he had gathered while preparing for his campaign: Hodge had a higher appropriation for his department than any of his predecessors, but even so he was going through the money rapidly, he was living on a high scale (he was supposed to be a millionaire), and he had borrowed a large sum from a Chicago bank to buy an apartment hotel in Florida. Also, he offered a list of 15 persons who were supposed to be on Hodge's payroll without doing any work. All of this material came from a prejudiced source, the auditor's political opponent. Even if true, it did not add up to anything much worse than rather shady but commonplace political activity in Illinois.

Nevertheless, the tip was relayed to Thiem at Springfield on a routine basis. The part he decided to check first was the payroll padding. He went to the auditor's office and examined the list of employees by counties, but none of the 15 names was there. Hodge was asked specifically about one woman who was supposed to be on the list, the wife of a state representative. He denied that she was on his payroll.

Faced by this denial, Thiem followed a good reporter's course. He tried a cross-check by going to another office, that of the state treasurer. There he went through the paycheck records and found that despite what Hodge said and what the auditor's records showed, several of the 15 had been drawing checks.

This was a small lie, and not much of a story, but it served to stir Thiem's suspicions of Hodge. More than that, he received a phone call from an acquaintance in the statehouse that Hodge was ordering everyone not to talk with Thiem.

The reporter also had been instructed to investigate Hodge's lavish living. He found that the state auditor had paid a $5200 hotel bill with a state warrant, issued by his own office, and paid $5000 to a Springfield night club for entertainment. There were other reports of large spending. Thiem's suspicion was only that Hodge was using state funds for personal entertainment.

Here his detailed knowledge of his beat helped. He knew that for each state check, or warrant, issued there should be a voucher in the files authorizing the check and stating its purpose. So he told Hodge that he wanted to go through all the auditor's vouchers. Hodge, still playing the genial politician but increasingly concerned about Thiem's probing, said that the files were far too voluminous for the reporter to plunge into like that. He stated, however, that if Thiem asked for any specific voucher by number, he could examine it. Vouchers were filed by serial number of the check.

Luck entered the investigation on Thiem's side at this point. Somebody in the auditor's office had seen the check for $5200 to the hotel going through the system and, thinking the item rather odd, had jotted down the number. Learning of Thiem's probing activities, he turned over this information.

After 11 long days of digging around, the reporter had only one solid piece of information—the serial number of a check which might prove that the auditor was using state funds for personal entertainment purposes. There was as yet no indication of a large-scale embezzlement operation. He had also picked up extensive gossip about conditions in the auditor's office and details of official procedure; all this was good background but not proof of anything irregular.

Next Thiem went to the office manager in Hodge's department and asked to see the office file of vouchers. The manager said there wasn't such a thing, that they only kept the originals, all of which were in a warehouse. This sounded strange to Thiem, but he went over to the warehouse with his only check number. A clerk quickly found the corresponding voucher. To Thiem's regret, it revealed nothing significant. The investigation might have ended right there, except for another bit of luck. Thiem got to talking with a career official in the warehouse, who proudly offered to show him exactly how the entire filing system operated. Among the things he showed Thiem was the record of all Hodge's appropriations, listing the serial numbers of checks written against the various accounts. The reporter had stumbled across information of great potential value, and from experience he knew what to do with it. He concentrated on one account for which $197,000 had been appropriated to last for two years; with less than a year gone, only $8.33 remained in it.

Thiem copied down the serial numbers of all checks over $2000 which had been written against the account. But he lacked an essential piece of information—the people to whom the checks had been drawn. Still, nothing illegal had been proven. At this point Thiem made his first contact with a law enforcement agency. He told the county attorney of Sangamon County, in which the state capital is situated, about his suspicions, and the attorney said he would take an official look.

Meanwhile, still trying to master the intricate accounting system, Thiem learned that in the state treasurer's office there was a file for warrant reconciliation. If an investigator has a check number, he can consult this file and learn to whom it has been issued. Thiem ran his check numbers through and obtained the names of firms and individuals to whom a dozen checks had been written. All the recipients appeared to be ones with whom the state might be doing routine and legitimate business.

Here the *Daily News* editors had to make a decision. How could they publish the material they had, hoping that it might touch off more conclusive developments and still not violate the libel laws? The *Daily News* solved the problem by running a story listing the checks, the recipients, and the amounts and saying in effect, "this is part of the story of how our state auditor is running through his funds so rapidly." This was published a month after the first tip. It made no accusation of crime.

Such a story is inconclusive and means little to the average reader, but it achieved its purpose. A Chicago attorney told the paper that a check for $9000 listed in the story as having been paid to him never reached him and that in fact he had no such sum due from the state.

That sent Thiem into still another state file. He remembered that at one time the state treasurer's office had been microfilming canceled state checks as a space-saving measure. He got out the proper roll of film and found the check in question. It had been endorsed by typewriter—and so had 14 others adjoining it on the film, all issued the same day. The total was $178,000. Here at last was the evidence that established a crime. The existence of 15 consecutive checks endorsed by typewriter was too unlikely to be a coincidence.

Hodge's secret had been uncovered. Tedious and persistent grubbing through the records by Reporter Thiem had revealed the simple scheme that was taking huge sums from the state treasury: Hodge and his associates were writing checks to pay nonexistent bills and then cashing the checks themselves.

The investigation had reached its climax. The *Daily News* editors assigned every available man to the task of tracking down the list of payees to make sure they had never received their checks and had none coming. Since no addresses were shown on the microfilmed checks, this was a difficult research job that had to be done in a hurry before Hodge had time to reach these people and try to buy their silence. The paper obtained copies of the microfilms. Unless it could print pictures of the checks, the *News* might have faced a major libel suit.

Six of those to whom the checks had been addressed made statements to *News* reporters that they had never received the payments and had none coming. These statements, along with pictures of the checks, were the foundation of the story that the *Daily News* broke all over its front page. Others came along later.

The editors faced another decision that must be made on an investigation story—whether to show it in advance to the person involved. The *News* decided to do so. Its political editor went to Springfield and gave Hodge the story that was about to be published. Hodge put on his jovial politician air and professed great surprise that anything was wrong in his department.

The same day that the *Daily News* story was published, the governor put armed guards around the state records. Hodge was arrested, tried, and sent to prison.

Perhaps no beginning reporter studying this account will ever be called upon to do such an intricate job of investigative reporting with such startling results. Yet there are several lessons in it that will serve him well in this type of work.

1. Thiem's dogged *persistence* in checking records. This was augmented by his detailed knowledge of the state house beat and the number of friends he had made who passed along helpful tips.
2. The *full backing* of his editors. They were willing to print a highly controversial story without having foolproof privileged documents and without any arrests having been made.
3. The reporter's *knowledge* of the significance of the evidence, once he found the facts in the records.
4. The importance of *physical evidence,* in this case the canceled checks, to give the story authenticity.
5. Willingness to invest sufficient *time.* Six weeks were spent in investigation before the story was published.
6. *Refusal to be deceived* by the suspect's genial manner, denials, and friendly gestures.

Chapter 13

Reporting for the Press Associations

The Function of Wire Services

Much of the news in the daily paper comes from the press associations which deliver it by teletype to the editorial department. These dispatches may carry datelines from the other side of the world, or from a city barely 50 miles away. Each story torn from the teleprinter by a copy boy and laid on the telegraph editor's desk has been moved through the wire service's complex system of editing and wire transmission. It is ready for publication if the editor chooses to use it, although there is no obligation for him to do so. He can print the entire story or any portion of it.

Since each wire service story is delivered to many newspapers and is subject to the varying desires and needs of many editors, the man who prepares it faces problems that do not exist for the reporter writing a story for his own newspaper. This chapter will explain the basic differences between reporting for a newspaper and for a wire service.

The function of a wire service story is to give the facts of a news situation in concise and tightly written form. The presentation must be neutral in such matters as politics and religion, since it will be printed in newspapers with different viewpoints, and it must not be slanted to express friendly or unfriendly attitudes toward personalities in the news. These restrictions leave little room for nuances. Since the wire service writer is serving many masters—the hundreds of newspapers which receive his service —he must lay especially heavy emphasis upon objectivity.

Opportunities in the Wire Services

The Associated Press and United Press International, the two American press associations, have been the training ground for thousands of newspaper writers and editors and for writers who have gone into such related fields as magazines, books, radio and television, and industrial writing. Their discipline, the emphasis on speed and accuracy, and the constant need to judge the relative importance of the day's news stories give young newsmen and women a rapid conditioning in the preparation and handling of news.

Some excellent writers and editors spend their entire careers happily in the press associations. But there is substantial turnover in manpower in these organizations and consequently a good opportunity for young reporters to obtain jobs. Naturally, fewer men can reach top positions in two wire services than can rise to superior posts on the many daily newspapers, and some talented press association men find other employers bidding for their services. After a few years, too, some wire service men become weary of desk assignments which necessarily make up a part of press association work. But virtually all who leave say their experiences were pleasant and extremely valuable.

The Associated Press and United Press International have large offices in the major cities and in the state capitals and one- or two-man bureaus in many smaller cities. After an initial breaking-in period as a minor member of a large bureau, a young man is often assigned to one of the offices in a small city and may soon have the title of bureau manager. He and his assistants are responsible for gathering the news of their assigned area, deciding which stories are of interest to newspapers outside that region, and putting the stories on the teleprinter circuit. Once a story has been transmitted, it is in the hands of all newspapers on that circuit and ready for publication. This puts a heavy responsibility upon the originating office to make sure that the dispatch is accurate and free from libel. The manager of a wire service bureau carries greater responsibility in many respects than a reporter of similar age and experience on a newspaper, because the latter's work is subjected to more frequent scrutiny before reaching print.

The newspaper reporter examining a piece of information asks himself, "Is this news interesting to the readers of my newspaper here in this community?" The wire service reporter, looking at the same information, asks, "Is this material of sufficient interest to the readers of our member newspapers in other cities to deserve space on our crowded wires?" The local reporter looks inward to his community; the wire service man looks outward to the rest of the world. For example, a restaurant holdup which makes a banner headline in a newspaper may not deserve even a paragraph on the press association wires because the newspapers to which it would be transmitted are much more interested in their own local holdups. This is one of the first lessons a beginning wire service newsman must learn.

Reporters working on small city newspapers often have an opportunity to earn extra money by serving as part-time correspondents for the press associations. This activity also enables the correspondent to develop his acquaintances in the wire service and may lead to a full-time job with it later. The stringer, as he is called, is paid a fee for each usable item he telephones or telegraphs to the wire service office. If his city happens to have an especially newsworthy industry or is otherwise the source of considerable news, the service may pay him a monthly retainer fee. The Associated Press is a cooperative newsgathering organization and has access to all news gathered by its member papers. United Press International sells its news reports to client papers under contracts. While these contracts include automatic news pick-up rights, this clause might be waived in the face of a client's prior contractual commitment (as to the AP). Thus the existence of string correspondent jobs in small cities depends upon the contractual arrangements of the local newspaper.

How Wire Services Get Their News

Much of the news report each press association bureau puts on the wire is rewritten from stories in the local newspapers.

It would be impractical for each bureau to have a reporting staff as extensive as the local paper's. The bureau manager assigns part of his staff to check the newspapers for stories and news leads. Sometimes these stories can simply be rewritten into wire form. More often they must be checked and developed by telephone calls to the news sources and examined with particular care for an "out-of-town" angle. These men also make independent checks of basic news sources like police and courts. The manager assigns staff men to cover stories of major statewide or national interest which originate in his territory, such as a sensational murder trial or catastrophe. In this role the wire service man functions exactly like a local newspaper reporter, gathering his material on the spot and either phoning it to a rewrite man, sending it in by telegraph to the bureau, or coming back in to write the story himself.

Each bureau is also responsible for creating feature material that can be moved during idle hours on the wires or incorporated in the printed supplementary service which the press associations mail to their newspapers. Much of this material is printed in Sunday papers, which need more timeless copy than the daily papers. Such features are developed by bureau men through interviews and research; they provide the beginning wire service reporter with an opportunity to show his bureau chief that he has initiative, ideas, and an ability to write.

The press associations have developed reporting by telephone. When a tip on a natural disaster or accident at a distant point reaches a bureau, long distance calls are placed immediately to police, hospitals, and other possible sources of information. If a local correspondent is available, he is also summoned into action by phone, but the story cannot wait for him to reach the scene. The essential facts obtained by telephone are moved on the wires first and are then supplemented by later details when available. If the situation is sufficiently important, a staff member may be dispatched by air or car.

The wire services have a graduated system of control points, from the small part-time bureau in a secondary city to the main news office in New York.

A story put on the Illinois wire at Springfield, for example, may be of interest only to other newspapers in that state. However, if the news agency's central division headquarters at Chicago, into which the wire runs, judges the story to be of interest in other midwestern points, it is relayed through the Chicago desk onto nearby state wires. If the story has general interest, Chicago puts it onto the transcontinental trunk wire for distribution all over the country. When it reaches the main New York office, it is again examined, this time for interest to readers abroad. The agency's foreign desk sends transmissions of American news to papers in many countries by wireless and cable. Thus the story datelined Springfield, Illinois, may get no further than papers in that state —or it may be printed in Tokyo or London. Its fate depends upon the judgment of the wire service relay editors and, subsequently, the client newspaper telegraph editors as to what makes news.

Techniques of Press Association Writing

A story which undergoes the vicissitudes mentioned above must be prepared differently than one intended for publication in the reporter's own paper. The story may be worth 300 words in one member newspaper, when judged in relation to other national and local stories in the news editor's hands, and only 100 words in another. Thus it must be written so that it can be cut without allowing any of the essential facts to be lost in the process. The writer must stick to the orthodox forms of presentation, packing the key information into his first few paragraphs, then adding detailed development of these facts in the order of descending importance. Thus a telegraph editor in a hurry to meet a deadline can trim the story from the bottom upward with the assurance that he isn't eliminating basic material. This means that much wire service writing follows the inverted pyramid style, although the services do encourage suspended interest leads and other devices for producing interesting feature stories.

The story may also be shortened by a relay editor when it is sent on from a local circuit to a larger one. Perhaps the editor at the relay point, a more experienced writer, may feel that a rewrite of the story emphasizing some unusual angle may make it more printable nationally. Or if it is something like a traffic accident story, of interest only to one or two clients in a distant part of the country, it may be reduced to an interbureau message containing only the skeleton facts. Wire time is a precious commodity for which many stories are competing, so brevity is essential. A seasoned press association writer gives freer rein to his stylistic individuality when his by-line is being used.

Unlike a newspaper, which has certain well-established deadlines to which all its newsgathering activities are pointed, the press association has a continuous deadline. Somewhere around the world one of its clients is about to go to press every minute of the 24 hours. Speed is a dominant factor. When a big story breaks, the press association must start moving it on the wires immediately in short segments, or takes. The writer cannot wait until all the loose ends are tied together and then write a comprehensive wrap-up story. When later developments warrant, a new lead is written which picks up suitably in the body of the earlier story. Experienced wire service rewrite men soon learn the trick of inserting a "platform" paragraph high in the original story onto which they can rest the pick-up paragraph at the end of the new lead, so the transition reads smoothly. They learn to avoid allusions whose meaning is lost if a new lead is placed on top of the story and to avoid burying an important angle from the early story under several paragraphs of new lead matter. Another trick they acquire is to keep the story in focus, so that the later but lesser developments do not smother the main elements of the news situation. Ideally, a developing story can be "topped" two or three times with new leads, yet will appear to the reader in his newspaper as though it was all written at one time.

Another unique editorial function in press association work is wire filing, that is, determining the order in which news stories are to be transmitted on the wire to the member papers. This is a task to which younger members of the staff are often assigned, under the watchful eye of the bureau chief. Techniques differ among the press associations, and even from one circuit to another within each organization, but the fundamental rules are the same: to send stories in a sequence that will serve the known needs and deadlines of as many clients as possible. Usually a circuit is opened with an editor's schedule of the major stories already in hand or anticipated. This helps the telegraph editor to plan his portion of the paper. When major stories develop un-expectedly, they take precedence over the scheduled stories for wire space, because the agencies are intensely competitive and pride themselves on being the first to deliver important bulletins. On a day when several big stories are running simultaneously, and other essential material like market reports and sports must also be moved, the proper filing of a circuit requires fast and hardheaded judgment on relative news merits. It is regarded as a sin to leave several stories "open" simultaneously—that is, lying incomplete on the telegraph editor's desk with "more" slugs on them. Wire filing is excellent training for any young press associa-tion man.

The agencies have developed a jargon of their own, partly a carry-over from the old days before teleprinters when all news was transmitted and received by Morse operators using hand sets. The object of such code words and abbreviations is to save wire time. Each office is called by code letters and signs all its messages that way. In the United Press International, Chicago is HX, New York is NX, Washington is WA, Los Angeles is HC, and Indianapolis is IA. The Associated Press calls San Francisco FX, Kansas City KX, Dallas DN, and Washington WX.

Here are some typical interoffice messages moved on the leased wires, with explanations of their full meaning:

95
NX
    CLI PRESSING PER OUR EARLIER MSG, AT 1242P.
WTR QUEEN CUT TAPE OPEN NEW HIWAY TDY OR
MERELY SIGNALED START CONSTRUCTION.
    SX HT213P. .

In the above United Press International excerpt, 95 indicates a priority, urgent message. Spelled out, the message reads: To New York. Client is pressing us for an answer to our earlier mes-sage, sent at 12:42 p.m., as to whether the Queen cut a tape to open the new highway today or merely made a signal to start construction. Signed San Francisco.

HT are the initials of the transmitting operator, 2:13 p.m. is the time the message was cleared. The two little dots after the

"P" signify that the San Francisco office is clear, with no further copy waiting to be moved on this wire.

This message moved on the Associated Press wire:

FX
FYI, NOW HAVE NIXON TEXT AND WILL ABSTRACT
WASHN VIA KX.

In full this means: To San Francisco. For your information we now have the text of Vice-President Nixon's speech and will write the story from it here. Signed Washington via Kansas City. The Vice-President was speaking in San Francisco, but as is often the case the text of his talk was given out to Washington reporters in advance.

KX FOR WASHN
POST ASKS PMS TMW STY MITCHELL'S DISCRIM-
INATION KFC WITH EMPHASIS ON COLORADO REP-
RESENTATIVE
DX

Spelled out, this says: Kansas City for Washington. Post asks for afternoon papers tomorrow a story on Secretary of Labor Mitchell's conference on discrimination with emphasis on Colorado representative. Signed Denver.

Press association dispatches are written in a more staccato, tightly worded style than coverage of the same events by correspondents of individual newspapers (called "specials" in the wire service language). A comparison between wire service coverage and a newspaper's reporting of identical events illustrates the "special" writer's more leisurely, conversational style.

We reproduce here two accounts of Queen Elizabeth II's arrival in the United States and her visit to colonial Williamsburg, Virginia, the United Press dispatch and that of the New York *Herald Tribune*. Each is well done for its purposes, but the contrast is easily discerned. The *Herald Tribune* story has more anecdotal material and dialogue giving glimpses of the royal visitors' personalities, and its paragraphs are interwoven in narrative style. The wire service dispatch, of approximately the same length, contains more material about the Queen's itinerary. Its paragraphs tend to stand alone so that some can be eliminated without leaving loose ends.

BY GAY PAULEY

UNITED PRESS STAFF CORRESPONDENT

WILLIAMSBURG, VA. (UP) —A BUOYANT, TIRE-LESS QUEEN ELIZABETH BEGAN HER FIRST STATE VISIT TO AMERICA TODAY WITH A PILGRIMAGE TO THE PLACE WHERE HER EMPIRE-BUILDING AN-CESTORS FIRST COLONIZED THE NEW WORLD.

SHUTTLING ABOUT IN PRESIDENT EISENHOWER'S BUBBLE-DOMED LIMOUSINE AND A HORSE-DRAWN CARRIAGE, THE SMILING QUEEN AND HER CON-SORT, PRINCE PHILIP, PUT IN AN EXHAUSTING DAY OF SIGHT-SEEING, SPEECH-MAKING AND HAND-SHAKING.

IT WAS LONG AFTER DARK BEFORE THEIR TOUR ACROSS THIS HISTORY-STEEPED CORNER OF THE OLD DOMINION STATE CAME TO A CLOSE. WHEN IT WAS OVER, BRITAIN'S BELOVED 31-YEAR-OLD ELIZABETH HAD PROVED THAT A QUEEN'S LIFE IS NO BED OF ROSES.

ARRIVING FROM CANADA, WHERE SHE ALSO PUT IN FOUR GRUELING DAYS, THE QUEEN MOTORED TO NEARBY JAMESTOWN ISLAND, WHERE THE FIRST PERMANENT ENGLISH-SPEAKING COLONY WAS ESTABLISHED 350 YEARS AGO.

AN ESTIMATED 50,000 AMERICANS CHEERED THE ROYAL COUPLE AS THEY MADE A ROUND OF CERE-MONIAL STOPS STRETCHING FROM PATRICK HENRY AIRPORT TO THIS RECONSTRUCTED CAPITAL OF COLONIAL VIRGINIA.

THE RECEPTION WAS EVEN MORE ENTHUSIASTIC THAN THE ONE ELIZABETH RECEIVED IN CANADA AND SHE AND PHILIP MADE THE MOST OF IT.

AS NIGHT FELL AND THE STREET CROWDS DI-MINISHED, ELIZABETH PLUNGED WITH HARDLY A BREAK INTO A ROUND OF SOCIAL FUNCTIONS,

CLIMAXED BY A DINNER GIVEN BY VIRGINIA GOV. THOMAS B. STANLEY.

TOMORROW, SHE AND PHILIP WILL FLY ON TO WASHINGTON FOR A NEW SERIES OF CEREMONIES AND A FOUR-DAY VISIT AS GUESTS OF PRESIDENT AND MRS. EISENHOWER.

ONE OF HER ESCORTS AS SHE SWEPT FROM HISTORIC POINT TO HISTORIC POINT IN THIS STORIED VILLAGE WAS WINTHROP ROCKEFELLER, WHO PUT UP MUCH OF THE MONEY USED TO RESTORE IT TO COLONIAL ELEGANCE.

IN THE RECONSTRUCTED PALACE OF COLONIAL GOVERNORS, THE QUEEN MINGLED WITH 1,200 GUESTS AND SIPPED A GLASS OF SHERRY. PHILIP DOWNED A SCOTCH HIGHBALL. FROM THERE THEY DROVE TO THE COLONIAL CAPITOL, LAST SIGHT-SEEING STOP OF THE DAY.

IN FIVE BRIEF SPEECHES AT VARIOUS POINTS, THE QUEEN SPOKE OF THE "ADVENTURES IN FREEDOM" MADE POSSIBLE BY THE PIONEERING SPIRIT OF "YOUR FOREFATHERS AND MY COUNTRYMEN."

ELIZABETH AND PHILIP LANDED AT NEARBY PATRICK HENRY AIRPORT AFTER A FLIGHT FROM OTTAWA TO THE ACCLAIM OF AN ESTIMATED 10,000 PERSONS. THEY PLUNGED IMMEDIATELY INTO A RIGOROUS SCHEDULE WHICH MATCHED THE PACE OF THEIR FOUR-DAY CANADIAN VISIT.

FIRST THEY VISITED JAMESTOWN ISLAND—A SWAMPY BUT CHERISHED LANDSPIT WHERE CAPT. JOHN SMITH AND HIS COLONIAL COMPANY LANDED IN THEIR THREE TINY SHIPS, THE SUSAN CONSTANT, THE DISCOVERY AND GODSPEED, IN 1607.

THEN THEY DROVE TO WILLIAMSBURG, COLONIAL CAPITAL OF VIRGINIA, FOR MORE CEREMONIES IN THE RECONSTRUCTED SECTION AND A NIGHT'S LODGING. HERE, SHE SWITCHED FROM THE PRESIDENTIAL LIMOUSINE TO A ROYAL CARRIAGE

WHICH CARRIED HER THROUGH THE ANCIENT
STREETS.

TOMORROW THE QUEEN AND PHILIP WILL FLY
ON TO WASHINGTON FOR A FOUR-DAY STAY AS
GUESTS OF PRESIDENT AND MRS. EISENHOWER.
THEIR U.S. VISIT WILL WIND UP MONDAY WITH A
NEW YORK TICKER TAPE PARADE AND A TRIP TO
THE EMPIRE STATE BUILDING.

HER MAJESTY AND PHILIP, BEHAVING AT TIMES
LIKE A COUPLE OF AMERICAN POLITICAL CANDI-
DATES, TROOPED TIRELESSLY ABOUT THE JAMES-
TOWN FESTIVAL PARK, SPREADING A WAVE OF
GOOD WILL IN THEIR WAKE.

AMONG OTHER THINGS, THEY SHOOK HANDS
WITH INDIANS, WATCHED GLASS-BLOWERS AT
WORK, CLIMBED ABOARD A REPLICA OF THE SUSAN
CONSTANT AND LISTENED TO A STORY ABOUT A
"MOTHER-IN-LAW" TREE.

THEY KISSED NO BABIES. BUT, JUDGING FROM
COMMENTS BY FEMALE SPECTATORS, THE HAND-
SOME PHILIP MIGHT HAVE FOUND HIMSELF BEING
KISSED HAD HE VENTURED INTO THE CROWD.

AT WILLIAMSBURG, THE COUPLE TOOK TEA
WITH THE PRESIDENT OF HISTORIC WILLIAM AND
MARY COLLEGE, ATTENDED A CEREMONY AT THE
WREN BUILDING ON THE CAMPUS, ATTENDED A
RECEPTION AT THE GOVERNOR'S PALACE, IN-
SPECTED THE CAPITOL AND—FINALLY—HAD DIN-
NER AT THE WILLIAMSBURG INN.

THE QUEEN EXCHANGED GIFTS WITH SOME OF
HER HOSTS. TO THE COLLEGE, SHE PRESENTED A
COPY OF THE STATUTES OF THE ORDER OF THE
GARTER. TO COLONIAL WILLIAMSBURG, SHE GAVE
A SMALL 17TH CENTURY CASKET.

AMONG THE PRESENTS SHE RECEIVED WERE REP-
LICAS OF THE CHALICE AND PATTEN IN BRUTON
PARISH CHURCH AND A PORTRAIT OF COL. AUGUS-
TINE WARNER.

"I CANNOT THINK OF A MORE APPROPRIATE POINT FOR US TO START OUR VISIT TO THE UNITED STATES," THE QUEEN SAID DURING HER JAMESTOWN VISIT.

SHE SAID THE FESTIVAL OF THE FIRST ENGLISH-SPEAKING SETTLEMENT ILLUSTRATED THE STORIES OF THE UNITED STATES AND THE BRITISH COMMONWEALTH—"STORIES OF EXPERIENCES AND ADVENTURES IN FREEDOM."

AFTER A 25-MILE DRIVE THROUGH AUTUMN-TINTED COUNTRYSIDE FROM THE AIRPORT TO THE FESTIVAL PARK, ELIZABETH GREETED A LARGE CROWD AT THE MODERNISTIC PAVILION.

Here is the *Herald Tribune* coverage of the same story:

Queen Elizabeth Is Kept Busy On First Day of U.S. Visit

By Judith Crist

WILLIAMSBURG, VA., Oct. 16.—Elizabeth II came to the United States today, but within an hour she had assumed the role and, in fact, the title of Her Britannic Majesty visiting the first British colony in the New World.

Welcomed by Wiley T. Buchanan, chief of protocol, on behalf of President Eisenhower; Gov. Thomas B. Stanley of Virginia and British Ambassador Sir Harold Caccia, as well as other officials, the English monarch was accorded full military honors on her arrival from Canada.

A twenty-one-gun salute, an honor guard of thirty-one men from each of the four armed services, and a color guard bearing the flags of the ten British Commonwealth Nations and the American flag, greeted the Queen and Prince Philip at their arrival in a Royal Canadian Air Force plane at Patrick Henry Airport, perhaps ironically named for the American apostle of freedom from the eighteenth century British colonial imperialism.

Then, with Gov. Stanley as her guide, the Queen, riding in President Eisenhower's bubble top limousine, with Prince Philip and Lady Caccia in the second car of the motorcade, set out for Jamestown to join in the celebration of the 350th anniversary of its founding by a hardy band of English colonists and to examine the relics and replicas of colonial life.

At Jamestown Island, the royal visitors attended brief services at the reconstructed Old Church whose original tower, built in 1639, still stands. Then as had the Queen Mother who visited here three years ago, they laughed heartily at the famous story of the "mother-in-law tree" in the church courtyard. Legend has it that the tree, which has grown up to separate the graves of a husband and wife, was planted by the wife's mother, who had disapproved of their marriage. The story, colorfully told in dialect by Sam Robinson, a Canadian-born Negro guide, is one of the major tourist attractions here.

Visit Jamestown Festival

At the Jamestown Festival, after greeting thousands in the Court of Welcome, the royal couple toured the Old World or British Pavilion, containing the Magna Carta and 200 other priceless treasures loaned to the Festival by the Queen, her government and private collectors. They walked through James Fort, a reproduction of the original Jamestown settlement, and boarded the 100-ton Susan Constant, the largest of the three full-sized reproductions of the Elizabethan sailing vessels that brought the 104 founders of Jamestown to the New World.

Elizabethan Costumes

Colorfully garbed pikesmen, halberdiers and musketeers were on hand to line the walks, while others in Elizabethan garb lent authenticity and life to the various reproductions. The royal couple paused before two men in stocks.

"Do they throw rotten eggs at you?" the Prince asked one, and the Queen inquired of another, whose arms were tied behind his back, "Does it hurt?" Both received blushing negative answers.

Aboard the Susan Constant crewmen climbed the rigging to add a lively note while the visitors examined the primitive navigational instruments. About 50,000 visitors had crowded the park for a glimpse of the Queen, who made a bright figure in a peacock-blue coat of heavy silk trimmed in black velvet, and wearing a hat of pheasant feathers, and black accessories. The crowd raced here and there across the park to keep up with the royal party.

Talk to Girl Scout

Twice the visitors paused to talk to private citizens, one a Girl Scout selected for presentation by officials because her late father had worn the Order of the British Empire and she was thereby eligible to be presented to royalty. Prince Philip congratulated her on her six badges. Then, observing a young woman and two children who were waving a British flag and "hip-hip-hoorraying" in British fashion, Philip left the royal party to chat with her. Learning that she was a British war bride from Northumberland, when she pointed out that the two wide-eyed youngsters at her side were hers, the Prince remarked: "Well, you're well in now. . . ."

Visit William and Mary

The Queen, who on her arrival had said that she and her husband were "going to have a wonderful time in the few hours at our disposal"— they leave for Washington in the morning—moved at a fast pace. From Jamestown the party proceeded to the President's House at the College of William and Mary, where the Queen presented to the college a copy of the Statutes of the Order of the Garter, which is presented to each knight of the order at investiture. This particular copy, the Queen said, had been presented to Prince William, Duke of Gloucester, the nephew of King William, three years before he and Queen Mary had granted a charter to their Royal College in Virginia.

The royal visitors toured Colonial Williamsburg in an open carriage with Winthrop Rockefeller, the chairman of the board of the community, and Mrs. Rockefeller. Tonight, in a regal white satin gown embroidered with crystals, diamonds and pearls in motifs of china-blue flowers mixed with moonstones and star sapphires, the Queen was honored at a dinner at the Williamsburg Inn.

The Queen received a series of bound booklets on seventeenth-century Virginia, a copy portrait of her Virginia ancestor, Augustine Warner, ninth great-grandfather of the Queen and Speaker of Virginia's House of Burgesses in 1676, and silver Church communion service of 1661.

The Queen gave Colonial Williamsburg a tortoise-shell casket of seventeenth-century Jamaican workmanship, constructed of oak and veneered with tortoise shell and mother of pearl and with silver mounts. Inlaid on the top in mother of pearl is an American Indian and the word "America." The casket is a little over a foot high and is two feet wide.

Writing for Radio Stations

Both the Associated Press and the United Press International operate special wires to radio and television stations over which they move the day's news stories rewritten for broadcasting. The copy is processed for spoken rather than printed use, emphasizing simplicity of sentence structure. Many paragraphs which are easily absorbed by the eye sound clumsy and stilted when read over the air by an announcer. The radio divisions of the press associations rewrite stories from the newspaper wires and offer supplementary radio features as well. They do only a limited amount of original reporting. This work, with its emphasis upon the ear rather than the eye, is splendid training for men and women who hope to write later for the stage and television.

Here is an example of a United Press Washington dispatch in its original form for newspaper publication and as rewritten for the radio wire.

BY CHARLOTTE G. MOULTON
        UNITED PRESS STAFF CORRESPONDENT
    WASHINGTON (UP)—TEAMSTER PRESIDENT DAVE BECK DEFIED AFL-CIO EXECUTIVE COUNCIL DEMANDS TODAY AND SAID THE GIANT UNION HAS NO INTENTION OF PURGING JAMES R. HOFFA FROM ITS RANKS.

    BECK, WHO IS SLATED TO BE SUCCEEDED BY HOFFA AS UNION PRESIDENT, SAID THE TEAMSTERS WOULD APPEAL THEIR SUSPENSION BY THE EXECU-TIVE COUNCIL TO THE AFL-CIO CONVENTION IN ATLANTIC CITY, N.J., IN DECEMBER.

    AFL-CIO PRESIDENT GEORGE MEANY SAID IN AN-NOUNCING SUSPENSION OF THE TEAMSTERS A WEEK AGO THAT HOFFA WOULD HAVE TO BE DROPPED OR THE EXECUTIVE COUNCIL WOULD RECOMMEND THE UNION'S OUSTER AT THE DE-CEMBER MEETING.

    BECK SAID THAT IF THE TEAMSTERS' APPEAL TO THE AFL-CIO CONVENTION WAS TURNED DOWN HE WAS SURE THE TEAMSTERS WOULD BE EXPELLED. ASKED IF HE THOUGHT THE APPEAL WOULD SUC-CEED, BECK SAID, "I CERTAINLY WOULD BE AN OPTIMIST IF I THOUGHT SO."

    THE UNION CHIEF TOLD NEWSMEN ASSEMBLED IN THE TEAMSTERS' FIVE MILLION DOLLAR HEAD-QUARTERS HERE THAT THE APPEAL WOULD BE BASED ON TWO POINTS.

    HE SAID THE UNION'S LAME-DUCK EXECUTIVE BOARD, WHICH MET FOR SEVERAL HOURS TODAY,

WOULD CONTEND THAT THERE WAS NO FACTUAL
EVIDENCE TO BACK ALLEGATIONS OF CORRUPTION
AGAINST BECK, HOFFA AND OTHER UNION OF-
FICIALS ELECTED AT THE TEAMSTERS RECENT
MIAMI BEACH CONVENTION.

HE ALSO SAID THE UNION WOULD ARGUE THAT
EVEN IF THE ALLEGED ACTS WERE TRUE—WHICH
HE DENIED—THEY ALL TOOK PLACE BEFORE THE
AFL-CIO CONSTITUTION WAS ADOPTED TWO YEARS
AGO.

BECK SAID EXPULSION MIGHT HELP THE TEAM-
STERS ORGANIZATION, THE AFL-CIO'S LARGEST
UNION, EVEN THOUGH SOME HARM COULD RESULT.

"IT COULD RESULT IN TREMENDOUSLY INTEN-
SIFIED ORGANIZING," HE SAID. HE DENIED THE
TRUCK UNION WOULD ATTEMPT TO RAID OTHER
AFL-CIO AFFILIATES IF IT WERE KICKED OUT.

BECK'S STATEMENT CAME AS THE TEAMSTERS
ASKED THE U.S. COURT OF APPEALS TO STAY A FED-
ERAL COURT ORDER BARRING HOFFA AND OTHER
NEWLY-ELECTED TEAMSTER OFFICIALS FROM TAK-
ING OFFICE.

IT DENOUNCED AS ENTIRELY UNJUSTIFIED THE
LOWER COURT'S FINDING THAT HOFFA'S ELEC-
TION WAS "RIGGED" AT THE TEAMSTERS' CON-
VENTION.

TEAMSTERS ATTORNEY MARTIN F. O'DONOGHUE
TOLD THE U.S. COURT OF APPEALS PANEL THAT HE
ALREADY HAD AGREED TO THE LOWER COURT
ORDER ON HOFFA AND THE OTHER OFFICIALS.

HE SAID HE WOULD NOT OBJECT TO ITS CON-
TINUANCE WHILE A TRIAL WAS HELD ON MERITS
OF THE CHARGES AGAINST THEM.

In the radio wire version of the same story, notice that much
background material has been eliminated, the phraseology made
more colloquial, and the story told in simple declarative
sentences.

(TEAMSTERS)

TEAMSTERS LEADERS WILL FIGHT A SUSPENSION ORDER BY THE AFL-CIO EXECUTIVE COUNCIL.

RETIRING PRESIDENT DAVE BECK SAYS THE UNION WILL CARRY ITS CASE TO THE LABOR FEDERATIONS' ATLANTIC CITY CONVENTION IN DECEMBER.

BECK SAID THE UNION HAS NO INTENTION OF COMPLYING WITH COUNCIL ORDER THAT PRESIDENT JAMES HOFFA BE DROPPED.

THE COUNCIL IS EXPECTED TO RECOMMEND THAT THE GIANT UNION BE DROPPED FROM THE AFL-CIO UNLESS HOFFA STEPS DOWN.

BECK INDICATED HE IS NOT OPTIMISTIC AS TO THE SUCCESS OF THE APPEAL MOVE. ITS REJECTION WOULD MEAN EXPULSION OF THE TEAMSTERS FROM THE AFL-CIO.

IN WASHINGTON, COUNSEL FOR THE UNION DENOUNCED RECENT TRIAL COURT FINDINGS THAT HOFFA AND OTHER OFFICERS CONSPIRED TO ASSURE THEIR ELECTION.

THE ATTORNEY URGED AN APPEALS COURT PANEL TO THROW OUT THE FINDINGS EVEN BEFORE A TRIAL CAN BE HELD.

Chapter 14

Washington, Political News Center

World's Biggest Dateline

The capital of the United States government has become the most important news center in the world. Under the dateline WASHINGTON, news dispatches report policy decisions which influence the lives of persons all over the earth. Every American citizen's mode of living and financial status are affected by actions taken in the national capital. The wordage filed daily from Washington about these developments is enormous.

The press corps includes hundreds of men and women from American newspapers, press associations, magazines, radio, television, and other publications; in addition, scores of reporters from foreign countries are based there. These Washington correspondents are a highly trained group of specialists in public affairs. A Washington job is the goal for many reporters who are especially interested in politics and find satisfaction in being close to the source of global decisions and in recording the interplay of forces which produces our national policy.

So many news sources exist in the federal government and the related groups which cluster around it that no reporter can cover them all. The press associations, which have dozens of men on their Washington staffs, provide coverage for most of the papers in the country. A few metropolitan newspapers, like the New York *Times,* have staffs large enough to produce their own special stories on at least a half dozen news developments each day. Even these newspapers, however, depend upon the press association reports for a substantial portion of their Washington news budget.

Papers which have small bureaus, from one to three men, frequently have their Washington men handle only the top general story of the day and devote the rest of their efforts to developing enterprise exclusives and stories of particular interest in their own circulation areas. Special news bureaus provide Washington coverage for groups of newspapers scattered across the country, or concentrated in a single state. These specialize in local angles for their client papers. Other reporters handle assignments for magazines, trade papers, and the newsletters which provide information on trends and supposed "inside" tips. Most of these news letters are prepared for businessmen or special interest groups. Also, there are syndicated columnists who write background and interpretive articles. The radio and television networks have news staffs which are smaller but comparable in organization to those of the press associations.

The Washington press corps has several organizations. One regulates membership in the Congressional Press Gallery, which totals more than 750 men and women. Others are the White House Correspondents' Association, the White House News Photographers Association, the Radio Correspondents Association, and the 50-member Gridiron Club. The National Press Club has a 14-story building which houses many news offices.

News Sources in Washington

Where does this swarm of reporters find its news? The biggest sources are the White House, Congress, the State Department, and the Defense Department, the places where the most important and newsworthy policy is made. During the months the Supreme Court is in session, its "decision days," on Mondays, produce many major stories. The other government departments, such as Agriculture and the Treasury, and administrative bureaus turn out a steady flow of information which occasionally makes banner headlines. The diplomatic corps, representing countries from all parts of the world, produces some spot news and extensive background material. Most embassies have officials responsible for press relations. Trade associations, labor unions, and other groups with direct interests in legislation and government decisions maintain offices in Washington. These are another important news source. So are the political party headquarters.

More fast-breaking major stories come from the White House in a year than any other single Washington source. The press room in the White House is staffed by some of the best-informed and most experienced reporters in Washington. They are called upon to handle stories full of complexities and nuances, and the way they handle them has a strong impact upon public opinion both in this country and abroad. A misconception of American policy, coming from a poorly handled news story, can have serious repercussions.

The President's press secretary meets the reporters as a group frequently to give them news of developments in the executive branch. Such news is usually labeled "the White House said" or is attributed to the press secretary by name. Between group meetings he undertakes to obtain answers to questions submitted by individual reporters. When the White House has a story of special interest coming up, it frequently puts out advance notification to enable attendance by other reporters in addition to the White House beat men. The White House reporters also obtain important stories by interviewing prominent visitors who come to talk with the President.

At stated times or at indefinite intervals, depending upon his schedule and inclination, the President holds a news conference. There is no legal obligation for him to do so, but this long-established custom makes him more available for personal contact with reporters than any other major government leader in the world. These conferences are attended by scores of reporters who hold White House credentials, in addition to the regular men on the beat.

Custom limits a presidential news conference to a half hour, at the end of which time the senior reporter present says, "Thank you, Mr. President" and the newsmen dash for the door. They are not permitted to leave during a conference, no matter how momentous the story they have to file.

Frequently a President will discuss so many subjects in a single news conference that it will produce several stories. There might be a story on a critical development in Russian-American relations, another on his plans for the political campaign, and a third about problems of the federal budget. The press associations carry a single dispatch including all these angles plus separate stories on the most important topics.

When the President travels, he is accompanied by reporters for the press associations and the radio and television networks and, within the limits of available space, by reporters of individual newspapers. The newsmen follow the President in separate automobiles or airplane. Rarely are the White House newsmen out of close touch with the President and his staff, no matter where he goes.

How Congress Is Covered

Coverage of Congress falls into two categories. The first is news the reporters obtain while attending public debates and committee hearings of the Senate and House of Representatives. The second is the material they gather in personal conversations with the lawmakers and their staffs. If a reporter develops good contacts and shows that he can be trusted, he can obtain many stories and news angles from these men, most of whom are publicity-conscious.

Some Senators and Representatives are the key figures in party strategy and in directing the movement of legislation through Congress; others are specialists in such fields as foreign affairs, atomic energy, and finance. Like a man on any beat, the experienced congressional reporter learns where to turn for certain kinds of information, which men are the best informed and most reliable, and which are merely trying to use him for their own purposes.

The following story, by a congressional reporter for the New York *Herald Tribune*, illustrates how a well-informed writer presents a news situation, even when he is not able to quote any source directly. Such a dispatch can be written only because the reporter has talked privately to men close to the situation.

House Under Pressure to Vote On Senate-Passed Labor Bill

By Rowland Evans Jr.

WASHINGTON—Backstage pressures are pushing the House toward a vote on the Senate labor-reform bill, it appeared tonight.

The Democrats, it can be stated, are fearful of the political hazards of permitting Congress to adjourn without at least a strong public effort to get the measure passed. A roll-call vote in the House is the minimum object of these powerful Democratic forces.

The Democrats are worried that their failure to get the Senate-passed bill to the House floor for a vote could tip the political balance against several Democratic candidates in key election races this fall. They also fear it could tag the Democrats generally as the party that lacked courage to stamp out labor union abuses.

Rayburn Is Target

For these and other reasons, Speaker Sam Rayburn, D., Tex., is under exceptional pressures to invoke a little-used parliamentary device to bring the reform bill to a vote. This device provides for a suspension of the rules on the first and third Mondays of the month, under which any bill can be taken from committee and voted on after forty minutes of debate in the House. To pass, a two-thirds vote is required.

This provision, contained in Rule 27, also provides for suspension of the rules during the last six days of a session, but precisely how that part of the rule could be used was uncertain because of the apparent impossibility to predict the exact day of adjournment ahead of time and thus assure that the action would be taken during the last six days.

The Senate bill was authored by Sen. John F. Kennedy, D., Mass., and Senator Irving M. Ives, R., N.Y. It passed the Senate 88 to 1 last spring, then lay on Rep. Rayburn's Speaker's desk in the House for forty days, when it was dispatched to the hostile Labor Committee.

Both Houses of Congress have press galleries where reporters can watch the floor debate and take notes. All statements made in the debate are privileged. Behind the galleries are long, bustling press rooms in which the reporters have their typewriters, telephones, and telegraph facilities.

Many of the biggest congressional stories come from committee hearings, held in special rooms some distance from the main debating chambers. Some of these sessions are closed to reporters, especially when members are discussing matters involving national security. However, by talking to committeemen after the meetings reporters at times can obtain printable information about the general trend of the discussion. Edited transcripts of the testimony, with secret material deleted, are sometimes made public later.

Public hearings on controversial bills and investigations held to determine the need for legislation are fast-breaking, exciting stories to cover. Among the spectacular ones in recent years are those involving labor, crime, unethical influences in government, foreign affairs, and alleged subversion. The hearing rooms are jammed with reporters, cameramen, and spectators. What the witnesses testify before the committee is privileged, but what they say to reporters in the corridors is not. Some refuse to answer questions from the committee, pleading the protection of the Fifth Amendment against incriminating themselves. At times this refusal leads to indictments for contempt of Congress.

Government Departments

There are press rooms in the government departments to which the press associations and larger newspaper bureaus assign men on a beat basis. The departments have public information men who issue handouts about activity in their offices. Reporters supplement these with personal talks with department officials and occasional press conferences with the cabinet member in charge. In recent years there have been charges by the newsmen that some public relations officials are more concerned with concealing legitimate news, which might be politically or personally embarrassing to their superiors, than in helping to give the public the information about its government to which it is entitled. Many stories with local angles come from the departments, such as those about construction of public works and awarding of contracts.

Typical of the stories which can be developed on a department beat is the following, written by the Associated Press reporter assigned to the Agriculture Department.

Farmers Union Urges Increase In Federal Aid Programs

WASHINGTON (AP)—The militant National Farmers Union is sounding a rallying call of those who believe the nation needs far-reaching federal farm programs.

The call comes when the government appears to be moving in the other direction—that of putting farmers more on their own than they have been for many years.

The Eisenhower administration, with which the Farmers Union has been at odds on policies and politics, has the upper hand in its drive toward reducing government's role in agriculture.

Hits Administration

The Farmers Union says that since the present administration took office in 1953 it has been weakening farm programs and putting farmers at an economic disadvantage.

For years, the Farmers Union has battled for legislation that would, it says, guarantee the family farm good prices and incomes. It has advocated measures to provide for government price fixing and government proration of farm income among all producers.

The administration, with the backing of the strong American Farm Bureau Federation, wants farmers to make their own way in a competitive market. It would emphasize efficiency of production, with the inefficient being encouraged, if not forced, to find other pursuits.

Under the administration theory, government would largely limit its farm aid to promotion of markets and research.

Book Is Challenge

The Farmers Union has challenged the administration program in a new booklet, "The Farmer's Share."

Holding that the administration's policies offer farmers no hope of equitable shares of the national income, the Farmers Union says bargaining power is the producer's only hope.

"The strong bargaining power possessed by industry has been acquired by strenuous efforts to expand exports and domestic consumer demand while at the same time controlling supply and thereby controlling prices," the book says.

"In self-protection, farmers must learn to build similar devices which they can use to operate a workable market protection system of farmer-controlled private and public farm commodity marketing operations."

Notice how the reporter has combined a spot news element, the issuance of a new book, with a background summary to build his story. He has woven in an impartial sketch of the two opposing viewpoints and added a reportorial conclusion—that the Eisenhower administration "has the upper hand."

Interpretive Reporting

Not all stories coming from Washington involve urgent, exciting developments. Many of the most important discuss evolving situations and trends. Here is a primary function of the public affairs reporter: to look beyond the day-by-day developments and keep his readers posted concerning the deeper currents of political thought and action. What he says in such stories cannot be pinned entirely upon quotable sources; he must gather views and facts from several places, examine his material for a pattern, and present it to the reader in a cohesive, meaningful form. This is interpretive reporting, as contrasted to the hard-and-fast factual presentation of the police beat. His own integrity and experienced judgment are important factors in giving such stories significance. The farm policy story just quoted falls into the interpretive category.

Interpretive political reporting is a challenge to a reporter's newsgathering and writing abilities, and inherent in it are several dangers. The peril of injecting his personal views, or those of his publisher, into the story is great. It is easy to give a political situation a partisan slant, since so many intangible factors are involved. Perhaps the reporter has assembled a substantial body of information—public opinion polls, the reports of campaign workers, the private views of leaders in both parties—that indicates that the Democrats are likely to win control of the Senate in the next election. Yet he happens to be a vigorous Republican. If he is a good public affairs reporter he will write his story so that the reader cannot discover whether he is pleased or displeased by the trend he is recording.

Another pitfall is caused by laziness. Since political writing involves generalities, a glib reporter can turn out stories about what he thinks will happen, without doing the research the

Top: Washington columnists Doris Fleeson, United Features, and Marquis Childs, St. Louis *Post-Dispatch*. Center: news commentators Eric Sevareid, CBS, and Joseph C. Harsch, NBC and *Christian Science Monitor*. Bottom: reporters who became executive editors, James Russell Wiggins, Washington *Post and Times Herald*, and James S. Pope, Louisville *Courier-Journal*.

Washington newsmen in action: above, John Hightower (left), Associated Press chief diplomatic correspondent, and AP's John Scali make notes as a Secretary of State, John Foster Dulles, talks at Washington airport. Below: Merriman Smith, White House correspondent for United Press International, interviews a controversial figure, Bernard Goldfine.

stories should have. Some political reporters have an unfortunate habit of interviewing each other, instead of going to the real news sources. The speculative stories they write, leaning on background instead of legwork, are known sometimes as "writing it off the west wall." Background knowledge is essential, but it is not a substitute for hard reporting effort!

With hundreds of Washington reporters scrambling for the available news, grossly exaggerated stories of political quarrels and disputes are sometimes published. Because conflict makes headlines, some political reporters strain too hard to create feuds and disagreements. Both political parties are constantly seeking campaign issues, too, and some of their members (not all!) are quick to seize upon any apparent discrepancy in the other side's actions or some fancied slight to whip up a quarrel. In reporting legitimate disputes and the clash of conflicting viewpoints, the political reporter must constantly guard against becoming an overeager sensation-monger or a tool for self-seekers just to make a story. The result of too much crisis-and-quarrel reporting is to give the public a false impression of how the machinery of government actually functions.

Covering Political Campaigns

The presidential election every four years and the congressional elections at two-year intervals are busy periods for political reporters. Politics in Washington never ceases, because officeholders and those who seek their jobs always have an eye on the next election. They know that many voters make their decisions upon an accumulation of issues and events, not last-minute campaign oratory. So in a sense, most stories out of Washington are political stories. In a campaign, however, the task of the political reporter reaches its climax.

The presidential nominating conventions of the Democratic and Republican parties receive coverage from hundreds of reporters, radio and television commentators, and cameramen. Newsmen circulate in the convention hall, through hotel corridors, committee rooms, state delegation headquarters, and social gatherings, seeking information about the line-up of delegate votes for the contending candidates. Since a televised picture of convention proceedings is now brought into millions of homes, the reporters for the printed media must search harder than ever for backstage stories, interpretation of developments, and human interest feature stories. A large press workroom is provided at the convention hall, and additional facilities are available in some hotels.

For many years the presidential candidates toured the country in special trains making "whistle stop" tours of large and small cities, showing themselves to the voters. A campaign train assignment was much sought after because of the big stories it produced and the excitement of traveling, but it was hard work. A special press room car was included in the presidential special. Recently, presidential candidates have been doing most of their traveling by airplane and depending upon television to bring their images close to the voters in many regions.

National headquarters of the two political parties in Washington become major news sources around election time and turn out a barrage of press releases, speech texts, and statements. Senatorial and congressional candidates have campaign offices in their home cities, and election activities dominate the Washington headquarters of those already in office.

A single word describes the reporter's goal in campaign coverage: balance. When a prominent candidate makes an accusation against his opponent, no matter how fantastic, it must be reported, so long as it isn't a glaring piece of libel; but the other man deserves equal space for his defense and for presentation of his charges.

During every election there are partisan cries of a "one-party press" (because the editorial policy of the majority of American newspapers is Republican) and of distortion and unequal political coverage. While there is some basis for these charges, the general level of fairness in political coverage in American newspapers has been rising steadily. Some newspapers continue to distort their news for partisan purposes, but most contemporary editors are aware of their responsibility and do their best to keep their news columns balanced. They try to keep editorial opinions where they belong, on the editorial page and in signed columns.

Because news ebbs and flows, and political stories must compete with other events for the available news space, one party or the other may have an edge in wordage printed on any single day. This is unavoidable. The real test is to add up the total space after a campaign is over and to see whether the statements of all candidates are printed with equal objectivity or whether some stories are peppered with innuendo and derogatory or laudatory phrases.

State Capital Reporting

Coverage of state capitals is similar to Washington reporting, but it is on a smaller scale. Reporters have press conferences with the governor and his leading officials, attend debates and committee hearings of the legislature, and make the rounds of government offices, building their contacts and hunting for news leads.

Some newspapers have a staff man covering the state offices at all times, especially if the capitol is in the state's largest city. Others send a reporter there only during sessions of the legislature, or on special assignment, and depend upon the press associations for daily coverage. The story of George Thiem and the Hodge scandal in Illinois, described in an earlier chapter, shows what a state capital reporter can accomplish.

Summary

Reporting of public affairs is specialized, responsible, and rather glamorous work. Much information is obtained at social functions. Those engaged in such reporting come to know the prominent personalities of the political scene, often on a first-name basis, and get an insight into the workings of government obtained by few other citizens. The opportunities for enterprise and interpretive reporting are large, and so are the perils of personal prejudice and of publishing misleading information, intentionally or unintentionally. The principles involved in public affairs reporting are identical with those on other beats: Know your sources, keep your coverage objective and accurate, and look beyond the obvious for the real story.

Chapter **15**

Becoming a Foreign Correspondent

The Role of the Reporter Abroad

The most glamorous sounding of all newspaper jobs is being a foreign correspondent. Young reporters dream of drawing such an assignment, of living in faraway places, mingling with diplomats and men of world renown, and flying from one global trouble spot to another for by-line stories.

The foreign correspondent does have extremely interesting work. But like all jobs, there are unpleasant sides to it, and frequently there is as much unexciting routine as in covering a local city hall beat. The purpose of this chapter is to give students a realistic look at these overseas assignments and perhaps help them to decide whether they wish to point their efforts toward one.

Since the United States has assumed a dominant place in world affairs as an outgrowth of the second world war, the role of the American correspondent overseas has taken on additional importance. He is not writing about something remote and of only academic interest to the average newspaper reader; the things he sees and reports have a direct effect upon every taxpayer's pocketbook and perhaps upon his survival. The impact of foreign news upon the reader is much greater today than it was a few decades ago. The coming of the jet airplane has reduced travel time to all parts of the earth, and development of nuclear and missile warfare has almost wiped out the Atlantic

244

and Pacific oceans as barriers protecting our country from attack. Thus the American reader today has a personal stake in the news he receives from abroad.

Also, the foreign correspondent is writing for a much better informed public than he did earlier in this century. If his dispatch carries a dateline from one of the major world capitals such as London, Paris, or Tokyo, he can assume that many of his readers have been to the city themselves. Thousands upon thousands of American military men were sent abroad during World War II and the Korean conflict. In most cases this was their first contact with countries other than their own. The swift expansion of commercial air service has also made foreign travelers of far more Americans than ever before. It follows that the better informed his readers are, the better prepared the correspondent must be.

The first requirement for a foreign correspondent is to be a good reporter. All the attributes of accuracy, persistence, objective judgment, and ingenuity which help make a good police reporter are necessary for a foreign correspondent. Also he must have a sense of history; that is, a realization that the events he is reporting are part of a continuing stream and the factors which govern today's developments may lie far in the past. If possible he should be well versed in the history and economy of the country to which he is assigned. This cannot be expected in all cases, but at least he should have a strong general preparation and interest in world history. Closely coupled with this, he must possess political awareness. Much of his work will involve diplomacy—that is, international politics—and the domestic political affairs of his assigned country.

Another desirable bit of equipment is a knowledge of at least one foreign language. Many correspondents abroad have functioned quite successfully without having a command of any language beyond English, yet all of them would agree that their work would have been easier had they known at least the rudiments of French, Spanish, or German for reading and conversation. If the reporter does not know the language of his assigned country when he first goes there, he should immediately set about learning it. Perhaps his news sources speak English better than he can learn to speak their tongue; nevertheless, his willingness to try makes them more sympathetic to him. Ability to read the country's newspapers without the delay and expense of a translation also speeds his work.

How extensive are the opportunities for a well-qualified reporter to become a foreign correspondent? Unfortunately, they are rather limited. The cost of maintaining a staff reporter overseas, both his living expenses and his cable bills, is so great that only a few wealthy and internationally minded American newspapers have their own men abroad. Most newspapers depend upon the press associations for their foreign news, and it is with these organizations that the greatest opportunity lies overseas.

The press associations have offices throughout the world, frequently with the double function of gathering foreign news for American readers and delivering a news report from the United States to foreign newspapers. The latter task requires a substantial number of men, some of them Americans, but much of the work is unexciting desk routine. For the more stimulating and exacting task of reporting foreign developments back to the United States, the press associations depend primarily upon American reporters in the major capitals. Part of this work, too, is handled by men who are citizens of the foreign countries. In more remote and less newsworthy cities, the staff of the American news agency consists of native citizens, possibly with one American as head of the office. Thus the number of jobs for American reporters abroad in the press associations is less than many persons believe.

The men whom the press associations send abroad have been trained in the domestic service and are usually given a period of preparation on the foreign news desk in New York, editing and doing rewrite on the dispatches coming in from overseas. The best way to get overseas with a wire service is to do an outstanding job in a domestic bureau and make known to the management your desire to go abroad when the opportunity arises. Sometimes a press association will hire an American newsman who applies in person at a foreign bureau.

Among the newspapers which maintain staffs of their own men abroad are the New York *Times,* New York *Herald Tribune,* the

Chicago *Daily News,* Chicago *Tribune,* Baltimore *Sun,* and the *Christian Science Monitor.* Some of these sell their foreign service to other American papers as a valuable supplement to the press association dispatches. Other American papers may keep one man on roving assignment overseas or send men abroad periodically on short trips. The newspapers usually fill their foreign jobs with men who have spent several years on the local staff and are well informed as to the paper's news coverage needs.

How Foreign News Is Gathered

An American reporter working abroad has fewer firm, easily tapped news sources than his colleague on the police beat at home. He is less able to obtain flat statements of fact or policy and has more difficulty in reaching the men whose opinions really count in international affairs. He must lean more heavily upon his background to interpret the significance of what has happened because his distant audience cannot be expected to catch the implications of events as it does when reading a local political story.

On the other hand, the foreign correspondent must guard against losing his reportorial instincts and depending more heavily upon pompous "heavy thinking" than upon determined legwork.

American reporters are generally more forthright in questioning high officials than foreign newsmen are, largely because they have less awe of the offices these men hold. But the reporter must conform with the pattern of the community in which he is working; if he tries to push his news sources too hard or trap them into making statements, he may find himself receiving little information. The principle of making friends on the beat is just as important in foreign reporting as on the local staff.

The workings of the British parliamentary system afford a good example of the peculiar limitations newsmen encounter abroad. London is more like an American city from a news and language standpoint than any other foreign post, yet even there the rules for reporting are different.

In the United States our federal government department heads and cabinet members hold press conferences to report their views and decisions. Sometimes they contradict each other and their President. British cabinet members cannot do so. They are ministers of the crown and members of Parliament and must make all their policy statements to the legislative body. An on-the-record policy statement by a British prime minister or cabinet member to a newsman is a severe breach of protocol not to be tolerated. This has given rise to the "informed source" system, especially in the Foreign Office. Sometimes the foreign secretary wants the world to know his government's views on a news development quickly, without waiting for a meeting of Parliament. So one of his assistants gives the word to reporters, who credit the information in their stories as having come from a reliable or informed source. Thus the foreign secretary stays within the bounds of parliamentary etiquette and still makes his views known. The London newspapers get many of their stories on this "leak" basis, both from the government and from Buckingham Palace. Each foreign capital has its own set of coverage rules, and the American correspondent must learn to play the game accordingly.

Among the chief sources of news leads in a foreign city are its newspapers. The correspondent must watch them carefully. Sometimes he can write a story quoting a paper as his source; in other circumstances he must seek confirmation for the story through his regular news sources. Many newspapers abroad are controlled by political parties, a fact which colors their views and often their news stories. The correspondent must learn which journals he can depend upon for accuracy. In some countries there are domestic news associations, comparable to our Associated Press and United Press International, whose services he can buy. But much of his work must be accomplished, just as it is at home, by legwork and a constant eye for angles.

In Moscow, where much news of world significance is made, foreign correspondents are largely limited to reporting what is published in the government-controlled newspapers and magazines. On rare occasions they may talk with a high Soviet official at a diplomatic reception, but interviews, press conferences, and the other newsgathering devices common in this country are rarely permitted. Government censors allow little speculation and background discussion in dispatches.

The foreign correspondent's job can be dangerous. When a war threat develops he must be on the spot, up in front seeing for himself. Overnight he can change from a foreign diplomatic correspondent to a front line war correspondent. Many newspapermen lost their lives in pursuit of their assignments in the second world war and in Korea. The scroll in the Overseas Press Club in New York listing the names of American newsmen killed on the job is long and filled with famous names.

With our American armed forces spread widely around the world, the correspondent does extensive reporting business with military officers. He needs a general knowledge of how our army, navy, and air forces are organized and how to obtain stories without violating the security restrictions.

Another aspect he must watch is to reflect the thinking and moods of the country to which he is assigned without becoming a spokesman or propagandist for it. To avoid this peril, the press associations and newspapers bring their correspondents home on leave from time to time, to refresh their American viewpoint and keep them in touch with their readers' interests. Men are moved from one country to another for this same reason. Thus any foreign correspondent lives an uncertain life, ready to move on from one post to another as the news situation dictates.

Censorship is one of the foreign correspondent's recurring problems. In peacetime there are no restrictions on filing dispatches from most free world capitals. But the heavy hand of the government censor is constantly at work in Moscow and intermittently at work in sensitive areas where unrest develops. Some foreign governments clamp on such restrictions whenever the situation in their countries becomes unstable, frequently as part of a martial law proclamation. Sometimes censorship is open, that is, the reporter submits his story to the censor, is permitted to see what that official cuts out, and perhaps can argue against the decisions. Blind censorship is more insidious; the reporter turns in his copy to the censor and is not allowed to see what is removed. A third type is indirect censorship. The host government gives the correspondent a set of general censorship principles and informs him that if he fails to obey them he will be ousted from the country. No actual blue penciling is done, but the government may tell the newsman at any moment that he has violated the spirit of the code and must leave the country immediately.

Getting his dispatches back to his home office presents a challenge to the foreign correspondent under some circumstances. Cable, commercial wireless, and overseas telephone are the three methods for fast transmission, all of them rather expensive. When working in a major world capital the correspondent has easy access to these fast transmission services, but when he goes out into an obscure region to cover military action or political developments he must often depend upon facilities that are subject to delay and uncertainty. A cardinal rule that the press associations hammer home to their men abroad is that no story is better than its transmission. The correspondent must become a communications expert as well as a reporter, a problem that does not exist for his colleagues at home where the telephone is always available. The press associations have developed such elaborate radio communications systems that urgent news can be transmitted to newspapers around the world in a few seconds.

Changing Trends in Foreign Reporting

The role of the foreign correspondent has been changing as the American people become more aware of world affairs. Editors are demanding more background stories to give breadth and meaning to the spot news developments and more stories about the way people abroad live and think. The correspondent must move outside the restricted fields of diplomacy and politics into the lives of ordinary people. Some of his best stories may be obtained while sitting in a sidewalk cafe or browsing in a store. What the people are saying and what they are buying, if suitably reported, can be of much interest to his readers. The foreign dateline adds enchantment, and people everywhere are intrigued by the affairs of another human being.

The development of radio and TV reporting from abroad has

contributed to this shift in the newspaper correspondent's role. Frequently the man on the scene is beaten on the spot break of a major story by an official announcement broadcast to the world. While his dispatch, reaching his paper a few hours later, may not be first with the news, it puts the developments in perspective and fills in the background. The correspondents for individual papers often leave the urgent reporting of fresh developments to the press associations and concentrate in their own dispatches upon the significance of the events.

Reporting the United Nations

Recent decades have seen a change in the major bases for foreign reporting, reflecting the shift in the centers of political power. Before the second world war the most important datelines were London, Paris, Berlin, and Tokyo because it was in these cities that decisions affecting the entire world were made. Today the prime centers of global power are the United States and Russia. Thus Washington has become a key dateline and gathering place for the newsmen of the world. Moscow would be, too, except for the severe restrictions placed upon reporters there. The European capitals remain important as news centers, of course, although the stories originating in those cities are frequently reactions to American developments rather than reports of great decisions taken there. Tokyo is the most important news center in the Far East.

A new dateline of much importance has come into being since the second world war—the United Nations. At this modernistic structure in New York is gathered a large and polyglot press corps from all corners of the earth. The American press associations maintain bureaus there, and many newspapers have correspondents accredited to the world organization. The UN is a fertile field for reporting, since spokesmen for a large majority of the world's countries mingle in its corridors. In the lounges and conference rooms the newsmen can talk informally with eminent statesmen. While the United Nations dispatches which receive the most attention are those involving debates in the Security Council and General Assembly, there is a rich vein of material available not only in the political field but in economic and social matters as well. The broad activities of the United Nations have made it a clearinghouse for valuable statistics and source material in dozens of fields. The reporter fortunate enough to draw the United Nations assignment for his paper has taken an encouraging step toward becoming a foreign correspondent.

Part Four

VARYING THE
WRITING

Chapter 16

Different Styles of News Writing

Variations in Presentation

We turn now from the discussion of newsgathering techniques to an examination of the many ways a news story can be written. Earlier in this book you were instructed in the traditional pyramid method of telling a news story and were told briefly that variations of this method are sometimes employed. In this and the next three chapters you will learn more about these variations in writing technique and the forms of specialized news writing and reporting widely used in contemporary newspapers.

Examine any daily newspaper and you will discover quickly that most news stories are written in the pyramid style. But if the paper you are studying is well edited, it will also contain some stories which do not follow the pyramid rules. In fact they may be written in just the reverse manner. The purpose of these variations is to make the paper more interesting, to give it zest the way a clever chef includes tangy seasoning in some of his dishes. Just as the chef must exercise good judgment in deciding which foods should receive that extra pinch of spice, so the newswriter must use caution in deciding which stories will profit from the application of unorthodox writing techniques and which will suffer.

Presentation of the day's major news developments, the "hard" news that readers need if they are to be kept abreast of important world and local developments, is usually in the pyramid form. It is easier to use, faster to write, and more easily revised if developments require. The variations of writing to be discussed in this chapter are used most frequently for stories of a feature nature. When handling these the writer usually has more time to work. Often he is concerned almost as much with telling his story in an interesting, and possibly entertaining, manner as in delivering to the reader a set of facts.

The Chronological Story

When the reporter writes of events in the order they happened, letting one action or statement lead into another, he is following a narrative technique of the storyteller. Some editors call this a running story. This method can be used effectively when extensive physical action is involved, and hence it is often seen in the sports section in reports of football and baseball games. Reports of disasters and controversial public meetings also can employ this technique, at least in a modified form. The reporter who uses the chronological method needs assurance that his story will have ample space, because editing down a chronological account to meet space limitations is more difficult than cutting a pyramid story.

A chronological story may open with a short lead, summarizing the basic facts of what happened, and then go into a detailed running account. Or it may start in the middle of the action and go on from there; this form is a feature treatment. In an account of a series of incidents which conclude in a climactic action—an argument at home, a few drinks, a car ride, an arrest by police who tell the man the wife he argued with earlier has slashed her throat—the reporter who has the space lets the story tell itself just as it happened, without attempting any sort of summary lead opening.

Notice in the following story from the Cleveland *Plain Dealer* how the chronological method is used to catch the reader's attention in the opening paragraph and then carries him along into an explanation of the "why" of the action.

New Eight-Ton Gun Carrier Will Be Built Here

Tests Prove Durability of Weapon Which Is to Be Air-Dropped

By Ted Princiotto

An eight-ton, tank-like gun carrier, the M-56, was dropped 10 feet to the concrete floor of a hanger here one day last week with a terrific, ear-blasting whoomp.

Instrument dials fluttered and a cloud of dust rose as the olive-drab monster, mounted with a 90-millimeter rifle, bounced heavily and settled with a crunching noise.

The impact of the free drop, from an overhead electric crane, was softened by thick, stiff sheeting of honeycomb cardboard strapped to the bottom of the vehicle.

In places the honeycomb sheeting showed no sign of the terrific pounding.

Moments later engineers at the Cleveland Ordnance Plant, sometimes called the tank plant, moved in to run their eyes and hands over the gun carrier.

Looking for "Goofs"

They were looking for engineering "goofs."

Then an Army sergeant in coveralls climbed inside the vehicle, switched on the ignition key and listened to the motor lurch into action. Satisfied, he switched it off again.

The drop was another in a series of successful tests as the M-56, the Army's new lightweight gun carrier, goes into production here. It's a versatile weapon designed to be airborne and dropped.

Officials of the General Motors Corp.'s Cadillac Division, which operates the tank plant, say they are ready to start production under a 17-million-dollar contract for the M-56, which had its birth on drawing boards five years ago.

Cadillac received its order last March for the revolutionary vehicle—built of aluminum except for its gun and recoil system.

Dropped with 'Chutes

The M-56, which resembles a tank in appearance, also has passed its actual flying drop tests, sailing safely to the ground beneath six parachutes from 1,200 to 1,500 feet high.

Latest of these tests, the first with a honeycomb cardboard pallet, or bed, was made Friday at Jefferson Arsenal in southern Indiana.

The dead drop at the hangar, according to Capt. Louis Perterka of the Army Quartermaster Evaluation

Agency at Fort Lee, Va., simulates the actual aerial drop with parachutes.

At the hanger, engineers estimated the M-56 was dropping at a rate of 25 feet a second when it hit the floor, which, incidentally, was undamaged.

The crane and aerial drops have been going on the last few months before Cadillac starts producing the M-56 in large numbers.

Some have been turned out as new tooling and production lines are being completed at the mammoth plant, used in World War II to make bomber parts.

The honeycomb cardboard pallet is a new feature of the tests. The sheeting consists of hundreds of small cardboard sections, much tougher but similar in construction to packages used for eggs.

It is lighter and uses up less space than bags of kapok, the lifejacket material, out of which earlier pallets were made.

The M-56 contains about 8,000 pounds of aluminium, bolted in sections similar to aircraft construction, rather than welded as is steel armor. Unlike the tank, it is not armored. Its alumium skin cannot take heavy fire.

It is designed to furnish mobile, powerful firepower to airborne troops, who in the past have been forced to fight without heavy artillery.

Its speed has been rated at 30 miles an hour, but may be higher. Its performance data are classified in many respects. It will be handled by a three-man crew of driver, loader and gunner, who parachute down on their own.

When dropped the M-56 will carry about 1,000 pounds of ammunition.

The Suspended Interest Story

This kind of news treatment is similar to the chronological technique as illustrated above. In that story the reader's interest was kept in suspension, waiting for the purpose of the action to be explained. He did not obtain all the basic facts from reading the first two paragraphs.

In most suspended interest stories, the writer holds back a key fact until the very end, just as writers of short fiction sometimes do. It is the unexpected twist or "kicker" at the close which gives the entire story its point. The mood of suspended interest is difficult to maintain without some giveaway clues; therefore it is used most commonly on brief quirk stories.

Here are two short examples of the suspended interest technique, the first one successful and the second only partially so.

DETROIT (AP)—Elmer Larson, a Southern Michigan Prison guard, brought inmate William Thomas to attend the funeral of Thomas' sister yesterday.

"I just hate to take a man wearing handcuffs to a funeral," Larson said later.

He had taken handcuffs off Thomas so the inmate could attend the funeral unencumbered. A minute later, Larson turned his back and Thomas fled the funeral and the prison term he was serving for carrying concealed weapons.

The writer's secret, the point of the story, was not disclosed until the final sentence. However, in the following example the writer gave away his point in the first paragraph. By more careful writing, he might have kept the reader guessing until the end.

CANBERRA, AUSTRALIA (AP)—Four escaped convicts, two officially described as "desperate and dangerous," surprised Mrs. Jimmie Kolp, wealthy airwoman of Wichita Falls, Tex., with their gallantry.

Mrs. Kolp, driving at night with two Australian airwomen, was stranded on a lonely country road with a flat tire and a broken jack.

"We were looking helpless when four young men drove up," Mrs. Kolp said today.

"Three of them lifted our car while the fourth fitted a jack under the axle. They seemed pleasant enough—but later we found their descriptions tallied exactly with the four escaped convicts."

Police are still seeking the convicts.

Sometimes skillful writing can sustain the suspended interest mood throughout a longer story, as in this example from a press association wire. Note that the headline and the opening paragraphs tell the reader the character of the story—impending tragedy—but do not clearly indicate the outcome. Note, too, how sentence length and paragraphing convey the mood of the story. It appeared on front pages of newspapers throughout the country because the writer successfully maintained suspense.

Tot Dies 'in Traffic'

Estate Built on Fear Fails

PASADENA, CALIF.(UPI)—A year ago, mural artist J. H. Zorthian read of how a tiny boy had been killed in traffic.

Zorthian became obsessed with the fear that the same thing might happen to one of his own children. The more he thought about it, the more fearful he became.

At last he cancelled his negotiations for a home in Pasadena and sought a place where his children would be safe.

He put aside all his work while scheming means of keeping his children safe from harm.

He thought of everything. First he bought 12 acres perched on a mountain at the end of a winding, narrow road. At each turn along the road he posted signs: "Children at Play."

Before starting work on the house itself, Zorthian personally built and fenced a play yard for his three children.

He built it in such a way that it was impossible for a car to get within 50 feet of it.

Then he built the house, putting into it all the careful design that he concentrated in the murals he has hanging in 42 public buildings in eastern cities.

Only this time, the design was for safety as well as beauty.

Finally he built the garage. Only one auto ever drove up to it. That was Zorthian's.

Then he surveyed every possibility of danger to the children. He could think of only one remaining hazard. He had to back in and out of the garage.

He might back over one of the children.

He immediately made plans to build a protected turnabout. He was going to pour the concrete for it last week.

However, the first rain fell in many weeks of a long California drouth, preventing him from doing so.

If it had not rained, the turn-about would have been completed by Sunday when Zorthian's 18-month-old son, Tiran, squirmed away from his sister's grasp and ran behind the car as Zorthian backed it from the garage. The child was killed instantly.

The Humorous Story

Humor in a news story is an uncertain commodity. Everyone enjoys a laugh, and the reporter who can give his readers some chuckles is a fortunate man. However, many writers are not as funny as they believe themselves to be. Forced, artificial humor is painful to the reader. If you have a whimsical touch, or a clever turn of phrase, use it; but if such writing does not come easily, leave it to someone else. A writer trying to be humorous without the natural instincts for it causes much the same reaction as a young girl seeking attention with a false attempt at cuteness: "isn't that silly?"

In most cases the newspaper writer should let the facts tell themselves. If they are funny and well presented, the reader will laugh. When writing humor, it is well to remember the technique of most successful professional writers in this field—underplay it. The reader's imagination is strong, and he will add details and nuances to a humorous situation as he reads. They need not be spelled out for him to the last detail.

Remember: Most puns are much funnier when spoken than they are in print.

There is a big market in newspapers for brief humorous quirk or "brightener" stories, those little items tucked away at the bottom of a page or in a feature box. They add variety to the news. These involve situation humor rather than funny writing—unexpected twists in events, incongruous situations, misunderstandings, or anachronisms. They may have nothing to do with a traditional news situation.

A press association carried this two sentence story which was printed on dozens of front pages across the country.

> One of Florence Schroeder's new white shoes had a squeak, so she stepped into a puddle by the curb to soak it out. The puddle was tar.

The incongruity of this story amid the reports of politics and disaster struck the fancy of telegraph editors. Thousands of women readers, visualizing the situation, thought either "That might have happened to me" or "How could she be so stupid?" The writer had produced a funny story because the situation was humorous. A reporter should keep his eyes and ears open for short items of this sort as he goes about his beat and his daily assignments. They can be found in unexpected places.

For example, here is a whimsical little story which developed from the custom of sending Christmas cards to teachers:

SAN BERNARDINO, CALIF. (AP)—Teachers in a grade school here are agreed that at Christmas time the spirit's the thing, especially since many of their pupils come from families of foreign extraction who have a little trouble with their English.

Among the greetings received by the faculty yesterday were cards bearing these messages:

"For you, Grandma, on Valentine's Day."

"Thanks a million."

"Sincerest sympathy."

Building a Story with Direct Quotations

Almost every story of more than a hundred words is improved substantially if it contains direct quotations. From a visual standpoint, they break up the solid body of type and vary the reading pattern. They add authenticity, especially when the reporter is handling controversial matter. The reader feels that he is receiving the information precisely as the news source gave it out and not screened through the writer's mind with a possible shift in emphasis.

Use of the direct quotation at every possible moment is not good practice, however. It is pointless to base your lead upon what somebody said and then quote him directly in a later paragraph saying the same thing. The quotation should add something to the story.

A reporter's summary can pack more facts into a hundred words than a direct quotation of the same length can do. A writer experienced in handling speeches, public meetings, and similar stories in which many words are spoken learns to alternate summary and quotation. Unless the speaker has done so himself, and few of them do, the reporter summarizes the main points in his own words, then uses direct quotations to substantiate and expand the summary. The reporter can bridge long unimportant passages with a paraphrasing sentence or two of his own and then return to direct quotations for the speaker's next essential utterance.

Some writers, especially in the press associations, fall into the bad practice of using fragmentary direct quotes in their lead paragraphs in an effort to add authenticity. Rarely does this achieve its purpose, unless it points up a distinctive bit of the speaker's phraseology that is likely to stick in the reader's mind. Usually the result is merely a choppy lead. Partial quotations are sometimes necessary, however, to distinguish the source's words from the reporter's.

If a reporter were writing an account of Sir Winston Churchill's memorable wartime speech, it would be good technique for him to use a lead like this:

> LONDON—Prime Minister Churchill, praising the work of the R.A.F. fighter squadrons in the Battle of Britain, said today that "never in the field of human conflict was so much owed by so many to so few."

But the snatches of direct quotation in the following lead add nothing and only block the flow of thought.

> Governor Johnson warned today that the legislature must act "swiftly" in appropriating funds for flood control or the state will face "grave danger" of a disaster.

Another variation is to let a brief quotation standing alone serve as the entire lead.

> "I am prepared to fight all the way to the Supreme Court to prove my innocence, and I have plenty of friends to back me."
>
> That was Chester Sorenson's reply today to his conviction by a county court jury on two charges of embezzling funds from the Community Chest, of which he was treasurer until his resignation last month.

This form should be used sparingly. Its success depends upon the eye-catching quality of the quotation used.

The Off-Beat Lead

The writer can sometimes draw his readers into a story by using a lead that at first glance seems puzzling or irrelevant. He provokes the reader's interest, draws him into the story, and then explains his meaning in the second or third paragraph.

A rewrite man on the Detroit *Free Press* used that approach to handle the second-day lead on an accident report. His story is reproduced here not only because of the unusual lead, but because of the excellent detail and smooth chronological style used to develop the story.

Injured Boy Warns Other Young Bomb 'Fans'

'Drop It,' His Pal Shouted, *But Paul Seemed Dazed*

Paul Granaas wanted his picture taken Thursday. It wasn't the common desire of many to have their pictures in the paper.

Paul wanted other youngsters to see the danger of home-made bombs.

Paul, 14, of 4429 Tonawanda, Royal Oak, made a bomb. Wednesday evening he touched it off.

It blew off his left hand at the wrist. His right hand was badly injured. The blast shredded his clothing. His face was battered.

Paul was in William Beaumont Hospital Thursday.

Lt. James Soule of the Royal Oak Police was able to reconstruct the accident after he talked to Paul's two companions, Richard Dudchik, 15, of 4522 Elmwood, and Frederick Fritzman, 15, of 4620 Elmwood.

They and some of their friends have been making the bombs out of gunpowder and saltpetre. Paul made a big one, filling a piece of pipe eight inches long and 1½ inches in diameter. The ends were stuffed with cotton. A hole was drilled in one side for the fuse—a cigaret and a piece of string.

Wednesday evening they were walking along the Grand Trunk Western tracks on their way to the Kimball High School to go swimming. Paul pulled the powder-filled pipe out of his pocket.

Frederick was frightened. He ran off a little distance. Paul lit the fuse.

Richard screamed, "drop it, drop it." But Paul seemed in a daze.

The bomb burst with a roar that was heard for two miles. Paul, blackened with smoke, was left with the tatters of his clothing burning.

Frederick ran to him and tried to beat out the flames. Patrons at a nearby drive-in theater were stopped by a high fence from coming to Paul's aid, although they could see him running toward them and calling for help.

Finally they managed to boost one man over the fence. He got to Paul, put tourniquets on the boy's mangled arms and stopped the bleeding.

The man disappeared when police arrived to take Paul to the hospital but doctors there said he did an excellent job of first aid, and may have saved Paul's right hand.

Neighbors described Paul as a fine boy, an Air Scout and extremely interested in airplanes. He is a member of the Walther League at Our Shepherd Lutheran Church, 2225 E. Fourteen Mile, Birmingham.

The Use of Slang

Newspaper writing reflects the events and moods of the current day and is therefore more colloquial than that found in books and most magazines. This fact, however, should not be taken as a signal to use slang words indiscriminately in your stories.

True enough, from the slang of today come the new dictionary words of next year. But the men who elevate the words into acceptance in our ever changing language are selective. So should you be in using slang in news stories. We all use more colloquialisms in our conversation than we realize, and it is easy to write them into our stories. Slang has its place, and sometimes such a phrase is just what is needed to give a story the simple, direct, tart feeling it needs.

Use of slang should be intentional, to achieve a purpose, and not merely a written reflection of our colloquial speech habits. In most cases the use of the straightforward, accepted word is more effective. Overuse of slang is a greater danger for the headline writer than for the reporter, since the space limitations he faces force him to search constantly for brief ways of expressing a thought, and the slang phrase often offers that alluring brevity.

Slang is elusive. Such expressions mean different things to different people or may have no meaning at all to some readers. Thus much restraint should be exercised in its use.

Chapter 17

Writing the Feature Story

A Definition of Feature News

In earlier chapters we examined some aspects of developing feature ideas and interviews and techniques of reporting that are helpful in gathering the information for feature stories. Now we will discuss the methods of preparing this material in newspaper form.

The term "feature story" is open to many definitions. Perhaps each editor has a slightly different concept of what he means when he tells a reporter to write a feature. In simple definition we can draw a distinction between (1) "Hard" or "spot" news—the daily budget of local, national, and foreign stories a reader needs to keep informed about what is happening in the world and (2) Feature news—stories that the reader may not really need but which he finds interesting, informative, or entertaining and which give him an insight into how people live and think.

In practice the line between the two types is very thin. As we have seen, a hard news story can be given a feature treatment at times and become much more effective. Also, especially in foreign affairs, a feature story will provide background knowledge that adds significance to the spot developments. Much of the newspaper's function of reflecting contemporary civilization is carried out through its feature content.

There is no fixed formula for writing a feature story. The reporter has more freedom in this kind of writing than in hard news, and his stories tend to reflect his style and personality. Speaking broadly, feature writing shows much more of the writer's individuality than spot stories do, although the latter are frequently more challenging and difficult assignments.

The spot story moves from the general to the particular—a lead summarizes the fundamental facts of a situation and is followed by development in detail, substantiating and expanding the lead. The feature story often moves in the opposite direction, from the particular to the general. The lead may be based upon an eye-catching detail; then, having attracted its audience, the story broadens out into a statement of reasons and principles.

An excellent example of this technique is found in this story from the Tulsa (Okla.) *Tribune*. (Note incidentally that the reporter writes in the first person, a device sometimes used in feature stories when it adds to the effect. In this case it does.)

Ford Success Story —
It's the Women Again! —
Sketched On Diner's Napkin

By David Corbett

We had the Ford success story sketched for us on a napkin over lunch in Detroit the other day.

"Women," said the artist, "they're the ones who decide the styles for us these days."

George W. Walker, a Puckish man with small, smiling eyes and greying hair (a rarity in the youthful Ford hierarchy these days), grinned around the table at us. He is a Ford Motor Co. vice-president and director of styling.

"Do you realize that 80 per cent of the nation's merchandise is bought by women these days?" he demanded. We confessed we didn't.

"Or that one out of every three women drives an automobile?" We feigned surprise that we haven't really felt since the day the wife passed her driving test.

"The fact is that we design our cars to please the buying public," he continued.

"Now it used to be that the buying public was the men. In the old days they used to buy a car by looking under the hood and tinkering around, even though they didn't know what it was all about.

"And what sort of car did they get?"

He answered his own question by reaching for the napkin and deftly sketching on it an angular automobile of the 1927 era. Alongside he drew an almost equally angular siren of the "flapper" days, accompanied by a pugnosed bulldog.

"Now what does the new style car look like?" he continued. "Why, it's slip-streamed, like the women."

The charcoal pencil created what Walker described as a "modern doll," leading a poodle. In the background was a long, low Ford.

Some guy next to us had the nerve to say he didn't like the new Edsel anyway. "My wife does, though," he conceded.

"That's what counts," Walker quipped back. "You'll buy it."

Our luncheon session with Walker came at the end of the press preview of the new Ford.

The company's publicity men cleverly climaxed the two-day program by sliding back a partition at the end of the long dining room to reveal for the first time the new Thunderbird.

The timing was masterly—and no one has yet been able to figure out how they got that brand new beauty up to the fourth floor of the Sheraton-Cadillac Hotel under the noses of several hundred newsmen without being detected.

However, there it was, sweet and low as ever, and 23 inches longer and 5 inches wider.

It was a four-seater this year. Sales of the highly successful two-seater have totaled about 53,000 in the past three years, but the company this year is bowing to "overwhelming public demand for more room coupled with the Thunderbird features."

The new model has a wheelbase of 113 inches, 11 inches greater than last year. The car's over-all length is 205.4 inches, and the width has been increased to 75.4 inches.

Other features are more head room, greater ground clearance and an increase in trunk capacity of more than four cubic feet.

As to the standard Ford model itself—which was primarily what we went to see—company executives were almost apologetic about making so many radical changes to a model as successful as this year's.

"By past standards, we could be expected to shift a few pieces of chrome and call it a new model," conceded Vice President J. O. Wright.

Instead, the company has spent $185 million on the new power train and styling.

The reason for this (and we quote), is that "this major policy change is not only sound business, but it incorporates real benefits to the customers and to the economy.

"By bringing unprecedented newness to the market each year, Ford improves its sales position and spreads its cost over a wider base, thus helping to take some of the disadvantages out of a rising cost trend."

Asked if this *really* means a completely new model every

year, a spokesman replied, "Yes."

The company made great play during the preview of a new administrative technique which it calls the "quality audit." The system permits the tracing of any poor workmanship right back to the individual on the assembly line who permitted the flaw.

Plant auditors daily choose a random group of cars that have cleared the assembly line and report on their quality to the plant manager as well as to the head office in Dearborn.

If a plant does not establish and maintain a standard for quality which ranks with the best plants in the system, a team of experts is sent to find the reason why.

The system already has been in effect four months, and the company claims it has achieved a 50 per cent improvement in quality ratings during that time.

The authoritative word is that the auditors are soured employes who will take the kick out of any customer's complaint.

This story deserves our attention not only for its clever opening but for the smooth way in which the reporter blends in mechanical statistics along with a touch of personal opinion. His use of direct quotations adds substantially to the pace of the story. What might have been a routine business page story was turned into a report that attracts general readership, masculine and feminine alike.

A feature writer can build a story by using the reverse twist, as in the following example. Many accounts are written about how it feels to win a large amount of money in a contest or to inherit unexpected wealth. This reporter in the Los Angeles *Mirror-News* looked up a man who almost won, but didn't; the result is a feature with a chuckle.

Relative Bliss

Loses $64,000, Takes It Like Real Nonentity

Here's a man who prefers to be a nonentity.

Al Einfrank, who missed the $64,000 question on television a month ago, returned home to 8911 S. Hobart Blvd. yesterday after six days in a Tucson hospital getting over an attack of hypertension.

"I've got my health back

and I'm thankful my phone won't ring all day and half the night," said the 56-year-old Douglas Aircraft Co. truck driver.

Einfrank got himself in the family doghouse when he went for broke on the TV show. His wife was "struck dumb" when he lost the pot, but has recovered from the shock and "all is forgiven."

"I'm way ahead," said Einfrank. "I sold the $6000 car they gave me as a consolation prize and bought a $3000 automobile.

"All I lost was eight weeks' pay and a lot of relatives, and I'm a lot better off without them. If I'm called back for the '$64,000 Challenge' show, they won't be holding their hands out.

"I'm glad it's over. I don't want to be a celebrity. Let the actors have their glory. I want to be a nonentity."

The Feature Interview

In the chapter on interviewing we discussed the technique of preparing for and obtaining a feature interview. When the time comes to write his story, the reporter's first problem is to organize his material in such a way that he can include all of the source's major points. He must then decide which of these makes the most attractive lead and build his story around that point, weaving material about the interviewee's personality into the fabric of the interview.

Such an interview can be used to present an organization's point of view, making the material more attractive by focusing upon the personality and words of an organization leader—telling the story through an individual. It may be desirable to build such a lead around a characteristic of the person rather than any statement of views. There is only a small step from such a treatment to the outright personality sketch which some papers like to print.

Here is the first portion of such a feature interview in the St. Louis *Post-Dispatch*. Notice that the writer starts by giving the reader a pen sketch of the interviewee but soon broadens the story to make it a statement of her organization's policy given in her words. The reader who would not be inclined to spend time on a story which appeared to be solely about the organization is carried along by the human interest appeal of the headline and opening paragraphs.

Mrs. Annalee Stewart —
Portrait of a Peace Battler

By Mary Kimbrough

Mrs. Annalee Stewart is quite accustomed by now to her place on the unpopular side of many a national question. And when you talk to her, you know somehow that she thrives on it.

Not that she wants to fight. In fact, the only thing she will fight for is peace—between races and between nations. She's a pleasant, enthusiastic, dedicated and ladylike battler against war in all its forms.

One of the first five women in America to be ordained as a Methodist minister, back in 1924, Mrs. Stewart has devoted her life to concern over social and moral issues, more often in the congressional halls of Washington than in the pulpit of a church. Long an active worker for international peace, disarmament and civil rights, she is now national legislative secretary of the Women's International League for Peace and Freedom, and came to St. Louis last week to address the local branch of the 42-year-old institution.

Vehemently indorsing the league's stand for total disarmament, Mrs. Stewart is convinced that only this way lies security and ultimate peace.

"In the process of building up stockpiles of bombs, you create only hate and fear," she said. "The more one side builds, the more the other must build to keep pace. Where, then, is the answer, where is the security?"

The dark-haired, Illinois-born Washingtonian spends much of her time giving statistics-backed arguments to legislators about such controversial issues as conscription and the ending of nuclear tests. She frequently appears as a witness in congressional committees and rarely fails to make her point.

Recently Mrs. Stewart headed a delegation of 10 women leaders of the league to take a letter and petitions bearing nearly 10,000 signatures to President Eisenhower calling for an end to nuclear tests.

"We believe we represent millions of American women who view with deep disturbance any continuation of tests which may wreak incalculable hazards on the innocent unborn," she said. "We are against war and the preparation for war. We are against production, testing and use of nuclear weapons to any and all governments. We make no exceptions. We are not scientists and we are not competent to offer scientific judgments on the extent of the danger. But we can make moral judgments. We believe that as long as there is any question of danger to life anywhere, or real or possible menace to children yet unborn, no argument can justify such risks." However, Mrs. Stewart pointed out, the league would not end military production and the building of stockpiles of missiles without a companion plea for a redesigned economy to ward off financial depression.

The "Made" Feature

Nothing pleases a city editor more than a story which demonstrates a degree of imagination and the inquisitive nature of one of his reporters. A reporter is given a routine news release announcing a meeting of bee-keepers at an agricultural college campus; he interviews the professor in charge and comes up with a feature story describing exactly what it means to be "busy as a bee." A nightside reporter gazes at the lighted windows in downtown buildings; he wonders who is working in the predawn hours and finds a clean-up crew which moves from building to building while others sleep. A stamp-and-coin dealer is interviewed about the peculiarities of his customers. The chief operator for the telephone company in town tells a woman reporter how many times the switchboard operators have helped save lives in the past decade.

In this type of story there has been no immediate news event. The reporter, interested in his fellow humans, and inquisitive about what he sees or hears, is imaginative enough to say to himself, "Might be a story in this." For the beat reporter, such inquisitiveness is developed by familiarity with the people and scenes involved. The real "pay-off," insofar as catching the eye of the city editor is concerned, comes from thinking constantly, "This might make a story." A feature developed out of an off-hours experience demonstrates the professional news sense of the young reporter and his willingness to work. City editors, needless to say, like this.

Such was the case with Paul Cunningham, a beginning reporter for the Minneapolis *Star*, who later became an NBC television news and feature writer. Two "made" features helped carry him through the probationary period for young reporters and won for him preferred status in the eyes of the city desk. They were simple stories, but they were run with large illustrations on the front page of the local news section—with by-lines. The first story involved a minimum of reporting; Cunningham merely used his time profitably while sitting in the waiting room of a hospital maternity ward and turned in his story just before Father's Day.

Diary of Those Who Wait

Dads-to-Be Pen Own Tribute

By Paul Cunningham

Those who joke about nervous expectant fathers pacing up and down outside a maternity ward never thumbed through the "fathers' book" at Swedish hospital.

You'll find some humor in the "fathers' book," and some drama and simple philosophy, too. But mainly, the comments in it represent a tribute to Father's day, to be observed Sunday, and to the nervous ones who "waited."

The comments vary from the laconic jottings of the "old timer" to the jittery scrawl of the "first timer."

Placed in the waiting room of Swedish hospital's maternity ward, within earshot of the nursery, the book provides escape for pent-up emotions of fathers who have read all the magazines on hand and who still can't fall asleep in the big leather chairs.

Those awaiting the "big news" are invited to write their reactions and to compare them with others.

* * *

Dad may recognize the feelings of the fellow who wrote, "If ever there was a time when a man feels clumsy, helpless and meaningless, it is now."

Or of the man who said: "It is 3 a.m. and the last guy just left when he heard it was a boy. Gee, it is lonely here. I'm counting on you, Doc, to do your best as fast as possible."

Tension mounts with waiting.

A recent arrival wrote, "What a beautiful day I can tell my youngster it is."

The same fellow added, hours later: "All night and still no word. I'm getting so impatient I don't care whether it is a boy or a girl, just so it happens soon."

Not a few arrive in the waiting room out of breath, like the man who wrote, "Just got here and not much too soon. Sure gave the cab driver a scare. Next time I'll call the taxi a week ahead of time."

Others, like the soldier just home from Japan, had more

fortunate timing: "I was greeted at the door by my wife, who told me to hold the taxi. Some homecoming!"

* * *

More fathers are writing in the book personally now than during the war years covered in the book's early pages. Then the messages were written by relatives and friends doing the waiting for a soldier or sailor away in service.

Grandmothers, aunts, sisters, brothers, uncles, the woman next door or even the landlady of "that nice young girl whose husband is in France" have attested to the difficulty of "just waiting."

When they are there with Dad, they find his reactions good material for writing.

"I hope it is the real thing this time as I hate to see my brother go crazy for another week," one youth wrote.

* * *

The nurses at Swedish say they actually have less trouble with nervous fathers than with their mothers-in-law.

Last year, the hospital had its all-time high in births, 2,664, and the nurses report that "they didn't lose a father."

According to Mrs. Anna Lunde, who has just completed 18 years as obstetrical department supervisor, the greatest satisfaction in her job has come from seeing the look on a father's face when she tells him that everything is over and all right.

"You never tire of showing babies to them," she said, "for you are sure to see the only expression of its kind steal over a man's face. It's wonderful."

Perhaps Dad remembers what she means.

For the other "made" feature, Cunningham visited a milk drivers' union meeting room with a friend and came up with a story combining the experiences of drivers on different routes and over the years. A commonplace feature, it illustrates that newspapers are always interested in people and what they do as well as in "great events."

Jack of All Trades

Deliver Milk? Why That's Just 'Sideline' for Local 471

By Paul Cunningham

Delivering milk often seems like a sideline for men who are called upon from time to time to diaper babies, apply first aid, fire furnaces, rout burglars and halt domestic spats.

At least, the tales swapped in the back room of Milk Drivers and Dairy Employes union, local 471, could put a pulp story writer to shame.

"What would you do if a young girl with her throat cut dashed into your arms some morning?," inquired Art Miller of Franklin creamery.

It was two years ago when a young man stabbed his wife after she told him she was leaving him. The girl died in Miller's arms.

Another morning he was held up in a dark alley by two men. He drove them off by hurling milk bottles at them.

Miller has helped fire furnaces which have gone out overnight, he has released persons from locked bathrooms and basements, and often has been called upon to minister to youngsters on his route.

A "natural" for children's difficulties, however, is Mike Rusinko of Clover Leaf creamery, a grandfather. He is adept at changing diapers, he admits.

"I went into a home one morning and found a young mother and her baby crying," he said. "Seems she didn't know how to change her baby's diapers. For me it was a cinch."

It is commonplace for customers to ask the milkman to "please feed the dog" while they are away. One family left bottled instructions to feed the gold fish, forward the mail, check the oil burner and care for the cat for four weeks.

Like others in service industries, milkmen have saved a number of lives.

Thomas Thompson, a driver for 10 years with Ohleen dairy, once found a woman suffering from a heart attack lying on a kitchen floor. He got help in time to save her.

Another driver wondered why a car motor was running in a closed garage at 4 a.m. He saved a despondent man already unconscious from monoxide poisoning.

Milkmen soon develop a philosophical attitude which they say comes from seeing too many people who have just gotten up in the morning. At any rate, they refuse to arbitrate discussions on politics, religion or marital problems.

They often are asked to help raise funds for charity and have hung up some records for responses.

During the recent Sister Kenny Foundation campaign they collected $26,000 in donations.

Now if people would only train their dogs not to scare the lives out of them in the dark hours of the morning, the milkmen might be able to get on with their tasks—just delivering milk.

The Color Story

Many reporters find more satisfaction in writing a memorable color story than in almost any kind of assignment. Well

they may, because a story of this sort requires a sensitive eye and
ear plus the ability to catch a mood in words without overflow-
ing into mawkishness.

When a disaster, a conflict, or a large meeting such as a political convention occurs, newspapers frequently supplement the
main dispatch on the latest news developments with a second,
or color, story. This article concentrates on the sights, sounds,
and smells, the vignettes and intimate details that bring the scene
to life for the reader. The color story is undistilled human interest. Its success depends in large part upon the writer's sympathetic understanding of the people about whom he is writing.
Details that may seem too small to be included in the main story
are just the thing the color story needs. A little girl searching
through the wreckage of a train for her doll may have little
significance when 30 persons have been killed, but a skillful writer's description of the girl's reactions as she finds it can be a
poignant commentary upon the tragic scene of destruction, the
symbolic finding of life (though imaginary) in a scene where
death rules.

One of the critical issues in the United States during the 1950's
was the effort to end racial segregation in Southern schools. This
boiled up to a climax at Little Rock, Arkansas, when a small
group of Negro students sought to enroll in the previously all-
white Central High School with the support of a federal court
order. The rioting which followed caused President Eisenhower
to enforce the integration order with federal troops.

Associated Press reporter Relman Morin was at the scene
when the rioting broke out. His color story, dictated under conditions of tension, is a brilliant example of this kind of on-the-
spot reporting. His dispatches won Morin the Pulitzer Prize for
distinguished national reporting. Notice especially how he
caught the surge of emotion in the throng and the terse natural
tone of the dialogue. Morin dictated his spot news coverage from
the outdoor telephone booth mentioned in the story, carefully
limiting himself to reporting only what he could actually see and
hear. Throughout the country readers felt they themselves had
seen the action and had heard the emotional outbursts of the
crowd.

Hate and Tears Stream Forth at School Barricades

By Relman Morin
Associated Press Writer

LITTLE ROCK, ARK., Sept. 23—It was a frightening sight. Women burst into tears and a man, hoisted up on a wooden barricade, roared, "Who's going through?"

"We all are," the crowd of whites shouted. But they didn't.

The drama-packed climax of three weeks of integration struggle in Little Rock came just after the buzzer sounded inside the 2000-pupil Central High School signaling the start of classes.

Suddenly, on a street leading toward the school, the crowd spotted four Negro adults marching in twos down the center of the street.

A man yelled, "Look, here come the niggers."

I jumped into a glass-windowed telephone booth on the corner to dictate the story. The scene was clearly visible. As the crowd surged toward the four Negroes, they broke and ran.

Fleeing Negroes Caught

But they were caught on the lawn of a home nearby. Whites jumped a Negro with a camera from behind, rode him to the ground, kicking and beating him. They smashed the camera to bits.

Then someone yelled— "Look, they're going into the school."

At that instant the eight Negroes—three boys and five girls—crossed the schoolyard toward a side door of the school.

The girls were in bobby sox and the boys were dressed in shirts open at the neck. All were carrying books.

They were not running, not even walking fast. They simply strolled up the steps and were inside before all but a few of the 200 people outside knew it.

"They've gone in," a man roared. "Oh, God, the niggers are in the school."

A woman screamed, "Did they get in? Did you see them go in?"

"They're in now," some other men yelled.

"Oh, my God," the woman screamed. She burst into tears and tore at her hair.

Hysteria swept the crowd. Other women began weeping and screaming.

At that moment a tall, gray-haired man yelled, waving his arms:

"Who's going through?"

"We all are," the people shouted.

They broke over and around the wooden barricades, rushing the dozen policemen.

Police Raise Billy Clubs

The police raised their billy

clubs. Some grabbed men and women and hurled them back. Two chased a man who slipped through their line like a football player. They caught him on the schoolyard, whipped his coat down his arms, pinning them, and hustled him out of the yard.

Another man, wearing a construction worker's hard hat, suddenly raised his hands high in front of a policeman.

I couldn't see whether the officer had a gun in the man's stomach, but he stopped running abruptly and went back.

Order was restored for a moment when the state troopers arrived but the weeping and screaming went on among the women.

A man said, "I'm going in there and get my kid out."

An officer gritted, "You're not going anywhere."

Suddenly another roar—and cheering and clapping—came from the crowd. A white student, carrying his books, came down the front steps.

He was followed by two girls. In the next few minutes other students came out. Between 15 and 20 left the school within the next half hour.

Each time they appeared, the people clapped and cheered.

The crowd heckled the police and state troopers, hurling insults and some obscenity.

"How you going to feel tonight when you face your neighbors?" a man shouted.

The officers stood pokerfaced, making no move or response.

Then the crowd turned on the newspapermen and photographers.

Someone said, "We ought to wipe up the street with these Yankee reporters."

"Let's do it right now," another replied.

But it was only words. Nothing happened. A woman buttonholed a reporter and said:

"Why don't you tell the truth about us? Why don't you tell them we're peaceful people who won't stand to have our kids sitting next to niggers?"

The story above was prepared under extreme pressures of time and emotion. Its terse, lean style reflects the pace and mood of the events it was recording. Here is another kind of color story, done at a more leisurely pace by a reporter of the Louisville *Times* assigned to cover a flood of the Kentucky River. All the action at Little Rock was concentrated in a small area and happened swiftly. To gather his material for the following story, Reporter Bill Woolsey had to move about through an entire town and talk with many people, picking up a paragraph here, a quotation somewhere else. Morin's story is concentrated drama; Woolsey's is a warm and rather humorous aftermath report of a catastrophe.

No Tears Wash Mud

Hazard Folk Salvage Little But Pluck and Wry Humor

By Bill Woolsey
Louisville Times Staff Writer

HAZARD, KY., Feb. 4—Nobody in this flood-devastated town is trying to wash off Kentucky River mud by crying into it.

But pluck and a certain wry humor are about the only things folks in and around Hazard salvaged from last week's record high water.

A teen-age volunteer at the high school gymnasium where food and clothing is being issued asked a woman applicant for her address.

"I don't have one," came the reply. "Last I saw of it—'twas floating."

Another woman in line wanted shoes. The pair she had on were caked with mud.

"I've been up and down the river bank all day," she said, "looking for my cook stove."

"Where We Started"

By noon last Tuesday the waters of the rampaging Kentucky River were lapping at the rooms of the frame house on East Main Street where Police Chief Robert Heath and his wife have lived all their married life.

Yesterday, when the last mud and silt had been shoveled out of the home Mrs. Heath took the garden hose inside the house and washed down the walls and floors. When I talked with her she was scrubbing away at the high water mark on the clapboard exterior of her house.

"Mr. Heath and I are right back where we started 23 years ago—with an empty house," she said. "There wasn't a stick of furniture we could save."

"Best Place in Town"

A week ago Mike Chrisovergis had a thriving restaurant in downtown Hazard. By last Tuesday night it was a watery ruin.

What did "Mr. Chris" do? He went over to the First Presbyterian church and volunteered to be the cook for the emergency kitchen set up there for the flood victims.

"He's made the church the best place in town to eat," said one of Chrisovergis' fellow citizens.

The muddy waters surged into $20,000 homes and riverside shacks alike. Probably two thirds of Hazard was hit.

"I can see most of the things that were in my closets before the flood, now strewn in treetops down by the river," said Mrs. Johnnie Robinson.

She's a Red Cross home service worker. "And I'm too busy to go back home and start the cleanup job," she said.

Candle Warmed Bottle

Those who were flooded out moved in with friends or relatives or went to emergency shelters set up in some of Hazard's churches. They are still there.

Only the buildings in what is called "The Backwoods"—Hazard's name for the hilly section overlooking Main Street—were out of the flood zone.

One resident of The Backwoods is reported to have taken in 40 refugees last week, including a 2-week-old baby. During the several days right after the inundation when power was off, the baby's bottle was warmed over a candle.

The two color stories reprinted above concern extraordinary situations. Scheduled events such as parades, conventions, and games are also subjects for such coverage. The following story from the St. Paul *Pioneer Press* is an excellent example of what can be done.

Cold Keeps Spectators Hopping—

Parade Watchers on Move, Too

By John R. Finnegan

It was a bouncing, hopping, hand-slapping crowd that watched the Winter Carnival parade Saturday.

Only the hardy, the well-wrapped or the well-insulated braved the 4-degree temperatures the entire two hours as the parade wound its way through St. Paul streets, swept by a cold, 20-mile-an-hour wind.

The cold muffled the cheers and spectators were often too frozen to applaud favorite units or floats as they went by. Earmuffs, scarves, overshoes and blankets were the foot-stamping crowd's uniform.

Much of the parade route was sparsely settled, affording spectators in parked cars a good view of the marchers. Cars were jammed into every available vantage point—used car lots, street intersections, filling stations and vacant lots.

Others Beat Cold

Spectators in stores and downtown buildings also beat the cold and benefited from the lack of heavy throngs on the curbstones.

Hotels, apartments, stores and bars were crowded with persons who had comfortable seats during the parade. It wasn't uncommon to see a tiny nose pressed against a huge window beneath a neon sign reading "Beer."

Many of these who braved the elements, like Robert Marcroft, 5½, of 1603 Bohland, and his parents, arrived at spots along the route about 1 p.m. Robert, wrapped tightly in a blanket, was chilly and had cold feet not long after the parade got under way.

"But he wants to stay," said his father, Robert Marcroft. "He has to see all the clowns."

The youngster's face was wreathed in smiles a moment later when clowns Don Wosuaski and George Abbott came up with a step ladder and a huge yo-yo.

Mr. Marcroft looked over the small crowd near the Cathedral and remarked, "I guess they're all home watching on television."

Actor Pleases

Janet Mellin, 14, of 3431 York, Minneapolis, and Audrey Melander, 14, of 2108 Carroll, weren't suffering from the cold after Robert Cummings, television and screen star, rode by.

"I like Cummings," wailed Audrey. "Best part of the parade."

"What a dream," sighed Janet.

Jamie Boileau, 11, of 177 Marshall, beat the cold wind by bringing a huge cardboard box with him. He climbed inside it as soon as the parade started and kept comparatively warm.

Not all the spectators came dressed for the show. E. J. Rutter, representative of the Square Dance Federation of Missouri, who was taking pictures of the marchers at Sixth and Minnesota, had to pause and stamp his western-booted feet to keep them from becoming numb.

"It was 80 degrees above when I left Tuscon," he said. "And 56 in my home town of Kansas City. This is my first trip to this country, and I'm cold."

Hot coffee brought from home helped thaw frostnipped watchers. Those who failed to bring it shouted gratitude to the Eibert Coffee Co., which provided a float and attendants to pass out coffee to as many spectators as possible along the route.

Hand warmers were carried by some persons, but one man in the vicinity of Rice and Summit found he had to refill his often. He was seen dashing from his curbside location into a nearby apartment building carrying a hot water bottle.

"Darn water doesn't keep warm long enough out here," he muttered.

Chapter 18

Special Types of News Writing

The Newspaper's Feature Sections

Many opportunities for reporting and writing exist on the daily newspaper outside the jurisdiction of the city editor. These are in the special and feature sections which together form a substantial part of the paper. The heads of these sections usually report directly to the managing editor.

Some of the best reporting and writing is done in these pages. The material is largely of a feature nature and thus gives the reporter a wider range of writing techniques. Work in these departments may be less exciting than on fast-moving cityside stories but it provides a good showcase for the reporter's abilities.

The largest special sections are those covering sports, woman's interest, entertainment, and business. All of these appear daily. Many papers also have weekly sections on religion, books, real estate, and travel. If they have Sunday editions, these usually include extra features such as a weekly news review and a Sunday magazine.

News of Science, Education, Labor, Religion

Even though he is not assigned to one of these sections, the young reporter is wise to develop a specialty in which he can become known as the office expert. This brings him to the attention of the city editor more rapidly and gives him stature on the staff that may speed his promotion. On most newspapers the staff isn't large enough to permit a full-time man on science, religion, labor affairs, or education. Yet all of these fields are essential in well-rounded news coverage, and the reporter who takes a special interest in one of them may soon find himself winning by-lines and choice assignments.

Much of the work in these fields is of the self-starting variety. There aren't so many obvious spot assignments as on the police or municipal beats, but excellent stories are lying around untouched because nobody on the staff has had the interest or knowledge to develop them.

Science is an especially good field. With the world more conscious than ever of the opportunities and challenges in scientific work, the general reader has developed a strong appetite for easily comprehended stories about it. New developments, problems, and products are all of interest if the reporter can write about them in popular terms that are also scientifically sound. If his writing is too technical, he loses his readers; if it is too casual and weakened by errors in detail, the scientists will not talk freely with him. News of medicine is included in the science beat.

For simplicity of presentation and the relating of complex material to the reader's own experience, the following story from the New York *Times* merits close examination. Notice the brevity of its sentences and the broad scope of the material covered. This is a roundup, or survey, type of science feature story handled in a manner easily comprehensible to all.

Industry Puts Heavy Strain On Natural Resources

By Richard Rutter

America is living dangerously. Every time a car is driven, a coal fire is made, a meal is cooked with natural gas, a tin can is thrown away, something is gone forever.

That something is a bit of a natural resource.

Day by day, year after year, the bits add up to an enormous drain on supplies of vital raw materials.

The survival of the nation is involved.

An assured supply of iron ore, petroleum, natural gas, metals, coal and a host of other materials is essential to the strength of the American economy. Without these, the great industrial machine would come to a halt.

Picture Gloomy

What is the natural resources situation of the United States? Are we self-sufficient? Are we faced with critical shortages? Can new sources be found and developed?

The picture is not very bright.

In almost every resource area, U.S. industry's demands continue to grow.

Run down the list of the 26 most important materials ranging from antimony to zinc. The 1975 outlook: U.S. dependence on foreign sources will range from 100 per cent to 25 per cent.

All supplies of such minerals as chrome, corundum, industrial diamonds, graphite, quartz, nickel and tin will have to come from overseas. This is largely the situation right now.

But will foreign supplies prove sufficient?

Experts believe there are no critical shortages now. But they believe such shortages are inevitable if the present rate of consumption is maintained—let alone stepped up.

Gone Forever

For instance, more than 2½ billion tons of 30 leading minerals, including coal, iron, copper, lead, zinc, magnesium, are mined annually throughout the free world.

This amount can never be replaced; once removed from the earth, it is gone forever.

There are no exact figures on world-wide mineral resources or on how much is being consumed. But there is no doubt about the extent at which irreplaceable raw materials are being depleted.

In the first half of this century, the amount of mineral products consumed far exceeded that during the entire preceding period of man's existence on earth.

There is the problem of getting the materials from their sources to this country during a war. The free world's lifelines are long and exposed.

Turkey is the chief source of chrome. Copper comes from Africa and South America, tin from the Far East and Bolivia.

Petroleum comes from South America and the Mideast, iron ore from Liberia and Labrador. Only military strength can keep the routes open.

What Can Be Done?

But how about the long-range supply situation? Can anything be done? Yes:

The most obvious is to develop and expand foreign sources. America's foreign aid program helps. So do such organizations as the World

Bank, the Export-Import Bank and the International Finance Corp. Private investment helps, too.

Much can be done at home, too.

The sheer physical waste of resources is enormous.

About 50 per cent of commercial grades of coal are left in the ground during the process of mining.

More than half of the petroleum in a pool is never recovered.

Enough natural gas is wasted each year to supply the needs of millions of homes. New techniques are being developed that will ultimately reduce these losses.

And it's generally agreed that undiscovered mineral sources in the United States may be far greater than those already found and exploited.

There is the makings of a trend toward using lower quality resources.

Only a handful of known minerals play a part in modern industry. Technology eventually, no doubt, will find uses for many of these untapped materials.

Synthetic materials are coming to the fore. Plastics, artificial fibers, manmade rubber are in themselves major industries.

More use can be gotten out of the present methods through reclamation. It's almost impossible to overestimate the potential of scrap of all kinds.

All of these approaches add up to a form of conservation.

Another realm offering opportunities to the enterprising reporter is education. This means much more than reporting the routine actions of the school board. Parents are anxious to know how their children are being taught and why, the problems of discipline a teacher faces and how she deals with them, and the reasons for the school board's policies on such matters as size of classes, bus service, and grading systems. As a whole our newspapers have not done as good a job as they might in reporting this important field of interest.

Closely linked to education is the recent trend in newspapers toward more news about teen-age interests. Some editors have come to believe that they must try harder to make teen-agers habitual newspaper readers so that they will remain customers in their adult years. These executives have been experimenting with record columns, picture features about party-giving, advice columns for young people, and similar material aimed at the teen-age market. Here is another opportunity for the young reporter to specialize. He is more conscious of what teen-agers care about than are many older men on the staff. Perhaps your paper is ready for a weekly teen-age page, if somebody on the staff would come forward with a well-organized plan.

Labor news comes closer to being a regular city desk assignment because there are periods of major spot developments in it. But between the recurring strike threats and contract negotiations there is much news of the labor movement that goes uncovered in some cities. Relations between organized labor and management aren't all strife and tension, as a reader of some papers might well believe. There are many constructive cooperative efforts, especially in the health and welfare fields. A reporter who develops a part-time beat of his own around union headquarters, and writes his material objectively, will be able to get many additional stories into the paper. He may soon be known as the office authority on labor.

Some papers, especially those in state capitals, have columns and feature stories aimed at special groups of workers, such as state or federal employes. If one company dominates the industrial life of a city with a large factory, the activities of its employes can be given special coverage.

Two other fields in which a city staff expert is frequently welcome are aviation and religion. Many metropolitan papers, especially those situated near aircraft factories or air bases, give special attention to aviation. They need someone to write about it who possesses a moderate knowledge of aircraft fundamentals and the intricacies of commercial and military aviation.

"Doing the church page" was for many years a much-disliked chore around the city room, often handed to an errant reporter as punishment. Fortunately this attitude has been changing. Editors are aware of what a factor religion is in contemporary life, and they are conscious of the need to give it better coverage. Almost every newspaper in its Saturday edition gives editorial space to announcements about the next day's services in the local churches, illustrated perhaps by a photograph of a visiting minister. This material is important. But much more can be done by the paper fortunate enough to have a man on the assignment who comprehends the dynamic nature of his material. He can find many angles for interviews with ministers on current religious issues, stories about how men and women apply religion in their daily life, and similar enterprise materials. Properly done, some of his stories may find their way into the daily news columns, too.

Some editors long held the view that it was unwise to permit religious controversy in their newspapers. This attitude has been changing. The widely held view now is that reporting debate and dispute on religious matters is a newspaper's function, so long as the material is handled with scrupulous objectivity and suitable restraint. The personal views of the reporter and editor should not be visible in the selection and writing of religious news.

Perhaps your newspaper has a man specializing in one or more of these fields already. But it is unlikely that all of them are in the hands of specific staff members. After you have been on the staff for a while and feel that you are well grounded in its routine work, let the city editor know of your interest in developing a specialty as a supplement to your regular job. If the field is currently being neglected, he will probably tell you to go ahead and see what you can do with it. Editors are always on the lookout for fresh ideas and enterprise.

Working in the Special Sections

The specialties we have been discussing are mostly part-time portions of the city staff reporter's job. Now we turn to an examination of the daily special sections mentioned at the start of this chapter, each of which operates in a jurisdiction of its own.

The principles of good reporting apply everywhere, whether in describing a football game, covering a fashion show, or writing a story about the trends in the stock market. Accuracy, balance, and a keen eye for facts are important; so are the reasons why things happen. In addition, each of these special sections has problems which are peculiar to it.

Sports

Many beginning reporters want to work in the sports section. They have taken part in athletics themselves, know the games about which they will be writing, and have a fondness for them. Sports writing is, in fact, a splendid training ground for the newspaper reporter if he is fortunate enough to work under an editor who enforces the same discipline that the reporter would encounter at the city desk. The sports writer covers both spot news and features, and there is more latitude of writing style permitted in the sports section than in the news section. He has an opportunity to meet people, develop contacts on a friendly basis, and attend, free of charge, many of the sporting events he would want to see, anyway.

Given all these advantages, it is unfortunate that many young sports writers do not develop the reporting skill and writing technique that they should. Sports editors as a group are individualists, writing columns and exercising a very subjective approach to the news. On too many smaller papers, at least, they do not spend the time they should in grounding their assistants in the fundamentals of sound reporting.

Excessive use of clichés is one of the worst faults of American sports writing. Hackneyed phrases in distressing numbers can be found on many sports pages. As a test, take sports pages from two or three newspapers and circle all the overworked terms and strained expressions you find on them. Sports headline writers in particular try so hard to find similes and language shortcuts that the result becomes almost ludicrous at times, especially on a Sunday morning in the football season when the sports staff seeks different ways of saying that one team won and its opponent lost.

A check of the sports pages in an otherwise well-edited newspaper one Sunday morning showed that the successful teams did these things to their opponents, at least in the headlines: whip, scuttle, nip, feast on, crush, roar back, rip, trip, humble, clip, and shade. Hardly anyone received credit for just plain winning.

Another common fault is using an adjective as a noun such as, "The teams meet in a crucial tonight."

The sports writer should exercise much self-discipline in his selection of phraseology. He is in greater danger of falling unconsciously into the trap of trite and overwritten prose than any other member of the newspaper staff. Also, he must guard against an overuse of jargon. Perhaps the reporter and the football players refer in their conversation to a TD instead of a touchdown, the belly series to describe a certain type of running play, and the Y and buttonhook pass patterns. That is trade talk, and the writer should put it in plain language for the casual reader. Beginning sports writers often try so hard to impress the athletes with their technical knowledge that they leave their layman readers confused.

Sports coverage gives the reporter a showcase for his descriptive writing. The difficulty is that so many others before him have done the same thing that seemingly they haven't left much room for originality. When seeking a fresh approach to the routine football game or horse race, he finds that almost everything he can think of has been used already.

Yet there are fine stylists in sports writing today, and there always will be. Most of them are men who have developed a philosophical outlook toward sports, remembering that these are only games they are covering, after all, and approaching their job with a sense of humor.

One of the very best for many years has been Harold "Red" Smith of the New York *Herald Tribune*. His columns are admired not only for their sound knowledge but for their relaxed and literate style. Notice in the following example how free his writing is from clichés, overemotional superlatives, and strained expressions.

How Much Will Series Pressure Affect Braves?

By Red Smith

Bowing from the waist, his plumed hat in hand, one of the knights of television greeted Fred Haney with Chesterfieldian grace when the dukes of the cheeselands arrived at Idlewild Airport. "Do you think," the man asked, choosing his words, "that the Braves will choke up against the Yankees?"

Fred Haney is a little man, physically the smallest manager in the major leagues, but given sufficient provocation he can contain more anger than the Cardiff Giant. His reply as quoted in the newspapers was phrased variously to suit the literary standards of each journal and the puritan conscience of the postal department. In essence, Fred said, "No."

Disregarding the singular tact with which the query was put, it was a valid question. Indeed, it may be the most valid of all those which fans are asking as the battle is joined for the rounders championship of the Universe.

By all the yardsticks by which athletic ability is measured, Milwaukee's personnel compares creditably with that of New York. Some competitors respond to unusual pressure and are the better for it. Others freeze. The Yankees' form in a competition of this class is clearly established in the past performance charts. The reaction of the Braves may be the factor that swings the balance.

Down Under the Flannel

No matter how insistently they may deny it, ball players are acutely conscious of the strain in a World Series. "Just another ball game," they say aloud, and everything they think and do and see and hear belies it. The crowds, the clamor for autographs and pictures, the distant relatives and childhood friends who crawl out from under the rocks whimpering for tickets, the bands and bunting, the politicians everywhere, the too-studied composure of playmates and manager—all these create an inner excitement that swells until even the veteran feels he must burst.

No game ever knew a fiercer gladiator than Frank Frisch, who played in fifty World Series games. You'd think his combative fires would have been banked along toward the end, yet he has confessed that he never went into one of these things when he wasn't weak with nervous strain. He got his strength back with the first pitch.

With Frisch it was an old story. With the Braves it is brand new, except for Red Schoendienst, Warren Spahn, Andy Pafko and Del Rice. It's not only new to the players, but to Milwaukee and Wisconsin. The phenomenal support which the Leiderkranz belt has given to the Braves in the past is likely to become a burden now.

Finally, those will be Yankees springing out of the other dugout. There is no chance for the Braves to forget that. They can tell themselves that they're playing just another big league team, no tougher than the Cardinals or Dodgers, yet they know the Yankees' record in World Series play, and they know the record wasn't compiled by accident.

Only the Braves, Etc.

The pressure is a real thing, and the belief here is that the Braves are real ball players. There is nothing in their record to support a suspicion that they're a pack of Alice Ben Bolts trembling with fear at Yogi Berra's frown.

They survived four months of cutthroat struggle against four other contenders, drew clear of their field in August, then came up with all the right answers when the Cardinals asked the question in September.

When their lead had been reduced to two and a half games, the Braves took off, closing out the race with seven consecutive victories. With the game in extra innings on the night of decision, Aaron stepped up and slammed the ball out of the park. There was nothing girlish about that finish.

Milwaukee has a sound team, ably staffed and happily balanced. Assuming that Haney's men know as much about the Yankees as the Yankees know about them, the chances are that the result will be decided by pitching. It usually is in a World Series, and it's usually the team with the "big" pitchers that comes through.

The sports section thrives on controversy. It is the realm of the second-guesser and the Monday morning quarterback, who always knows afterward what the players should have done. The famous long count of the Dempsey-Tunney heavyweight championship prize fight is still being debated three decades later. Every baseball and football season produces quarrels over close decisions and unusual plays. The arguments at the scene will be continued for days in the newspaper columns, to the pleasure of the ardent fans. A sports editor trying to build readership often emphasizes the controversial, taking arbitrary positions in his column and passing sweeping judgments. No other editor in the newspaper exercises quite such personal freedom in this respect. Since disputes make good reading, this is acceptable practice if not overdone—and if the writer is sufficiently well-qualified to offer his opinions. But he should be willing to acknowledge his more glaring errors of judgment, or bad guesses, in print, and with good grace.

In smaller communities the sports section provides a good way to get the names of men and women into the paper. Publication of bowling scores, local golf club results, high school game line-ups, and similar material attracts readers.

Many reporters and editors working on the general news staff and even in other feature sections started as sports writers. They drifted out of sports either by chance or because they found their interests shifting as they grew older. Others equally talented spend their entire newspaper careers in the sports department.

The Woman's Section

One of the revolutionary changes in recent years in American newspapers has been the revamping of the traditional society page. Belatedly newspaper editors realized that women were finding more useful reading in the magazines than in the woman's pages of their newspapers. Consequently there has been a shift away from routine coverage of parties and club meetings to stories and pictures about the problems a woman faces in running her home, grooming herself, and taking her place in the business world. The phenomenal growth in the number of working women has accelerated this trend.

The woman's section of many newspapers today offers a challenging field for women reporters and, in some cases, for men. Quite a few metropolitan newspapers have men as editors of their woman's pages. This has been done partly to give the pages more "news side" flavor in layout and partly to broaden the field of interest within the department. Some papers have gone so far as to drop the title "woman's section" and call the section a "family" page. No longer need the woman's department be a backwater of the editorial department. An increasing number of editors, too, are trying to get more stories with feminine appeal into their news pages.

Readership surveys have shown that the stories in the woman's section drawing the greatest attention are those dealing with beauty, fashion, and food. Society news in the traditional sense rates much lower, and club news rates below that. Each society and club story may be of much importance to those involved, but it does not have general appeal. The recent trend has been to play up the stories of broad interest but to retain sufficient coverage of social and club activities. In smaller cities, where people are well acquainted with each other, the woman's page continues to be a clearinghouse of community social information. The larger the city, the smaller is the impact of names.

In the autumn of 1957 the Miami (Fla.) *Herald* published an announcement indicative of the thinking now governing many woman's sections:

The women's department of The Miami Herald Tuesday announced a change in policy in publication of club news, effective immediately.

At the same time Club Editor Roberta Applegate called on publicity chairmen to consider themselves part of the Herald staff as "idea women" for stories.

Here are some of the changes:

Advance stories will be used on only those activities which are open to the public.

The calendar of events will be expanded to give more information.

The club staff will cover more meetings, special events and projects of all types which will be of general interest to the readers. . . .

The emphasis, it is evident, is upon story material of widespread interest, not merely that concerning a limited group.

Many papers have their own homemaking editor who writes about the ways to prepare food, prints recipes, and passes along suggestions for home management. With the development of editorial color photographs, some papers now supplement their coverage at least once a week with colored pictures of foods prepared for serving. This is an attractive field for a young woman writer with a flair for home economics. Personnel directors report difficulty in finding young newspaperwomen who have satisfactory writing ability coupled with a knowledge of foods to fill such positions.

The trend in woman's sections provides space for interviews —success stories, career women's stories, advice from experts in beauty and dress on how the reader can make herself more attractive, suggestions from interior decorators for brightening the home, and many others. Some of these interview ideas come to the woman's editor through publicity sources, but most of them depend upon the ingenuity of editor and staff. A woman reporter can also create participation stories in which she does somebody else's job for a day and then writes about her experience. Some of these stories may be humorous in tone because of her misadventures; others are quite serious. She might, for example, serve food in a school cafeteria and tell her women readers how their children picked the dishes they had for lunch. Or she might don a Salvation Army costume at Christmas time, as one clever newswoman did, and write a first person story about what kinds of people dropped money into the little Christmas fund pot and which ones ignored it. The possibilities are limited only by the imagination of the reporter.

Beauty and fashion material is provided to newspapers by the various syndicates. Papers in larger cities frequently have specialists of their own in the field who report on new fashions and products in the local stores. Metropolitan papers have their own fashion artists who illustrate the stories with sketches similar to those seen in the woman's magazines. In fact, the woman's section of many newspapers today is filling much the same service functions as the woman's magazine, but it is edited for faster reading and local interest.

Many papers also publish advice columns tailored for their feminine readers in which the columnist answers problem letters from readers, suggesting ways to handle such personal difficulties as an abusive husband, a love affair, or a snoopy neighbor. Nationally syndicated columnists provide this service to many papers, but others prefer to have advice columnists of their own to add the local touch. It is a quirk of human nature that women readers will write highly intimate details of their personal affairs to a newspaper advice columnist whom they know only through her writing.

A basic ingredient of the woman's section continues to be stories and pictures of engagements and weddings. Policies of papers vary as to how much space is given to bridal pictures; some run every one received, if possible, while others ration their space strictly to those girls who are prominent socially or have achieved distinction in other fields. Handling of this material requires tact, patience, and extreme accuracy. A mistake in the bride's name may be perpetuated in the family scrapbook and be a point of irritation for years.

Women preparing for newspaper careers should look at the woman's section in its entirety, for on many newspapers it offers a satisfying variety of writing and reporting work.

Business

The financial sections of our newspapers have also been undergoing a change of method and approach, being broadened from their former role as statistical reports on market conditions to a more comprehensive role as recorders of general business trends. They are being given a more popular tone.

The atmosphere of prosperity which prevailed in the country after the second world war brought much more extensive investment by the general public in stocks and bonds. The stock market reports which formerly were read primarily by businessmen became daily fare for housewives as well. This has been reflected in the appearance and content of newspaper financial sections.

Statistical information continues to be the core of these pages. All larger newspapers and many smaller ones publish daily closing prices for the entire New York stock exchange list. Most small papers print at least a selected list of the best known and most heavily traded issues. Depending upon the space they wish to devote, the newspapers carry an additional group of secondary market reports such as the American exchange, over-the-counter issues, the grain and commodity exchanges, and the livestock markets. Because the close of the markets each day comes near their edition times, afternoon papers must handle all this material with great speed. Most of it comes to them from the wire services, although local market reports are usually obtained by telephone.

The investor is also interested in dividend reports and news developments that may affect the value of the shares he holds. These, too, can be obtained from his newspaper's financial pages.

In recent years many newspapers have been adding to all this traditional material a layout of interviews with business leaders, success stories about the way individuals and corporations have built their business, backstage glimpses of what makes the business world function, and discussions of commercial trends. There has been a substantial effort to get the human element into these pages along with statistical data. As a result, readership in the sections has risen.

Much credit for this broadened approach should go to one newspaper, the *Wall Street Journal*. Long an institution in the financial market with its comprehensive statistical reports, the *Journal* began adding feature stories about the business world on its front page. These cover such diverse matters as the techniques of promoting impulse buying in department stores and the way large corporations distribute "success symbols" such as company automobiles and country club memberships to the executives on various rungs of the corporate ladder. Such stories are a far cry from the old-style, highly technical articles about market fluctuations. Newspaper editors around the country, noting what the daily trade paper of the financial world was doing, decided that they could use some of that technique to brighten their own business pages.

As a result, the young reporter assigned to a business section today has a much wider field in which to operate than his predecessor a few decades ago. The public's interest in business news has been whetted, and editors have discovered that much drama, whimsy, and entertaining information can be developed by a persistent and clever reporter. A reporter who wishes to work in this field, however, needs to have a strong interest in financial methods and commercial operations; the human interest feature material is only a supplement to the statistical matter, not a replacement for it.

Here is a typical page one feature in the *Wall Street Journal*, illustrating the type of material now finding its way into business pages. Note the informality of the writing style, which might well surprise anyone who did not know the character of the publication with such a rather misleading nameplate. During the 1940's the paper's coverage was broadened to include lucidly written summaries of important national and world news and comprehensive stories interpreting trends in industry, government, and world affairs. It twice won Pulitzer awards for its editorials. As a result, the *Wall Street Journal* quadrupled its readership during the 1950's and became a standard paper for study and reference in other newspaper offices, where expansion of business news reporting staffs and broadening of business page coverage were under way.

'Throat Cutting'

It's Risky, but It Still Helps Many Ambitious Executives Get Up Corporate Ladder

A Wall Street Journal News Roundup

A vice president of one eastern corporation not long ago plugged the carburetor in the auto of a new rival to make him late for his first executive meeting.

A high executive of a conservative Pennsylvania corporation planted rumors that his principal rival had "fallen for a New Dealish line," thus ruining his chances for the presidency.

An elevator company executive waited for his rival's special project to flop, then submitted to the boss a series of memos (carefully backdated) to show he'd opposed the project all along.

These businessmen were practicing that most delicate of all the arts of self-advancement—throat cutting. Most of the techniques of throat cutting have changed little with the years. The rewards for the skilled practitioners of the art remain high—and so do the risks for the inept.

One man who gambled—and lost—was a salesman for a rubber company. Scrambling for the vacant job of assistant sales manager, he spread rumors of his rival's addiction to wine, women and song. As he expected, the tales reached the ears of the boss. But they backfired; the boss, who liked to dally a bit, too, handed the job to the high liver. The more circumspect salesman, who had been careful to stress his own purity, fell from favor and eventually was fired.

More than 50 executives interviewed by Wall Street Journal reporters in 12 cities agreed throat cutters nowadays meet with disaster as often as with success. Still, the alluring example of those who are successful is keeping the art very much alive.

Throat cutting isn't the only route to promotion, of course; some executives advance simply because they're skilled at their jobs. But one leading San Francisco management consultant maintains, "The man who is competent and ruthless and combines this with skill at throat cutting will probably win out over the man who is just competent."

Most executives—after they think it over—concede the existence of throat cutting within their companies.

"There's no throat cutting around here," avers an officer of a big Southwest oil company. But after a moment's reflection he adds: "Of course, some people in this company will do just anything to get promoted." He claims one high official hired a staff of talented assistants to do all his work so he could devote more time to office politicking.

The Verbal Scalpel

Among the basic weapons of throat cutting, the verbal scalpel ranks high, whether applied at the conference table, in the executive lunch room or right in the boss's office. The interoffice memo is another traditional vehicle for demolishing a rival. Of more recent vintage: introduction of an "objective" management survey to undermine an opponent's project. Pacts with customers or competitors to do in an executive are not uncommon. Some overeager throat cutters have even placed bribes and rifled files to achieve their ends, but these coarser methods are scorned by the cognoscenti.

Most of these techniques have stood the test of time. Historians say underlings managed to bounce President Charles Schwab of U.S. Steel from his job 54 years ago by spreading tales of Schwab's Monte Carlo gambling expeditions. Chairman Elbert Gary, something of a moralist, started restricting the president's jurisdiction, so Schwab stormed out of the company.

What troubles many business leaders is that a surprising number of younger corporate recruits have taken a liking to these well-worn techniques. One Detroit business official says he's noticed many youngsters just embarking on corporate training programs who already are trying out their carving skills.

Internal Warfare

Another point of agreement among executives: throat cutting appears to be more prevalent in large companies which have achieved predominance in their fields than it is in smaller, still-growing enterprises. "Internal warfare is bound to be greater in a mature organization which isn't growing very rapidly," says one veteran manufacturing executive. In small, fast-expanding firms, he says, there are always new opportunities for meritorious young men.

Entertainment

Coverage of entertainment news in daily newspapers until a few years ago consisted largely of film reviews and publicity and reports of local theatrical performances, professional and amateur. The growth of television has changed this situation radically. It has opened a new field of reporting for men and women.

Television has transformed much of the entertainment-seeking public into a stay-at-home audience. Instead of going to the movies two nights a week, the people sit in their living rooms before their television sets and obtain their entertainment free. Whether the shows they see are better or worse than those they used to view in the local theater is open to debate.

Not that the film business has died out. It has shifted direction toward fewer and more spectacular films. The producers have decided that it takes something striking or unorthodox to coax the audience away from home. Many suburban theaters have closed because their audience disappeared.

As a result newspaper film critics have fewer new films to review than previously. Yet the public appetite for news about its favorite stars and Hollywood activities remains strong and the readership of such news high. This is partly because of a growing exchange of talent between films and television; the hero on the living room screen tonight may be starring in a major film at a local theater next week.

Most newspapers have met this changed situation by adding detailed daily television program logs, and in larger cities most papers print week-end supplements listing all the programs for the coming seven days. They have also added television columns reviewing new shows and discussing the activities and views of TV personalities. A majority of papers giving such coverage use nationally syndicated film and television columns from New York or Hollywood, usually supplemented by a column written by a local staff member. On larger papers, at least, the film and television reviews are not written by the same man. This is due in part to the work load and in part to commercial resistance from the film companies. While they are being forced to join hands with television, many film executives still look upon TV as a dangerous competitor and oppose having the film reviewer "besmirched" with a television title, too. Most publishers listen sympathetically to this argument, since motion-picture companies are large advertisers. Television executives, too, prefer to have the reporting of their medium and motion-picture news handled by different reporters.

The film critic also covers stage productions, except in New York and one or two other cities. To satisfy the demands of

film advertisers and the public's desire, the critic must print
a substantial amount of publicity material about the new pictures, most of which is provided by the publicity departments
of the motion-picture studios. The television networks provide a
similar "news" service to the TV editor.

News of radio programs in the newspapers has diminished as
news of television has increased, except in those rural areas
where television has been slow in becoming a major entertainment factor. There is less need for a complete radio log now
than two or three decades ago because of the changed nature
of radio programming. The elaborate network radio programs
of the 1930's and 1940's have moved over to television, and the
once intricate radio networks have been breaking up. In their
place has come the upsurge of the disc jockeys, who intersperse
recorded music with commercials for several hours at a time.
Thus there is less need for radio logs broken into detailed 15-
minute segments. Radio news is handled by the television editor.

Included in the area of entertainment is the newspaper space
devoted to news of books, music, and art—what might be termed
cultural coverage. A local musician of prominence usually serves
as the paper's music critic on a space or retainer fee basis, unless there happens to be a staff member qualified to handle the
work as a sideline. The same arrangement prevails in those papers
which feature art news. These columns normally appear on Sunday, in cases where the paper has a Sunday edition. A few, very
large metropolitan newspapers have full-time critics in these
fields.

Book reviewing is another part-time occupation, except in
a handful of metropolitan newspapers. Approximately 20 papers
from coast to coast have weekly book sections supported by
substantial amounts of advertising from the book publishers.
Some of these also have daily columns about new books. The
sections are usually edited by men with a background in publishing. If there is an established literary editor on your paper,
he may welcome short reviews from younger staff members.
Many other papers publish weekly book columns handled by a
staff member or outside contributor. Although smaller in scope
than the sections, the quality of their reviewing is frequently
high. There is a need for more book reviewing in our news-

papers, but editors must be convinced that the work is done sufficiently well so that it amounts to something more substantial than free publicity space.

The Editorial Page

The editorial page is the newspaper's heart; it, more than any other page, determines a newspaper's personality. Here the editor's opinions that have been kept out of the new stories are set forth concerning the issues of the day. Evidence of the paper's political philosophy and its attitude—aggressive, conservative, liberal, or fence-straddling—is found on its editorial page.

The editorials themselves are accompanied by an editorial cartoon, letters from readers, and perhaps the opinions of a columnist or two. The purposes of the page are to pass judgment and to stimulate thinking. Some large papers also have an opposite editorial page on which they group the views of several columnists, national and local, and also publish background articles. The writing on the editorial page may be brisk and provocative, or long-winded and dull, depending upon the men who prepare it.

Because the newspaper's policy is involved, and many intricate considerations often arise, most editorial page work is done by senior members of the staff. On many large papers the position of chief editorial writer carries much prestige. The way a younger newsman is likely to break into editorial page work is as a junior editor doing the partially mechanical tasks of editing the syndicated columns and preparing readers' letters for publication. However, editorial writers always welcome ideas from reporters who have run across an injustice on their beats or a situation which they believe needs correction. Frequently an editorial writer will turn to a reporter for facts and opinions about a situation he has been covering.

The Zone Sections

A recent development in large city newspapers has been the establishment of zone sections. These are designed to meet the outward population growth of metropolitan areas into spreading suburban regions. Residents of each suburb, or group of suburbs, develop local interests of their own in addition to their concern about metropolitan affairs. Local news that interests people living to the north of the city limits may have little meaning for those living to the south.

A growing number of large newspapers are trying to overcome this difficulty by publishing a section of the daily paper devoted to the interests and problems of the residents of one suburban zone. A separate section may be stuffed into the papers going to that zone or pages may be replated for the different zones. Regardless of the mechanical methods used, the purpose is the same: to give suburban readers a metropolitan paper plus their own community news.

Development of zone sections has in some cases created jobs for younger reporters. They have beats in the suburbs, gathering and writing community news just as they would if working on a small-town newspaper. In its own way that is just what a zone section is, a small-town paper within the framework of the metropolitan daily.

Chapter **19**

Writing a Column

The Columnist's Role

The newspaper column is the contemporary form of personal journalism. The editor's feuds, private feelings, and personal ax-grinding have been largely removed from the news pages, where they were frequently evident in the early days of American journalism. The paper's official opinions are, in most cases, confined to the editorial page. Yet the writer of a newspaper column has wide latitude to express his views on many subjects, to campaign for and against causes, and to shower praise or blame upon individuals. In many cases the columnist has become the ruler of a private kingdom within the newspaper's confines.

This sense of independence, power, and self-expression is one of the attractions that makes so many newspaper writers, especially younger ones, desire to become columnists.

Column writing takes many forms, and there are no firm rules to govern it. The columnist's subject matter may be in a special field, such as sports or television, or it may range the world. Some writers specialize in provocative revelations, others in personality sketches, whimsical anecdotes, nostalgia, politics, or gossip.

Local Columnists

A strong local column is an important asset to a newspaper's circulation. The writer develops a following and may become the best known personality on the staff. If he can make his readers chuckle, nod with appreciation, or perhaps shed a tear over events in his city, he is sure to become a figure in the community. He fills an important role by reflecting his neighbors' moods and manners. Readers appeal to him for all sorts of aid, believing that the mention of their names and plights in his column will bring magical results. Sometimes it does so, if the situation happens to stir the public's sympathy and sentiments.

Lowell Nussbaum in the Indianapolis *Star* tells in one of his articles about the odd assortment of inquiries the public sends to a local columnist. His experience is typical.

> A columnist can have a busy day even without writing a column. Some days mail and phone inquiries can keep him on the jump. For instance:
>
> Phone call complaining that while I recommend feeding birds in winter, I never try to help the squirrels. Okay, so squirrels like to eat, too. Go ahead and feed them.
>
> Letter asking about the rules for playing Bolivia. Gosh, I dunno. Now if it were tiddlywinks. . . .
>
> Phone calls and letters asking if I know of any children's organization that desires used greetings cards. I don't. Most get more than they can use from their own members. One individual has asked for some cards, but no organizations.
>
> More non-column business: Postcard asking if it is true that in Germany you are one-year-old the day you are born. I don't know. Maybe that's the origin of the expression, "I was born at an early age." One reference book says many of us confuse the two meanings of the word and regard one's first birthday as his second birth day.
>
> Postcard: "Was the dog shown in the Ken-L Biskit ad shown in the Indianapolis Star Magazine, Sunday, recently a Dalmatian?" No, I'd say it was a Great Dane.
>
> Letter: "Could you find the owner of a roll of films we found a year ago and just had developed?" I doubt it. (The films showed a couple at a Maine lighthouse, at Whiteface Mountain ski center and at College Notre-Dame.)
>
> Phone Call: "When's the cherry blossom festival in Washington, D.C.?" I don't know. The date varies with the weather. Last year it was the fourth week in April, according to the Hoosier Motor Club.
>
> And that's the way the time goes.

All this attention is flattering to the columnist. It also has its dangers. He needs a sense of balance and restraint or his ego can easily be inflated to unpleasant proportions—a fate that has befallen some practitioners of the art. Anyone who becomes a columnist and finds himself the recipient of abundant praise, invitations to parties, requests to make public appearances, and a flurry of fan mail should remember that much of this is self-serving. The flatterers want something from him, usually a mention in his column. Without his daily allotment of space in the newspaper, he might quickly be forgotten. Along this same line, the beginning columnist must be careful lest he fall into the habit of pontificating. His access to personal newspaper space does not qualify him as an expert on all things. The sports columnist on the college paper who tells the football coach in print how he should run the team may only be making himself look ridiculous.

The author of a column should remember, too, that the power of the printed word is greater than he knows, and he has an exceptional opportunity to abuse it. Hurting people in print is far easier than he may realize. A writer can be controversial and provoke lively discussion without becoming vindictive or vicious.

The columnist isn't always the best reporter on the paper, although many readers assume that he is. He may be selected for the assignment because of his flair for words or his wit. He would be wise to remember that he can learn things from other staff members, many of whom are probably more experienced in reporting than he.

Writing a column is not the easy task that many other newspapermen consider it. The columnist is always running into remarks about what a soft job he has—"only one column to write a day, all those parties and you can say anything you want." These comments are usually delivered in a half-whimsical tone but with a vein of jealousy underneath. If the detractors knew the difficulties of writing a good column day after day, they would not talk so. By the very nature of his exposed position, the columnist is subject to criticism and generalized observations that he isn't as good and interesting as he used to be.

The local columnist cannot write day after day entirely from the resources of his own mind. He must depend upon contributions. Some columnists receive quotable tidbits and anecdotes year after year from volunteer contributors who get no more for their efforts than an occasional mention of their names in print. The better the writer's group of volunteer contributors, the better his column.

Commercial publicity men look upon the columnist as a prime target. They know that an item about a client, whether it be a product or a personality, "planted" in a column is sure to be read. In fact synthetic celebrities have been created by clever exploitation of their names in nationally syndicated gossip columns. Some columnists keep such mentions to a minimum, using them only when the story has legitimate merit. Others, unfortunately, have been known to develop a pay-off system, the payment for a good mention usually coming in the form of favors rather than cash. Publicity men often try to keep on good terms with the columnist by supplying him with usable items in which they have no commercial interest. Some metropolitan columnists, exploiting this practice, have gone so far as to promise a commercial mention for the publicity man's client in return for every three printable items he submits.

The success of the nationally syndicated column from New York, Washington, and Hollywood is a phenomenon of contemporary journalism and not an especially wholesome one. Lacking staff coverage of their own in these centers of American interest, newspapers have purchased the columns written by men and women residing there. These daily articles are carefully contrived to be provocative, to be laden with glamour, and to give the impression that the columnist has access to much inside information. The columnists make flat unqualified statements that a client editor several hundred miles away would not accept in a locally written story, yet he has no way to check them. If he cuts the syndicated columnist's article sharply, some readers accuse him of exercising censorship. For this reason, and because they believe that much of the material in the columns is merely trivia made to look exciting, some editors refuse to run syndicated columns. Others believe that such "name" columnists are strong circulation builders and give prominence to their work. They believe also that these columns provide a challenging kind of writing that they cannot get from their own staffs.

Most syndicated Washington columnists deal more in political opinion than in hard news. They become known for their political point of view—conservative Republican, middle-of-the-road, or liberal—and are spokesmen in print for these viewpoints. Some editors will print only those political columns which parallel their own editorial policy. Others choose to publish columnists with conflicting attitudes to stimulate their readers' thinking.

Reporters in the early stages of their careers rarely find themselves cast as columnists. The column has become such an important part of our newspapers, however, that several examples of different column-writing techniques are included here. In most cases these are presented in somewhat abbreviated form to give an indication of the techniques used.

Among the most noted practitioners of the local short item column, full of names and vignettes, is Herb Caen of the San Francisco *Chronicle*. He uses the dot and dash technique, a breezy style with a sprinkling of plays on words and coined expressions.

One Man's San Francisco

By Herb Caen

The Beef Over Crabs—beef over crabs???—isn't the only war plaguing F'man's Wharf these days. There's also a parking war. Now at the point where Mario's Mobil Station at Beach and Taylor is charging only a nickel for all-day parking. His principal competitor, Nuncio Alioto, is down to 15 cents. Both started at a quarter. . . . W. P. Roth, Matson's chairman of the board, was so ill last wk-end (heart attacks) that the company's Brass was on an "alert." . . . The trouble with the State's Republicans, sniffs Lobbyist Don Cleary, is that "their machinery is showing!" . . . Nelly Gaffney, the historic Postreet dresshoppe, has to move in February—Qantas Airlines is taking over its space—but a new spot is being hunted in the Union Squarea.

Henry North, the Metropolitan Life boss who lives in an aerie high in the Clay-Jones Apts., sets his watch each morning by squinting at the big new clock atop—Equitable Life!

. . . Now the public is getting blahzay about free Cadillacs, fevvinsakes. Nobody showed up to claim the Cad given away by Regal Gas in its Nov. 7 drawing. . . . News to me: that Mission High, getting all wound up for a gala reunion Dec. 7, is the only high school in the nation that has graduated two Rhodes Scholars: Axel Gravem and the late Vincent Butler of Pillsbury Madison and Sutro. . . . If you'd care to hear the sexiest voice this side of the doll who does the weather on Monitor, dial Oakland's GL 2-3681. Her name is Janet Clark— and her delivery is whooo-wheeeee.

The current titanic struggle between the federal and state narcotics officers here—they're all acting kind of dopey, it seems to me—reminds Col. George White, the Fed'l chief, of the time he sent Agent Larry Wong to fetch an addict held by the state. "My boss, Colonel White, wants to question him," said Wong. "White or Wong," ans'd the state fellow, "we're keeping him." I tellya, folks, things are not in good shape.

Molloy's Springs, the 75-yr.-old saloon near the cemeteries in Colma (many a mourner winds up there to commune with the spirits), celebrates its birthday Sat. by reviving the Good Old Days for one day: draft beer for a nickel, 10 cent bottled beer, two-bit highballs. . . . "The Incident," the fast-selling new book by S. F.'s Marc Rivette, is bring peddled around the movie studios—but there's plenty of resistance on acct. most of the action takes place in an open boat. H'wood's last attempt along these lines, "Lifeboat," laid such a bomb that producers are still shuddering. . . . June Palmer, City Transfer's moving consultant, had her car stolen the other morning, took a bus to work, and as she was walking toward her office at 430 Main, What Did She See, parked right in front of her? Of course. If it *wasn't* her car, whereinell would we be?

A different approach to the local column is the essay method of Sydney J. Harris of the Chicago *Daily News*. Harris writes a daily contemplative piece on anything that interests him, from Russian political behavior to the following typical column about men's attire.

Strictly Personal

Loud Shirt Is Explained at Last

By Sydney J. Harris

"What are you wearing tonight?" casually inquired the lady with whom I lodge, as we were preparing to go out for the evening.

"Oh," I said, just as casually, "I thought I'd wear my basic black. It's always in good taste, you know."

She smiled tightly. "Don't give me any of your smarty talk; I just wanted to know whether you are going to wear a suit, or slacks and that ghastly striped sports jacket you're so indecently fond of. I don't enjoy dressing and then learning that you're going out looking like a bowler in a beer ad."

I bowed deeply from the waist (no easy trick, when you're attired only in a bath towel), and promised to wear my mourning suit. With the dark maroon tie that hints discreetly of untold wealth and lofty status.

As I showered, I thought of the curious transformation that has taken place in the world of finery. Until modern times, it was the man (like the male of all lower animal species) who adorned himself in resplendent fashion—with satins and silks and lace and ribbons, and no one to call him effeminate for it, while he still carried a sword in his scabbard.

But the beginning of the industrial revolution signified the end of all that. Man in the western world soon became as drab as the factories that were springing up in cornfields, and quickly he began to transfer his symbols of conspicuous wealth from his own person to that of his wife.

Today, of course, the bank president and the janitor look pretty much the same on Sundays—except that the janitor customarily pays more attention to his clothes. It is the wives of each who reflect their comparative wealth and social standing.

Regard the men at any party. Even if they are not wearing conventional black ties, they look as standardized and anonymous as background traffic in a movie. One dark suit is pretty much like another; there are distinctions in material and tailoring, but the net effect is scarcely dramatic to the eye. They all look like parts of the same man.

This modern repression, this break with the tradition of grandeur in male attire, has created its own unconscious resentments. Nothing else could explain the recent rise of the hideously flamboyant sports shirt, the vividly mottled tie, the odd jacket that would make a horse blanch with embarrassment.

Man is the naturally vainer of the two sexes, and when he put away his ribbons and his lace, he did not bury his dandyism, but simply shifted it to the golf course, the swimming pool and the backyard barbecue.

One of the oldest columns in American newspapers is the Chicago *Tribune's* "A Line o'Type or Two," conducted by a number of different writers through the years. It is typical of the anecdotal column, sprinkled with verse and quips from contributors.

A Line o'Type or Two

*Hew to the Line, let the
quips fall where they may*

Blessings and Aldermen

The time has come to count your blessings and your alder-men. Reporter Edward Schreiber, to show that all is not grim work for these statesmen, and that at heart they are just big bantering boys, has recorded a bit of council meeting, at which Police Commissioner O'Connor was being questioned about his budget.

Ald. Hartigan (49th) interrupted Ald. Sperling (50th), who was asking questions, to say, "Alderman, you are not very articulate."

"What he means, Alderman," interrupted Ald. Geisler (34th), "is that you should tell a joke once in a while."

*   *   *   *

Ald. Hoellen (34th), complained that squad car 187, assigned to Damen Ave. station, was wrecked last May, and had not been repaired or replaced. He had to pause while a siren wailed by city hall.

"There it goes now," said Ald. Corcoran (37th).

Ald. Hoellen went right on to deplore the lack of police post men in Damen Ave. district. He pointed out that a safe had been blown in a drug store, Irving Park and Damen, and the matter was not discovered until the next morning.

"That must be a quiet neighborhood," observed Police Commissioner O'Connor.

*   *   *   *

Then Ald. Hoellen discovered that the 1958 police appropriation for gasoline is $425,000 as compared with $460,000 in a previous budget. He asked if Police Commissioner O'Connor planned to lay by a few squad cars.

Police Commissioner O'Connor did not answer, but Ald. Joe Burke (14th) said, "No, they are going to have the carburetors adjusted."

Ald. Hoellen, noting the dog pound appropriation, asked, "What are you going to do about that dog flying around the world?"

Ald. Janousek (22nd) answered for the police commissioner. He said, "We'll appoint you a committee of one to go after him."

Well, of course, everyone like to have died at this sally. Then it was time to go to lunch.

Subject Change

Of Outer Space and moons and such
I wish they would keep still,
And let me think of Christmas and
How many days until!

Mable F. Browder

From Which Side?

Dear Line: I spotted this ad for the friendly tavern in the
Elgin paper: "So you're in a jam. . . . So you gave your wife
poison instead of pepper. So cops from five states are after
you. So what! Forget your problems in the friendly atmosphere of Clem's lounge." Do you suppose that is why the local
gendarmes are there glaring at the door?

Just Jane

Saith the Stoker

Life is real. Life is earnest
And quite pleasant on the whole,
So long as it is furnaced
With a due amount of coal.

Ellis O. Jones

A black and white dog, named Apache, was fitted for glasses.
Why couldn't they leave the poor dog alone? Now he'll find
out that all those pleasant blurs are really people.

Thomas Morrow

Washington Columns

The Washington political columns syndicated nationally
are written in a far graver tone than the whimsical local columns printed above. In fact most of these Washington writers
avoid any show of humor whatsoever in their columns, apparently in the belief that it would seem out of character. Here
are two examples of these columns. The first represents a viewpoint generally considered to be conservative in political outlook,
the second a pro-liberal position.

David Lawrence, a veteran commentator on the Washington
scene, has specialized in interpretation of economic news coming from the nation's capital. This sample column deals with the
problem of the federal budget.

Congress Priority Is Urged for Budget Defense Items

By David Lawrence

WASHINGTON—The headlines call it "Ike's Budget." Congress alone, however, can vote the money. The President proposes, but Congress disposes.

Whose budget, then, is it? Who takes the responsibility, especially when the Democratic party controls the legislative branch and the Republican party controls the executive branch of the government?

It's really the people's budget. For only they can tell Congress what to do and what not to do.

The pressure for specific appropriations is intense. It goes on here in myriad ways. Each group has its own special argument and special means of communicating it to Congress.

The Congress will have to go before the people with its decision next November, when the entire House of Representatives and one third of the Senate must be elected.

Will the budget be an issue? Certainly it will be, and the reasons are conflicting. Some people will be resentful that the budget has gone higher than before and that there has been no decrease in taxes. Others will worry because the Communists are supposed to be ahead of us militarily and presumably America hasn't spent enough.

Basically the people want peace—not war. They will approve any spending that assures peace. The President's determination is to keep the nation at peace by building up our military strength and by insuring the strength of our allies, some of whom have economic troubles that require American aid.

Indignation Last Year

Last year at this time a wave of indignation swept the country, because the budget recommended by the White House was $71.8 billion. It wasn't so much the size of the budget but the rate at which it was rising that excited many critics. For a runaway spending spree was condemned as meaning more inflation, higher prices and a drop in the purchasing power of the dollar.

Examining the new budget, which asks for $73.9 billion, it is important to focus on the non-defense totals. In the fiscal year ended June 30, 1957, all non-defense spending proposed was $25 billion.

In the fiscal year ending June 30, 1958, it is $27.9 billion.

In the fiscal year ending June 30, 1959, the non-defense items total $27.6 billion, which is a reduction of $300 million from the previous year.

This shows how little change there has been in the non-defense schedules, and it is to be noted that "non-defense" includes aid for our allies under development and technical assistance programs.

So it is apparent that federal expenses for non-defense items are being held down.

The big expense is on the armament, or security, side. From $44.9 billion in fiscal 1958, it has gone up to $46.3 billion for fiscal 1959.

Today the criticism may well be that the military side has not received enough funds. But the country hasn't as yet digested the fact that something has to give if military expenditures are to continue mounting. Either the dollar has to be depreciated and forced down from its 50-cent level or else economies have to be made on the non-defense side. The danger is in the addition by Congress of many non-defense items not in the budget that are wanted by special groups.

Another veteran political commentator, Drew Pearson, writes from a viewpoint reflecting liberal policies. His column works in more factual reporting than most Washington columns, but selection of material is done with a political purpose. Here is a brief sample of his method:

How a Scientist Was Hamstrung

By Drew Pearson

WASHINGTON—The manner in which McCarthyism and Nixonism have barred key scientists from missile-satellite research is vividly illustrated at the California Institute of Technology, where Dr. Fritz Zwicky, the first man to attempt an earth satellite, is now barred from all government research.

Dr. Zwicky is a Swiss, proud of being a Swiss, wants to remain a Swiss. But at the same time, he wants to help the United States and the free world, of which he is a part, get ahead in the missile race. He can't do it, however, under the security restrictions laid down by the Defense Department after McCarthy and Nixon started their scourge of scientists from the government.

"During the war," explains Dr. Zwicky, "I signed up to fight with you. I didn't have to. Switzerland is supposed to be neutral. But I joined the U.S. Air Corps and served on General Hap Arnold's scientific board.

"After the war I told the Air Corps that artificial meteors —or satellites—would be the next step in modern war. And on Dec. 17, 1946, we fired a V-2 rocket at the White Sands proving ground in New Mexico, carrying small meteors.

"We couldn't drum up enough interest to carry on, though we could have got earth satellites into the air if we had," said Dr. Zwicky. "Later, under the new Security Manual which the Air Force had to adopt, I was barred because I am Swiss.

"I can go to Washington and give them my ideas—which I do. But I can't stay to see if they are properly carried out."

(*Reprinted by special permission of the Bell Syndicate, Inc.*)

Guide for Columnists

While there can be no firm rules for writing local columns, because of their highly individual nature and wide range of subject matter, these principles are helpful:

1. Express your viewpoints firmly but not so blindly that you ignore the existence of differing opinions.
2. Use of anecdotes brightens the column and builds reader interest. Write in terms of people.
3. Check your facts just as carefully as you would in writing a news story.
4. Do not use your column to carry on personal feuds or attack others who have no way to reply.
5. Remember that possession of a column does not make you omniscient or qualified to pass judgment on every topic.
6. Volunteer contributors can supply much useful material. Encourage them.
7. Avoid becoming an "easy mark" for publicity men. Be sure that you print their offerings only on their news or entertainment merit, not as a favor.

APPENDIX

Preparation of Copy
Copy Reader's Symbols
Sample Style Sheet

Preparation of Copy

The following rules for preparing news copy are universally followed in all types of newsrooms:

1. Reporters type on one side of the copy paper only.

2. Stories are double-spaced, never single-spaced (some newspapers even ask for triple spacing). Double spacing permits editing between the lines of typing.

3. The reporter's name, a "slug line" identifying the nature of the story, and the date are typed on three lines in the upper left hand corner of the first page of copy ("Frank C. Jones/tenement fire/Nov. 18").

4. If the story runs more than one page, the word "more" is placed at the bottom of the first page, and is circled (all material not intended to be set into type is circled).

5. The reporter's last name, the "slug line," and the number of the succeeding page go in the upper left hand corner of additional pages ("Jones—tenement fire—2").

6. Start your story about one-third the way down the first page. Leave one inch margins at the left and right. Indent paragraph openings liberally—about ten spaces—for ease in copy editing.

7. Put a closing mark at the end of your story ("#" or "30" are the commonly used ones) and circle it. This tells the desk there is nothing more to come.

8. Use the lower case "x" key to strike over letters, words, or sentences you do not wish to have appear in your copy. In addition, draw pencil lines firmly through all "x"-ed copy so that your finished story is neat.

9. Read your copy over carefully. Make corrections or changes neatly with a pencil, using the copy reader's symbols. These marks are universally used by copy desks and print shops and the beginner should learn to use them correctly. They are explained on the following page.

Copy Reader's Symbols

Marks used in correcting copy are shown in the typewritten copy at the left. Explanations of the marks are given at the right. Transpositions can be marked only for adjacent letters or words; circling to indicate "spell out" or "abbreviate" is restricted to numbers and commonly abbreviated words.

James B. Reston, Pulitzer prize-winning Washington	Start a paragraph
bureau chief for The New York Times, will speak on	No capital letter
"Politics and the reporter"	Capital letter
at 8 p.m. Monday in Wheeler auditorium.	Deleting a letter
Reston's appearance on university campus is	Deleting a word
sponsored by Sigma Delta Chi, professional journal-	Insert letter
istic fraternity, as a part of Journalism Week.	Insert word
Winner of the 1945 and 1957 Pulitzer prizes for	Insert space
national reporting, Reston is widely known for his	Close up space
coverage of political and diplomatic news coming out	
of the many sources from the nation's capital.	Connect lines
A reception will be held at the Delta Tau Pi	Transpose letters
house Monday at 5 p.m. for Reston by the presidents	Transpose words
of 5 campus assns. and the board of the Student	Spell out
Publishing Company.	Abbreviate
Officials expect more than seventy-five guests	Use number

Sample Style Sheet

A style sheet is a guide to usage in matters of capitalization, abbreviation, punctuation, use of numerals, and handling of titles, names, times, addresses, etc. Every professional publication adopts a style sheet of its own for the sake of uniformity, readability and ease of editing.

The sample style sheet which follows is based on the style book of the Associated Press, which represents views of the majority of newspapers in matters of style preference. This style sheet covers situations commonly encountered by the reporter, but it is not as elaborate as many style books.

Capitalization

General rule: Proper nouns are capitalized. This means that this style sheet follows an "up-style" like that in magazines and books. Specific rules follow:

1. The common noun is capitalized when forming an essential part of a proper name but lower case when used alone as a substitute: University of California, Indiana University, the university; Roosevelt High School, Baker Hall, Wrigley Building, Ford Motor Co., Faculty Club, Methodist Church, Bach Society, Hotel Windsor, Lake Huron, Ohio River, Law School, History Department.

2. Titles preceding names are capitalized. Titles following names or standing alone are not capitalized (except that the title of the head of any nation—King, Queen, President, Prime Minister, Pope—is capitalized when standing alone if it refers to the person): President Frank C. Jones; Frank C. Jones, president.

3. Names of all formal branches of government are capitalized when specifically identified, both as nouns and adjectives: U.S. Senate, the Senate, Senate action; Congress, House, Cabinet, Supreme Court, Legislature, City Council, U.S. Air Force, Chamber of Deputies, Parliament, House of Commons, Board of Regents, Student Council.

4. Official names of federal and state departments, commissions, courts and legislative committees are capitalized when given in full: Department of Agriculture, the department; Federal Trade Commission, the commission; District Court, the court; Senate Labor Committee, the committee.

5. Specific names of political parties are capitalized: Republican Party, a Democrat, Socialist Party (*but,* a socialist form of government).

6. Descriptive terms for specific geographic areas should be capitalized, but not mere direction: Middle West, East, Midwest, Orient, Deep South; *but,* go 10 miles north.

7. Names of races, nationalities and religions are capitalized: Negro, Frenchman, Jewish; *but,* white, black.

8. Capitalize names of special events, holidays and religious observance days; all words denoting the Diety; titles of books, plays and songs (except for articles and prepositions of fewer than five letters which do not start or close the title); names of newspapers and magazines (but not preceding articles); names of wars and battles; names of flags; proper names of animals; trade names.

9. Do not capitalize names of seasons; proper names which have acquired common meaning (plaster of paris); kinds of animals; college degrees when spelled out; sun, moon and earth unless used in series with names of other bodies which are capitalized (Mars, Venus).

Abbreviations

General rule: When common abbreviations are unquestionably clear to the reader, they should be used. When they might puzzle the reader, they should not be used. This style sheet tends toward use of abbreviations. Specific rules follow:

1. Abbreviations may be used for names of widely known groups, agencies or organizations, thus: YMCA, FCC, AFL-CIO, AP, RCA; *but,* use periods with U.S., U.S.S.R., U.N.

2. Common nouns in names of business firms are abbreviated: Corp., Co., Bros., Ltd., Assn., Inc.

3. When used as part of a specific address, abbreviate: St., Ave., Blvd., Rd., Pl., Sq., Hwy., Pkwy.; use N., S., etc., for North, South. (2427 Wilson Ave. S.; take Dixie Pkwy. and Hwy. 101.)

4. Names of states are abbreviated when used with names of cities, except for Idaho, Iowa, Maine, Ohio, Utah, Alaska; also Hawaii: Fresno, Calif.; Ames, Iowa; Pittsburgh, Pa. Spell out all names of states when used alone.

5. Titles preceding names are abbreviated and capitalized: Dr., Prof., Gov., Sen., Rep., Gen., Adm., Col., Capt., Cmdr., Maj., Lt., Sgt., Pvt.; *but,* do not abbreviate president, commodore, field marshal, postmaster general and other longer or less common titles. Titles of two or more words and uncommon titles usually follow the name.

6. Abbreviate months of six or more letters when used with specific dates, but otherwise do not abbreviate months or days of the week: Monday, Jan. 4, 1960.

7. Abbreviate college degrees: B.A., M.A., M.S., Ph.D.

8. Spell out United States when used as a noun.

Names

General rule: Names should be used as their owners prefer. Ordinarily, first name, initial and surname are used for men. Specific rules follow:

1. The first time a name appears in a story it should be given in full: John C. Jones, Mrs. John C. Jones, Mr. and Mrs. John C. Jones, Mary Sue Jones (unmarried woman).

2. In subsequent mentions the same individuals become: Jones, Mrs. Jones, Mr. and Mrs. Jones, Miss Jones. (Mr. is not used except in the clerical title: the Rev. Mr. Jones.)

3. Use the full name of clergymen, with the proper title, in first mention: the Rev. William T. Smith, Rabbi James Wise, Francis Cardinal Spellman. In subsequent mentions, Protestants become the Rev. Mr. Smith; others, Rabbi Wise, Cardinal Spellman, Father Smith ("the Rev." is used in first mention for a Roman Catholic priest, but never use "the Rev. Mr." in a subsequent mention of him).

Numerals

General rule: Spell out all numbers from one through nine; use figures for all numbers of 10 or larger. Specific rules, and exceptions, follow:

1. The general rule is not followed in a series of related expressions: He had 5 suits, 27 shirts and 105 ties.
2. Ordinal numbers follow the same general rule: third, 12th, 22nd, 33rd (*but,* They ranked 3rd, 12th, 22nd and 33rd).
3. Round figures may be written this way: one million, 20 billion, 180 million dollars.
4. Exact sums of money should be expressed in figures: 6 cents, $1.25, $1,745,318, $25 (no zeros with even sums).
5. Use figures for scores: New York won, 10 to 5.
6. Use figures to give precise measurements including ages, distances, height, weight, per cent: John C. Jones, 28; 5-year-old; 6 feet 2 inches, 8 pounds, 7 per cent.
7. Use figures for time: 7 a.m., 2 p.m., 11:27 p.m. (except for noon and midnight, where words are used). Note that "a.m." and "p.m." are not capitalized.
8. Fractions are spelled out except for: $\frac{1}{8}$, $\frac{1}{4}$, $\frac{3}{8}$, $\frac{1}{2}$, $\frac{5}{8}$, $\frac{3}{4}$, $\frac{7}{8}$.
9. Casual, or nonprecise, figures are spelled out: six or eight pieces, about ten weeks, about thirty miles.

Punctuation

Regular rules for punctuation should be followed by the reporter—and should be learned. This style sheet lists three exceptions which are common among newspapers:

1. The comma is omitted before the conjunction in listing words or figures in series: Tom, Joe and Ed; 11, 12 or 13.
2. The comma is omitted between name and abbreviation of persons: John Jones Jr., Henry Ford III.
3. The comma and final period are placed inside quotation marks. Other punctuation marks are placed inside quotation marks only when they are part of the quoted matter.

INDEX

Index